# Living Geography

01-533

PRINCETON ■ LONDON

Published in the United States and Canada by
Two-Can Publishing LLC
234 Nassau Street
Princeton, NJ 08542

www.two-canpublishing.com

'Two-Can' is a trademark of Two-Can Publishing
Two-Can publishing is a division of Zenith Entertainment plc,
43–45 Dorset Street, London W1H 4AB

Hardback ISBN 1-58728-2542
Hardback   1 2 3 4 5 6 7 8 9 10 02 01 00

COVER DESIGNED BY PICTHALL AND GUNZI LTD
Photographic credits: FPG/J. Zehrt (hurricane/Earth & Moon) and Steve
Bloom (oil rig), Telegraph Colour Library; Tom van Sant/Geosphere Project,
Santa Monica (Earth: rectangular view), Science Photo Library; Larry Ulrich
(Carp River, Michigan), Tony Stone Images

WEATHER
Text: Barbara Taylor; Consultant: Tim Davie BSc PhD, Hydrologist,
Queen Mary and Westfield College, University of London, UK; Editor:
Robert Sved; Art Director: Carole Orbell; Senior Designer: Gareth Dobson;
Senior Managing Editor: Christine Morley; Production: Leila Peerun;
Photography: John Englefield; Picture research: Lyndsey Price, Dipika
Parmar Jenkins; Model-makers: Melanie Williams, Peter Griffiths; Art
direction and model-making for experiments: Andrew Haslam;
Special thanks to Sharon Nowakowski and Patricia Ohlenroth. Photographic
credits: Tony Stone Worldwide: p.6 (top right); Still Pictures: p.7 (top right);
NASA: p.10 (top right); Zentrale Farbbild Agentur GmbH: p.17 (top left);
Doug Scott/Chris Bonington Library: p.21 (top left); Leonard Lee
Rue/Science Photo Library: p.30 (top right); Warren Faidley/Oxford
Scientific Films: p.34 (top right); E.R. Degginger/Oxford Scientific Films:
p.36 (top right); B. Harris/Zentrale Farbbild Agentur GmbH: p.43 (top left);
Still Pictures: p.43 (top right); Jules Cowan/Bruce Coleman Limited:
p.44 (top right); M. Nimmo/FLPA: p.46 (top left); Steve C.
Kaufman/Bruce Coleman Limited: p.47 (top right).
Maps: © The Meteorological Office, UK: p.6 (bottom left);
© Scan-globe A/S edition 1991: p.15 (bottom)

OCEANS
Text: Barbara Taylor; Consultant: Rachel Mills BSc PhD, Southampton
Oceanography Centre, UK; Editor: Jacqueline McCann; Managing Editor:
Christine Morley; Art Director: Carole Orbell; Senior Designer:
Gareth Dobson; Production: Leila Peerun; Photography: John Englefield; Model-
makers: Peter Griffiths, Melanie Williams. Photographic credits: Britstock-
Ifa/Bernd Ducke: p.53; Bruce C. Heezen and Marie Tharp © Marie Tharp,
1977: p.51; Dr Ken Macdonald/Science Photo Library: p.57; Mark Edwards/Still
Pictures: p.83; Oxford Cartographers: p.89 (map); Planet Earth Pictures/Gary
Bell: p.74; Planet Earth Pictures/John Bracegirdle: p.67; Planet Earth
Pictures/John Eastcott/Yva Momatiuk: p.72; Planet Earth Pictures/Robert
Hessler: p.76; Rex Features/Rob Howarth: p.71; Simon Fraser/Science Photo
Library: p.91; Tony Stone/Warren Bolster: p.64; Tony Stone/Randy Wells:
p.50; Tony Stone/Ted Wood: p.84; Zefa/M. Hoshino: p.60

RIVERS
Text: Barbara Taylor; Consultant: Dr Geraldene Wharton BSc PhD; Editor:
Jacqueline McCann; Art Director: Carole Orbell; Senior Designer: Helen
McDonagh; Managing Editor: Christine Morley; Deputy Art Director: Jill
Plank; Production: Joya Bart-Plange; Commissioned photography: Jon Barnes
and Matthew Ward; Picture Research: Debbie Dorman and Dipika Palmer-
Jenkins; Model-makers: Melanie Williams, Peter Griffiths, Paul Holzherr. Thank
you to the models: Matthew, Vanisha, and Zakkiyah. Photographic credits:
Britstock-Ifa/Jean-Pierre Vollrath: p.111; Britstock-Ifa/Jim Nelson: p.117; Bruce
Coleman/Atlantide: p.125; Bruce Coleman/Charlie Ott: p.99, p.104; Bruce
Coleman/Jeff Foott Productions: p.134; David Parker/Science Photo Library:
p.114; GSF Picture Library: p.101; Harvey Maps Ltd: p.94, p.103;
Nic Dunlop/Panos Pictures: p.120; Oxford Scientific Films/Paul McCullagh:
p.106; Planet Earth Pictures/Andre Bartschi: p.122; Robert Harding/Michael
Jenner: p.112; Survival Anglia/Tony Bomford: p.100; Zefa p.132

MAPS
Text: Barbara Taylor; Editor: Robert Sved; Consultant: Steve Watts FRGS; Art
Director: Carole Orbell; Senior Designer: Gareth Dobson; Additional Design:
Helen McDonagh; Senior Managing Editor: Christine Morley; Managing
Editor: Kate Graham; Production: Joya Bart-Plange; Photography: John
Englefield; Picture Research: Lyndsey Price; Model-makers: Melanie Williams,
Peter Griffiths. Photographic credits: British Library/Bridgeman: p.162 (bottom);
British Library: p.144 (top right), p.163 (top left); British Museum: p.162 (top
left); Dr Eckart Pott/Bruce Coleman: p.147 (top centre); Greenland National
Museum & Archives: p.138 (top right), p.162 (top right); NRSC Airphoto
Group: p.174 (top); Oxford Cartographers: p.172 (top right); CNES, 1994
Distribution Spot Image/Science Photo Library: p.179 (top right), p.155 (top
right); ESA/PLI/Science Photo Library: p.156 (top); Tom Van Sant/Geosphere
Project, Santa Monica/Science Photo Library: p.139 (top), p.140 (top); US
Geological Survey/Science Photo Library: p.179 (bottom right); JP
Delobelle/Still Pictures: p.147 (top left); Zefa: p.166 (top left).
Maps: p.138 © Quarto Publishing, © Zermatt Landeskarte der Schweiz,
© Geocart, © Crown 85069M/Ordnance Survey, © Crown/Courtesy HMSO;
p.154 © Slovenska Kartografia, © Crown 85069M/Ordnance Survey; p.159
© Instituto Geografico Nacional; p.161 © Arno Peters/Oxford Cartographers;
p.174 © Universal Press Pty Ltd; p.175 © Teito Rapid Transit Authority,
© Universal Press Pty Ltd; p.177 © Crown 85069M/Ordnance Survey; p.178
© American Express Publishing Corporation Inc

Printed in Hong Kong

Words marked in **boldface** in the text can be found in the glossary

# Contents

Studying the weather 6
Weather around the world 8
The atmosphere 10
Making the weather 12
Heat and climate 14
The seasons 16
Air temperature 18
Air pressure 20
Air on the move 22
Wind speed 24
The water cycle 26
Clouds 28
Rain, snow, and hail 30
Air masses and fronts 32
Storms 34
Tornadoes and hurricanes 36
Recording the weather 38
Weather maps 40
Weather forecasting 42
Weather and the land 44
The changing climate 46
Studying oceans 50
The world's oceans 52
Birth of an ocean 54
The ocean floor 56
Seawater 58
Frozen oceans 60
Ocean currents 62
Waves 64
Tides 66
Changing sea levels 68
Coasts 70
Coral reefs 74
Black smokers 76
Marine life 78
Deep-sea sediments 80
Ocean resources 82
Ports and settlement 84
Exploring oceans 86

Mapping the seabed 88
Oceans under threat 90
Being a geographer 94
Rivers of the world 96
The water cycle 98
Sources of rivers 100
Drainage patterns 102
Underground rivers 104
The upper river 106
Waterfalls and rapids 110
Energy from the river 112
Dams and reservoirs 114
Lakes and basins 116
River canyons 118
The middle river 120
The human water cycle 126
Farming on the lower river 128
River deltas 130
Flood control 132
Managing rivers 134
Being a mapmaker 138
A bird's-eye view 140
Scale and grids 142
Measuring height 144
Signs and symbols 146
Mapping the sea and sky 150
Human maps 152
Three-dimensional maps 154
The globe 156
Dividing up the world 158
Mapping the globe 160
Early maps 162
Surveying and measuring 164
Plotting maps 166
Making your own map 168
Finding your way 174
Changing maps 178
Glossary 180
Index 188

# Weather

# Studying the weather

Geography helps us to understand what happened to the Earth in the past, how it is changing now, and what might happen to it in the future. Studying the weather is an important part of geography. This job is done by **meteorologists,** who study all the things that make up the weather, such as wind, rain, clouds, and sunshine. They do this by looking at the changes in the layer of gases that surrounds the Earth called the **atmosphere**.

△ The weather can affect the type of home we live in. These houses in Singapore are built on stilts to protect people from floods that may happen when it rains.

## People and weather

Since earliest times, people's lives have been affected by the weather. Basic needs, such as growing food and finding shelter, have always been linked to the weather of a place. Nowadays, the weather still greatly influences our lives, from the clothes we wear and the homes we live in to the food we grow and the transportation and communication we use.

◁ Meteorologists use charts like these to help them to predict the weather. You can use a camera, **thermometer,** and notebook to keep weather records.

## Forecasting through the ages

People who can forecast the weather have always been important to society. During the Middle Ages, people made weather predictions based on the positions of stars and planets. Today, weather forecasters use new technology, such as **satellites** and huge computers. But anyone can begin to forecast the weather by taking a few measurements and looking at the clouds.

## Make it Work!

The Make it Work! way of looking at geography is to carry out experiments and make things that help you to understand how geography shapes the world in which we live. By studying the models and following the step-by-step instructions, you will discover more about how the weather works.

## Using this book

Meteorologists study a wide range of geographical subjects. Throughout this book, we have used symbols to show where information relates to particular topics. The symbols are:

 Recording and forecasting

 Land    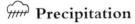 **Precipitation**

 **Temperature**  Air and wind

▷ *Weather satellites give us very clear pictures of the moving layer of clouds that lies above the surface of the Earth.*

## Recording the weather

It can be expensive to buy instruments to record the weather. This book shows you how to make simple models that can detect and measure changes in the weather.

▽ *The models in this book have arrows of different colors to show how air, water, and heat move around to make our weather.*

## Safety

You may need to use sharp tools for some of the experiments in this book. Ask an adult to help you. Some of the weather measurements have to be taken outdoors. Be careful in wet, windy, icy, or stormy weather.

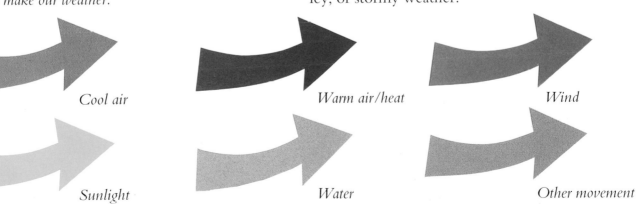

*Cool air*

*Sunlight*

*Warm air/heat*

*Water*

*Wind*

*Other movement*

# Weather around the world

The weather is different all over the world. In some places it's always warm and in others it's freezing cold. Some areas have violent, stormy weather while others have calm, mild weather. When we ask about the weather, we usually want to know how wet it is (rainfall), and how hot it is (temperature).

▷ *This map shows the annual rainfall and temperature ranges of places all around the world. It also tells us where violent storms most frequently happen.*

## 🌧 Rainfall

The highest amount of rainfall over one year is near the **equator**, where more than 79 inches (2,000 millimeters) of rain falls in a year. Areas just north or south of the equator, such as North Africa or Australia, are mostly very dry. Places farther away from the equator, such as Europe, have plenty of rain. In the Arctic and Antarctica, there is little rain and most of it falls as snow.

## 🌡 Temperature

Temperatures are highest at the equator and gradually decrease toward the Arctic and Antarctica. Some places, especially those near the equator, such as Singapore, have an even temperature all year around. Places farther away from the equator, such as Paris and Montreal, have warm summers and cold winters. Temperature is measured in degrees Fahrenheit (°F) or degrees Celsius (°C).

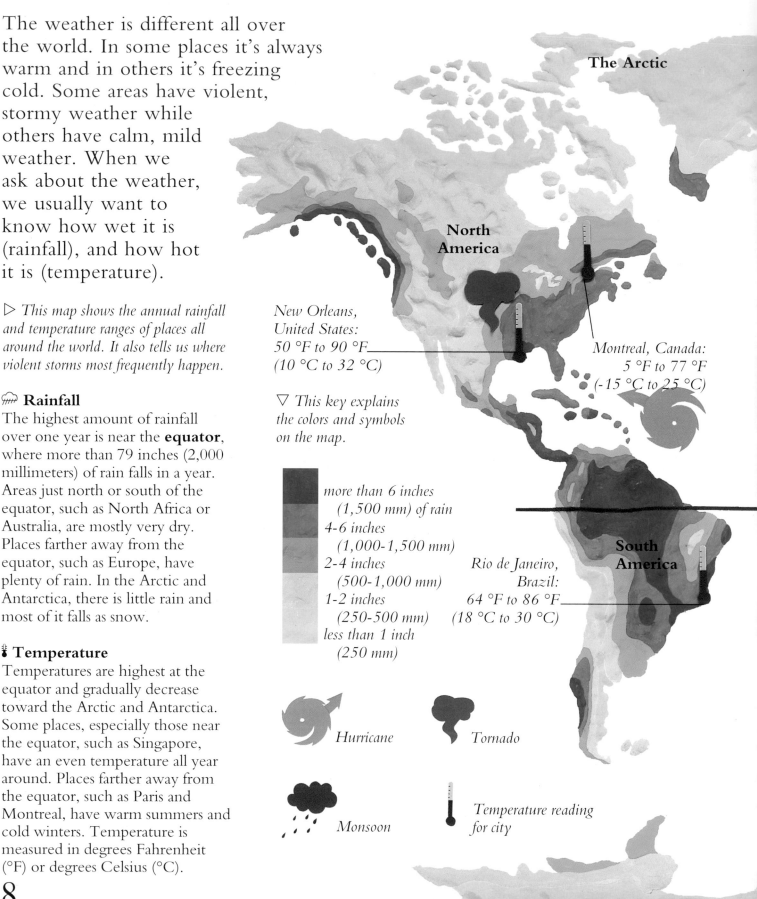

The Arctic

North America

New Orleans, United States: 50 °F to 90 °F (10 °C to 32 °C)

Montreal, Canada: 5 °F to 77 °F (-15 °C to 25 °C)

▽ *This key explains the colors and symbols on the map.*

more than 6 inches (1,500 mm) of rain
4-6 inches (1,000-1,500 mm)
2-4 inches (500-1,000 mm)
1-2 inches (250-500 mm)
less than 1 inch (250 mm)

South America

Rio de Janeiro, Brazil: 64 °F to 86 °F (18 °C to 30 °C)

Hurricane

Tornado

Monsoon

Temperature reading for city

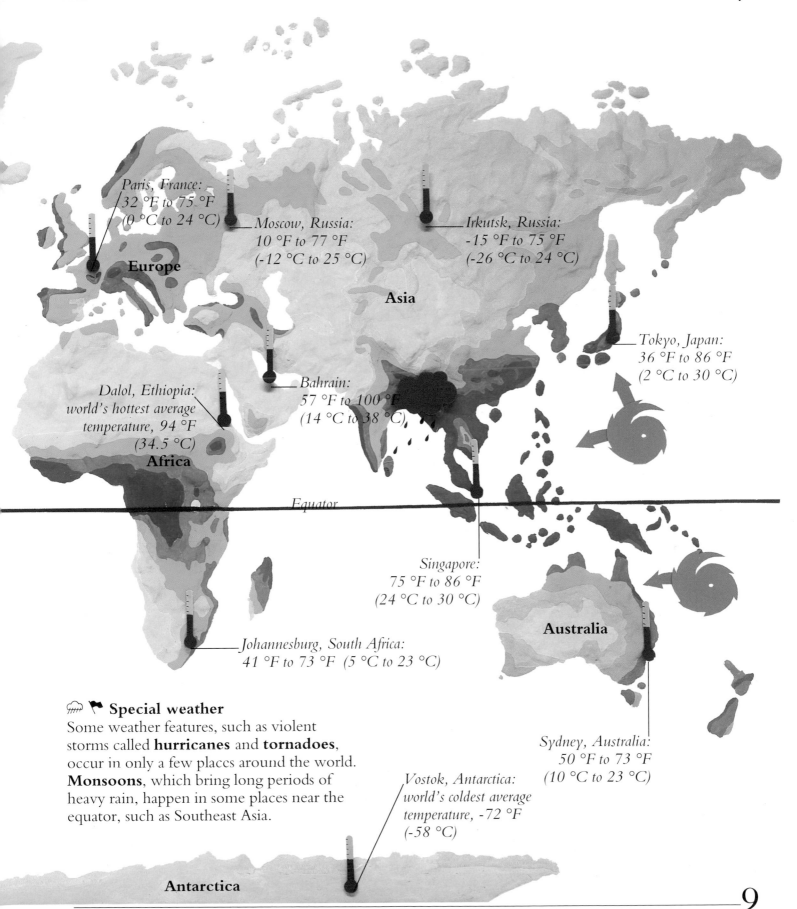

Paris, France:
32 °F to 75 °F
(0 °C to 24 °C)

Moscow, Russia:
10 °F to 77 °F
(-12 °C to 25 °C)

Irkutsk, Russia:
-15 °F to 75 °F
(-26 °C to 24 °C)

**Europe**

**Asia**

Tokyo, Japan:
36 °F to 86 °F
(2 °C to 30 °C)

Dalol, Ethiopia:
world's hottest average
temperature, 94 °F
(34.5 °C)

**Africa**

Bahrain:
57 °F to 100 °F
(14 °C to 38 °C)

Equator

Singapore:
75 °F to 86 °F
(24 °C to 30 °C)

**Australia**

Johannesburg, South Africa:
41 °F to 73 °F (5 °C to 23 °C)

**Special weather**

Some weather features, such as violent
storms called **hurricanes** and **tornadoes**,
occur in only a few places around the world.
**Monsoons**, which bring long periods of
heavy rain, happen in some places near the
equator, such as Southeast Asia.

Sydney, Australia:
50 °F to 73 °F
(10 °C to 23 °C)

Vostok, Antarctica:
world's coldest average
temperature, -72 °F
(-58 °C)

**Antarctica**

9

# The atmosphere

The Earth is wrapped in a layer of air, which is the mixture of gases we breathe. We call this layer the atmosphere. The atmosphere is thick near the surface of the Earth, where it is easy to breathe, but becomes thinner farther away from the Earth. About 560 miles (900 kilometers) away from the Earth, there is no more air left, only space. The weather only happens in the lowest part of the atmosphere.

△ *Seen from space, the atmosphere looks like a glowing, thin blue layer around the Earth.*

### ⚑ A mixture of gases

The atmosphere is made up of many gases. More than three-quarters of the atmosphere is nitrogen. About a fifth is oxygen, the gas that all living things need to stay alive. Other gases help keep out the sun's harmful rays, and some keep the Earth's heat in at night.

### ⚑ Layers in the atmosphere

The atmosphere is divided into five layers according to temperature. There are no solid boundaries between each layer – they fade into one another. The weather happens in the lowest layer, called the **troposphere**. This layer contains the water needed to make clouds.

## TEST THE ATMOSPHERE

**You will need:** modeling clay, a candle, matches, a shallow bowl, a tall glass, colored water

**1** Attach a candle to the center of a bowl using a lump of modeling clay. Pour water into the bowl, as shown above, and with an adult's help, light the candle.

**2** With an adult's help, place the glass over the candle so that no air can enter.

**Result:** As fire needs oxygen to burn, the candle flame will go out when all the oxygen has disappeared. The water rises about one-fifth of the way up the glass, replacing the oxygen. This shows us that about one-fifth of our atmosphere is oxygen.

### The lower atmosphere

The troposphere stretches about 6 miles (10 km) from the surface of the Earth. The next layer up is called the stratosphere. Fast aircraft fly here because the air is calmer than in the troposphere. The stratosphere includes a layer of a gas called **ozone**. This blocks out most of the sun's harmful rays that can make our skin burn. In the mesosphere, the coldest part of the atmosphere, temperatures fall to –148 °F (–100 °C).

### The upper atmosphere

Above the mesosphere lies the thermosphere, the hottest layer. High temperatures burn up all the debris, such as meteors and old satellites, falling toward the Earth. In this layer, gases collide with sunlight and make bright splashes of light called auroras. These can sometimes be seen from the Earth's surface. The top layer of the atmosphere is called the exosphere. Some satellites circle the Earth in the exosphere, but most are out in space.

▽ *This model shows the five layers of the atmosphere. You can also see some features of each layer.*

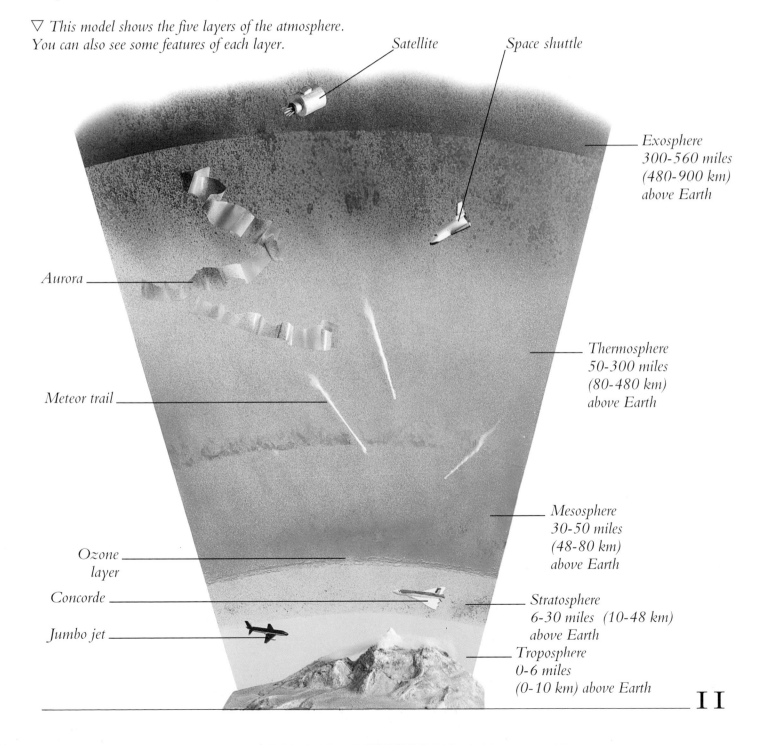

Satellite

Space shuttle

Exosphere
300-560 miles
(480-900 km)
above Earth

Aurora

Thermosphere
50-300 miles
(80-480 km)
above Earth

Meteor trail

Mesosphere
30-50 miles
(48-80 km)
above Earth

Ozone
layer

Stratosphere
6-30 miles  (10-48 km)
above Earth

Concorde

Jumbo jet

Troposphere
0-6 miles
(0-10 km) above Earth

11

# Making the weather

Three things are needed to make the weather: water, air, and heat. The sun's heat stirs up the atmosphere, making the air move. The moving air becomes wind, which carries heat and water around the Earth. This makes the weather happen.

**Water in the air**
When the sun heats up oceans, rivers, lakes, and plants, the atmosphere soaks up water from them like a sponge. The water turns into an invisible gas called **water vapor**, which stays in the air. Water vapor is a small but important part of the air. When the air cools down, the water vapor turns back into drops of liquid water again, forming clouds and rain.

**Air on the move**
When air around the Earth cools down or warms up, it moves. Warm air is lighter than cool air and it rises. Cool air is heavier and it sinks. Air rising and sinking causes winds all over the world, from such small winds as sea breezes to larger winds that circle the globe.

▽ *This model shows the sun, wind, and rain in action on the surface of the Earth.*

*Water droplets collect in clouds.*

*Air rising and sinking causes the wind to blow.*

*The sun's rays heat the ground which warms the air.*

*Water falls to the Earth's surface as rain.*

## ☀ The sun's rays

The sun sends out **energy** in the form of light and heat. As this energy enters the Earth's atmosphere, some of it is absorbed or scattered by gases. Further down, in the troposphere, clouds reflect more energy back into space. Only about half of the energy that reaches the atmosphere passes through it to heat the Earth's surface.

▷ *This model shows how the sun's rays lose energy as they pass through the atmosphere.*

## ☀ Heating the air

Although the sun's heat warms the air, it does not do so directly. The sun heats the ground or the sea, and the warm surface then heats the air from below. A radiometer is used to measure the energy given off by the warm air.

## MAKE A RADIOMETER

**You will need:** a glass jar with lid, cardboard, aluminum foil, a matchstick, black paper, thread, glue, tape

**1** Cut four 1-inch (2-centimeter) squares of cardboard. Cover both sides of two squares with black paper and two with foil.

**2** Glue the squares to the matchstick, as shown above. The silver squares should be at right angles to each other, as should the black squares.

**3** Tape one end of the thread to the end of the matchstick. Tape the other end of the thread to the middle of the inside of the lid. Put the lid on the jar and make sure that the cardboard cross can spin inside the jar.

**4** On different days, place your radiometer outside in the sunshine and note how often the cross spins in one minute.

**Result:** When the jar warms up, the black squares heat up more easily than the silver squares. Hot air bounces off the black squares and pushes the cross around. The cross spins more quickly when there is more sunshine.

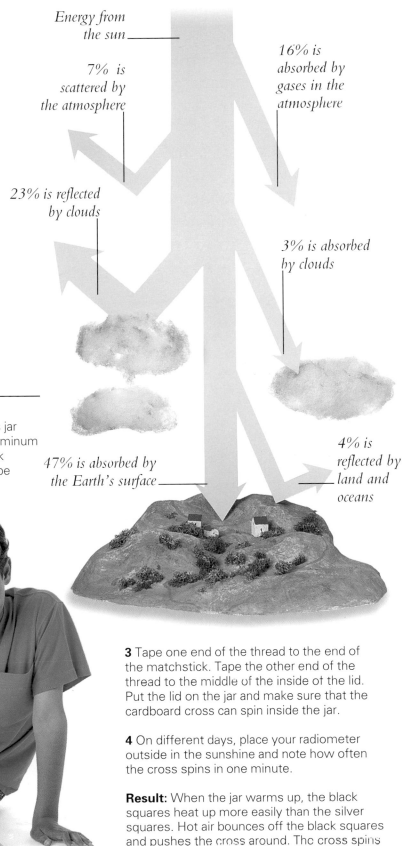

*Energy from the sun*

*7% is scattered by the atmosphere*

*16% is absorbed by gases in the atmosphere*

*23% is reflected by clouds*

*3% is absorbed by clouds*

*4% is reflected by land and oceans*

*47% is absorbed by the Earth's surface*

# Heat and climate

**Climate** is the pattern of weather for a place. This pattern is roughly the same each year. Some places have warm climates, some have cold climates, and some have medium, or **temperate**, climates. The climate of a place depends mainly on its distance from the equator. It is hottest at the equator and becomes colder toward the **poles**.

### Curved Earth
The Earth's surface is curved. This is why different parts of the Earth receive different amounts of heat from the sun. At the equator, the sun's rays hit the Earth directly. The sun is overhead at midday and its rays are concentrated on a small area. This makes areas around the equator very hot. At all other places, the sun's rays hit the Earth less directly.

▽ *This model shows how the sun's rays strike the Earth directly at the equator but are more spread out at the poles.*

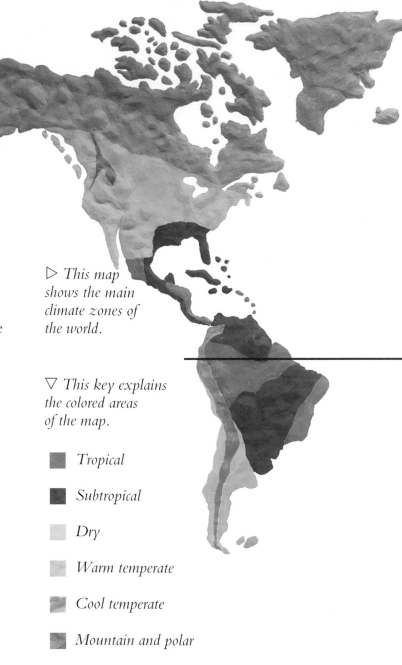

▷ *This map shows the main climate zones of the world.*

▽ *This key explains the colored areas of the map.*

- ■ *Tropical*
- ■ *Subtropical*
- ■ *Dry*
- ■ *Warm temperate*
- ■ *Cool temperate*
- ■ *Mountain and polar*

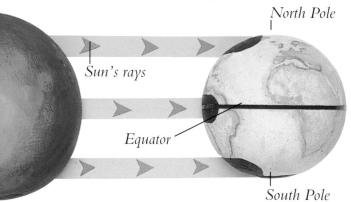

North Pole

Sun's rays

Equator

South Pole

### The cold poles
At the poles, the heat from the sun's rays is spread over a wide area, so the ground cannot warm up quickly. Here, the sun is always low in the sky, even at midday. The sun's rays also travel farther to reach the poles than to reach the equator. This means they lose more of their heating power.

### Mountains and coasts
Climate is also affected by how high a place is and how near the coast it is. The higher up a place is, the colder its climate will be. On mountains, it is possible to move through different climates as you climb from the base toward the snowy peaks. The climate of coastal places is affected by the temperature of sea water near the coast.

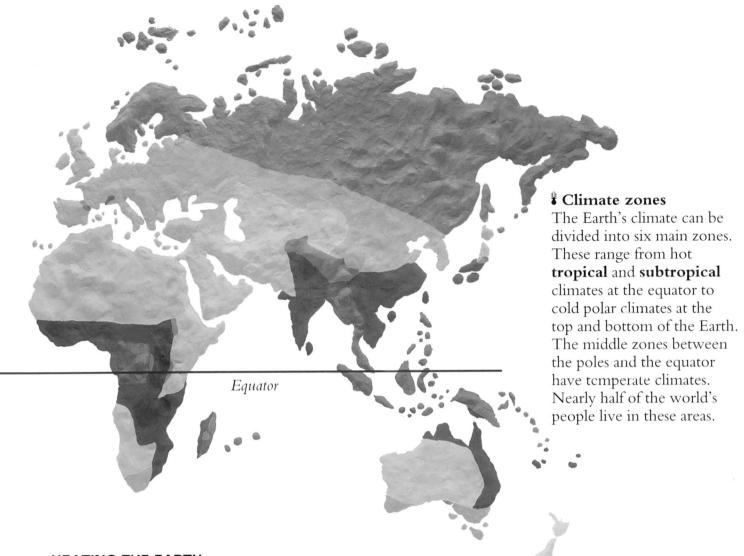

Equator

**Climate zones**
The Earth's climate can be divided into six main zones. These range from hot **tropical** and **subtropical** climates at the equator to cold polar climates at the top and bottom of the Earth. The middle zones between the poles and the equator have temperate climates. Nearly half of the world's people live in these areas.

## HEATING THE EARTH

**You will need:** a flashlight, a globe, cardboard, scissors, a large coin

**1** Place a coin on a piece of cardboard. Draw around it and cut out the circle.

**2** Shine a flashlight toward the globe through the hole in the cardboard.

 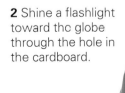

**3** Move the cardboard to direct a circle of light at the equator.

*Sunlight at the equator*

**4** Keep the flashlight still and move the cardboard up to shine light at the North Pole.

*Sunlight at the North Pole*

**Result:** The light makes a small, bright dot at the equator but is paler and more spread out at the poles.

# The seasons

In most parts of the world, the weather changes during the year. Each time of year with a particular kind of weather is called a **season**. Temperate areas have four seasons: spring, summer, autumn, and winter. Seasons happen because the Earth tilts at an angle as it goes around the sun.

## ᛞ Warm and cold

The Earth moves around the sun once a year. As it moves, places are tipped closer to the sun to make warm seasons and farther away from the sun to make cold seasons. Seasons are opposite in the Northern and Southern **hemispheres**.

▽ *This model shows how the Earth's journey around the sun produces the seasons.*

## ᛞ Changing seasons

**1.** From June to August, as shown below, the North Pole is nearer the sun than the South Pole. It is summer in the north and winter in the south.
**2.** From September to November, the North Pole starts to move away from the sun. This brings autumn in the north and spring in the south.
**3.** From December to February, the South Pole is nearer the sun, bringing summer in the south and winter in the north.
**4.** From March to May, the North Pole starts to move back toward the sun. It is then spring in the north and autumn in the south.

*Photographs on the next page show how this temperate region changes during the year.*

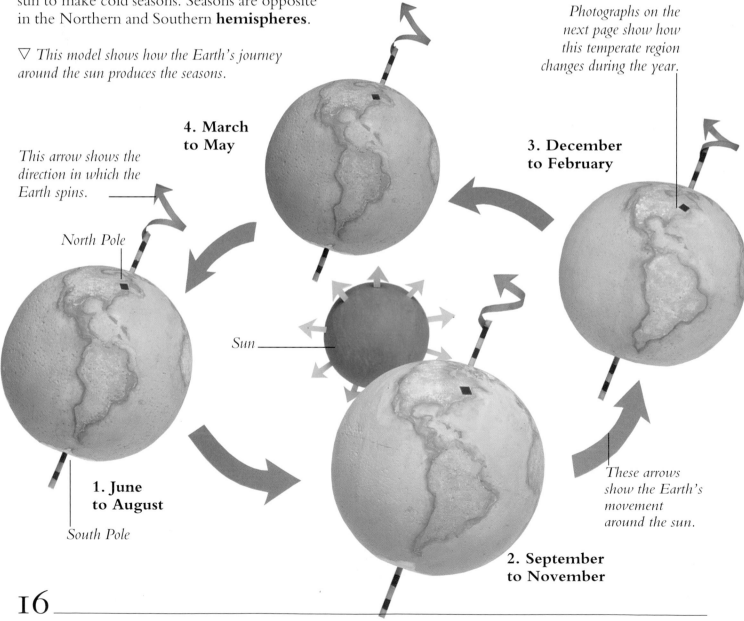

**4. March to May**

*This arrow shows the direction in which the Earth spins.*

*North Pole*

**3. December to February**

*Sun*

**1. June to August**

*South Pole*

*These arrows show the Earth's movement around the sun.*

**2. September to November**

16

▽ *These photographs show the seasons in Connecticut, marked as a red square on the model left.*

**1** *Summer*

**2** *Autumn*

**3** *Winter*

**4** *Spring*

### ☀ Polar seasons

Areas close to the poles are tilted nearer to the sun and farther away from the sun than other parts of the Earth. They have only two seasons — six months of summer followed by six months of winter. As the sun never sets in summer, these areas are sometimes called *lands of the midnight sun.*

### ☀ Tropical seasons

In tropical areas, near the equator, the sun's rays always hit the Earth directly, and the tilt of the Earth does not affect the weather much. It feels warm all year around. Although the temperature changes very little, some areas have wetter climates than others.

### ⌇ ⚑ Wet and dry seasons

In some tropical areas, especially in southern Asia, there are wet and dry seasons. These are caused by winds changing direction. In the summer monsoon season, the winds blow off the sea, bringing rain and floods. In the winter, they blow off the dry land, causing a hot dry season.

## WATCH THE SEASONS

**You will need:** a light bulb in a standing light socket, a rubber ball, pieces of ¼-inch (5-mm) and ½-inch (10-mm) dowel, two squares of soft wood, a drill, a bradawl, paints, glue

**1** Make a model Earth by painting a map of the world on the rubber ball. With an adult's help, use a bradawl to poke a hole into the North and South poles. Push the ¼-inch dowel through the Earth.

**2** With an adult's help, drill a ½-inch hole in the center of one square of wood. Push the ½-inch dowel into the square. Glue the Earth to the dowel so that it is tilted.

**3** Set up the Earth and sun—the light bulb—on a square of wood, as shown.

**4** Move the Earth around the sun to see how the position of the Earth changes during each season.

△ *Summer in north, winter in south*    △ *Winter in north, summer in south*

# Air temperature

The temperature of the air around you makes you feel hot or cold. Air temperature is affected by the climate and the season. It also depends on the time of day. Our days and nights happen because the Earth spins once every 24 hours. As it spins, the Earth receives different amounts of heat from the sun.

### 🌡️ ⚡ Thermometers

Thermometers are used to measure temperature. They are usually made with a narrow tube containing mercury or alcohol. These liquids expand when they warm up and contract when they cool down. So, as the temperature rises, the liquid moves up the tube.

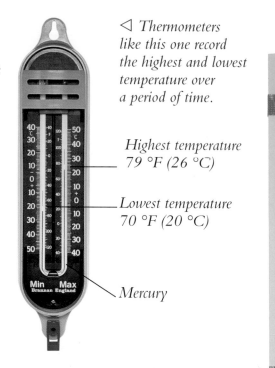

◁ *Thermometers like this one record the highest and lowest temperature over a period of time.*

*Highest temperature 79 °F (26 °C)*

*Lowest temperature 70 °F (20 °C)*

*Mercury*

## MAKE A WATER THERMOMETER

**You will need:** a glass bottle, colored water, a jug, a rubber stopper with a hole, rubber bands, modeling clay, a stick, scissors, cardboard, tape, a clear plastic tube, pens, an ice bucket and ice, glue

**1** Push the tube into the stopper and seal any gaps with modeling clay.

**2** Mark ½-inch (1-cm) divisions on a strip of cardboard and glue it to the stick. Fix the stick behind the bottle using rubber bands.

**3** Using the jug, fill the bottle with water up to the brim. Plug in the stopper so that the water rises about halfway up the tube. Tape the tube in place to complete your thermometer.

**4** Place the thermometer in an ice bucket. Fill the bucket with ice cubes.

**5** Water expands when it gets warmer and contracts when it gets colder. So the water level falls as it gets colder. Cut a small triangle out of the cardboard. After about 10 minutes, mark the water level with the triangle. This is zero on your scale.

**6** Take the thermometer out of the bucket and leave it outside in the shade. Wait for the water level to rise and count the divisions from zero. Make a note of this temperature.

**7** Let the thermometer sit a day and take the temperature once again. Has it gotten warmer or colder?

## ♨ Warming up

The sun's energy heats the land during the day. The air around the Earth takes time to warm up, so the warmest time of day is usually in the middle of the afternoon, not at noon when the Earth receives the most energy.

▷ *This model shows daytime in Australia. The sun's energy warms the land and sea during the day.*

*This arrow shows the direction in which the Earth spins.*

*Heat and light energy from the sun* —————

*Australia* —————

## ♨ Cooling down

Although there is no sunlight at night, the Earth continues to release the heat energy that it has absorbed during the day. If the sky is cloudy at night, the clouds trap some of the heat given off by the Earth, making the night warmer.

*Heat energy*

▷ *Now it is night-time in Australia. Heat energy is released from the Earth and it warms the air.*

*Australia*

## ♨ ⛰ Absorb or reflect?

Air temperatures near the Earth's surface depend on the temperature of the land beneath. Different surfaces absorb different amounts of heat. Snow reflects the sun's rays and absorbs very little heat, so the air above it stays cool. However, sand in the desert absorbs heat more easily, so the air above it becomes warmer.

## ♨ ⚑ Wind chill

Your body gives off heat, making a thin layer of warm air around you. But if the wind blows away this warm air faster than your body can replace it, you feel cold, even on a warm day. This is called wind chill.

### HEATING LAND —————

**You will need:**
sugar, sand, two small thermometers, two dishes, a lamp

**1** Fill one dish with sugar and the other with sand. Place a thermometer into each dish.

**2** Shine a lamp on the dishes. The thermometer readings will rise. Which rises faster?

**Result:** The sand warms up more quickly than the sugar. This shows that some materials can absorb heat more easily than others.

# Air pressure

The weight of the air pressing down on the Earth is called air pressure. Although you don't notice it, the air around you does not always weigh the same. When the air is heavy, it presses down hard and makes high pressure. This usually brings good weather. When the air is light, there is low pressure, which usually brings clouds and rain.

### ⚑ Warm and cool air
Air pressure varies from place to place. This is mainly because the air temperature is always changing. When air is warm, it is light and rises, leaving behind an area of low pressure (see below). When air is cool, it is heavy so it sinks, making an area of high pressure (see right).

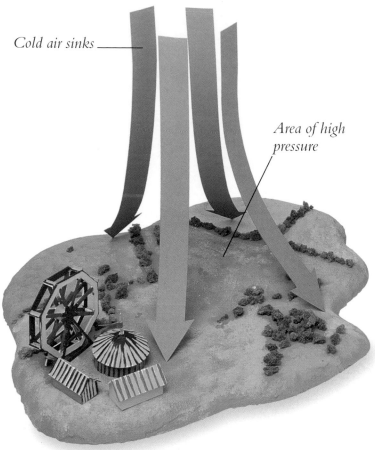

*Cold air sinks*

*Area of high pressure*

△ *This model shows cold air sinking, forming an area of high pressure.*

*Warm air rises*

*Area of low pressure*

△ *This model shows warm air rising, forming an area of low pressure.*

### ⚑ Pressure and rain
In areas of low pressure, rising warm air starts to cool down. When warm air gets cooler, the water vapor in the air **condenses** and becomes liquid water. This is why there is often rain in low pressure areas. In an area of high pressure, air sinks and starts to warm up. Warm air can hold a large amount of water vapor without making rain, so areas of high air pressure usually have clear, dry weather.

### ⚑ Pressure and the wind
The atmosphere is always working to balance areas of pressure. So air moves into areas of low pressure from surrounding areas of high pressure. This movement of air creates the wind. Strong winds happen if there is a big pressure difference between two areas.

20

### ⚑ Changing height

Air pressure decreases as you rise. This is because there is less air pushing down on the Earth's surface at higher levels, such as a mountaintop. Air pressure is measured with a **barometer**, in units called millibars.

◁ *High up in the mountains, the air pressure is low, so the air is light and contains little oxygen. Climbers may carry oxygen tanks with them to help them breathe.*

### ⚑ Feeling air pressure

If you travel by plane, you may feel a change in air pressure when your ears pop. The air pressure inside your ears is higher than in the plane and it pushes your eardrums out. As you swallow, the air pressure inside your ears goes down and your eardrums "pop" back into place.

## MAKE A BAROMETER

**You will need:** a glass bottle, a bowl, cardboard, colored water, glue, pens, scissors

**1** Fill the bottle with the colored water. Place the empty bowl over the bottle and carefully turn them upside down. Make sure the bottle is standing securely on its neck before letting go.

**2** Gently let some water out of the bottle until it is about two-thirds full.

**3** Draw very small divisions on a piece of cardboard and glue the cardboard on the bottle. Cut out a small triangle and glue it on the cardboard to mark the level of the water, as shown below left.

**4** Leave your barometer in the shade. Make a note of how much the water level rises or falls each day.

▽ *Here the barometer shows that the air pressure has dropped.*

**Result:** When there is high air pressure, the air pushes down on the water in the bowl. This makes the water level rise in the bottle. The higher the level, the higher the air pressure.

# Air on the move

Wind is moving air. Air always moves from an area of high pressure to an area of low pressure. Winds that blow around the world are called global winds. Smaller winds, that may happen near coasts or mountains, are called local winds.

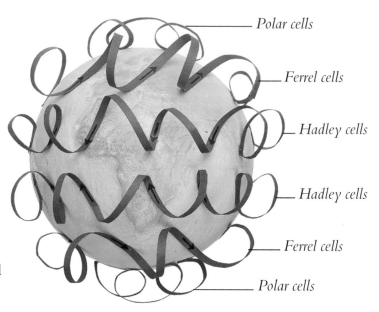

Polar cells

Ferrel cells

Hadley cells

Hadley cells

Ferrel cells

Polar cells

### 🏴 Global winds

In each hemisphere, there are three circles of wind, called cells, as shown right. At the equator, warm air rises and begins to move toward the poles. The air cools, sinks, and moves back toward the equator, forming Hadley cells. At the poles, cold air sinks. As the air moves away from the poles, it warms up and rises, forming polar cells. The middle cells, called Ferrel cells, are pushed around by the moving air to either side of them.

△ *This model shows the huge patterns of global winds that snake around the world.*

▷ *This model shows the directions of the world's prevailing winds.*

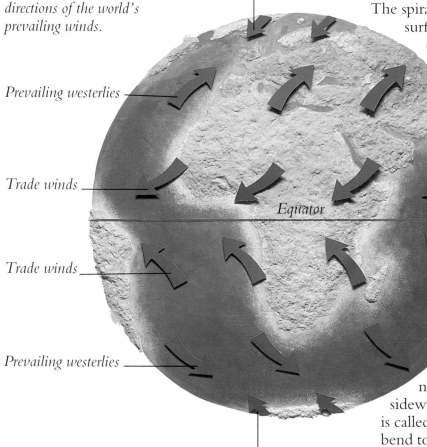

Polar easterlies

Prevailing westerlies

Trade winds

Equator

Trade winds

Prevailing westerlies

Polar easterlies

### 🏴 Prevailing winds

The spiraling cells create winds on the Earth's surface that blow mainly from one direction. These are called prevailing winds. Prevailing winds that blow toward the equator are called trade winds because they were used by sailing ships carrying goods to trade around the world. In temperate areas, there are winds from the west called prevailing westerlies. In polar areas, there are winds from the east called polar easterlies.

### 🏴 Why do winds spiral?

If the Earth did not spin, all the winds would blow directly from north to south or south to north. Instead, winds are dragged sideways by the spin of the Earth. This is called the **Coriolis effect**. It makes winds bend to the right in the Northern Hemisphere and to the left in the Southern Hemisphere.

## MAKE A WEATHER VANE

**You will need:** Some ½-inch and ¼-inch (12-mm and 5-mm) dowel, cardboard, tape, a push pin, a compass, a bead, a drill, scissors, colored pens

**1** With an adult's help, drill two ¼-inch holes, at right angles, through a long piece of ½-inch dowel. Push two dowels through these holes to make a cross.

**2** For the vane, ask an adult to help you drill a small hole through the halfway point of a ¼-inch dowel.

**3** Stick the pin through the ¼-inch dowel and bead, as shown right, and push it into the top of the larger dowel.

**4** Cut out pieces of cardboard and color them, as shown. Tape them to the ends of the dowels.

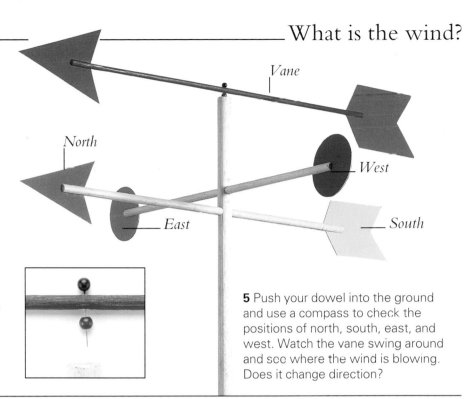

*Vane*

*North*

*West*

*East*

*South*

**5** Push your dowel into the ground and use a compass to check the positions of north, south, east, and west. Watch the vane swing around and see where the wind is blowing. Does it change direction?

### 🏴 Sea breezes

Local winds that happen at the coasts are called land and sea breezes. During the day, the land heats up faster than the sea, so warm air rises off the land and a cool breeze is sucked in from the sea. This breeze replaces the rising warm air.

▷ *Sea breezes occur during the day when land is warmer than the sea.*

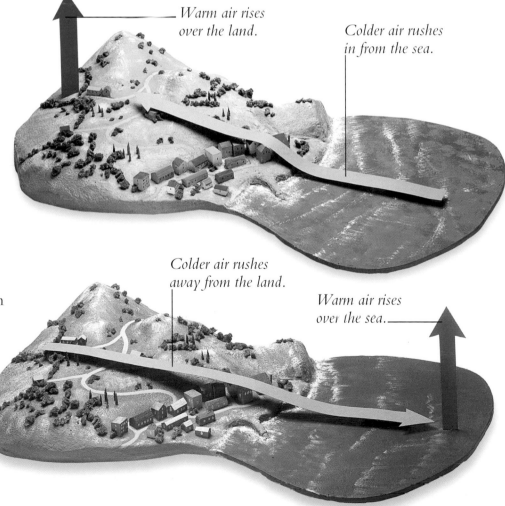

*Warm air rises over the land.*

*Colder air rushes in from the sea.*

*Colder air rushes away from the land.*

*Warm air rises over the sea.*

### 🏴 Land breezes

During the night, the land cools down faster than the sea, so warm air rises over the sea and cool air sinks over the land. Cold air from the land is drawn out to the sea to replace the rising warm air. This creates a breeze blowing from the land to the sea.

▷ *Land breezes occur at night when the sea is warmer than the land.*

# Wind speed

The speed of the wind depends on the difference in air pressure between two areas. A slight difference produces a gentle breeze. A huge difference can cause a violent wind, such as a gale or a hurricane. Wind speed is measured with an instrument called an **anemometer**.

🏴 **Breeze to hurricane**

In 1805, Francis Beaufort, an admiral in the British Navy, invented a scale to measure the speed of the wind. It described the effect of the wind on ships and waves. This scale, called the Beaufort scale, has been adapted for use on land. The scale goes from zero (calm) to 17 (hurricane force) and shows how different wind speeds affect people and their surroundings. On the models below, the 13 commonly used stages of the Beaufort scale have been grouped into six stages.

**The Beaufort scale**

**Force 0-2**
These are light winds that blow up to 7 miles per hour (11 kilometers per hour). Smoke rises or drifts gently and leaves rustle.

**Force 3-4**
These are gentle breezes that blow at 8-18 mph (12-28 kph). Small branches move and flags flap. Dust and paper blow about.

**Force 7-8**
These are gales that blow at 32-46 mph (50-74 kph). Twigs break off trees and whole trees may sway. It is hard to walk against the wind.

**Force 9-10**
These are strong gales that blow at 47-63 mph (75-102 kph). Branches break off trees and there may be slight damage to houses.

## ▰ ✍ Mapping the wind

On weather maps (see page 40), symbols tell us about the wind. A long pointer shows wind direction, and lines on the pointer show different wind speeds, based on the Beaufort scale.

0  1  2  3  4  5  6  7  8  9  10  11  12

△ *These symbols are used on maps to show the different forces of the Beaufort scale.*

### Force 5-6

These are strong breezes that blow at 19-31 mph (29-49 kph). Small trees sway and there are small waves on lakes. It is also hard to use an umbrella.

### Force 11-12

These are violent storms, such as hurricanes, that blow above 64 mph (103 kph). There may be widespread damage to buildings and the landscape.

## MAKE AN ANEMOMETER

**You will need:** three pieces of corrugated cardboard [(two 5 inch (12 cm) x 8 inch (20 cm), one 3 ½ inch (9 cm) x 3 inch (7 cm)], colored paper, two 4 inch (10 cm) x 8 inch (20 cm) wooden blocks, thumb tacks, a wooden skewer, a straw, a drawing compass, a matchstick, a utility knife, glue, a pen

**1** Glue colored paper to one side of each piece of cardboard. With the skewer, poke a hole through a corner of each large piece of cardboard 1 inch (2 cm) from each edge, as shown above.

**2** Use a compass to draw two arcs on each of these pieces, one 3 inches (7 cm) from the hole and the other 2 ¾ inches (6.5 cm) away. With an adult's help, cut out these curved slots with a utility knife, as shown above. Mark equal divisions along these slots.

**3** Glue the box together. Glue the straw to the long edge of the small piece of cardboard and push a matchstick into the short edge, as shown above.

**4** Place the cardboard in position so that you can push the skewer through the holes and the straw, so that the cardboard hangs in place. Secure with pins, making sure that the matchstick pokes through one slot. Glue a paper triangle to the end of the matchstick.

**5** Now point the flap towards the wind to measure its strength. Try measuring wind speed in different places outside. Does it vary?

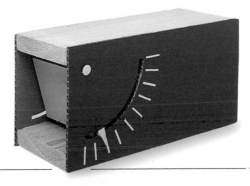

# The water cycle

Water moves up into the sky and back down to the ground in a never-ending cycle called the water cycle. To do this, water has to change from liquid water on the ground into an invisible gas called water vapor. This process is called **evaporation**. Up in the sky, water vapor changes back into liquid water again. This process is called condensation.

▽ *On this model of the water cycle, blue arrows show the movement of water. Green arrows show how clouds move, often carrying rain toward the land.*

### Clouding over

It is the sun's heat that makes liquid water on the Earth evaporate and mix with the air. As the air moves higher up in the sky, it cools down because temperatures are cooler higher up. Cool air cannot hold as much water vapor as warm air, so some of this water vapor condenses into droplets of water or freezes into tiny ice crystals. These gather together to make clouds.

### Rainfall

When clouds cool down, rain may fall and collect in rivers, lakes, and oceans. Water also soaks into the soil and is taken in by plants and animals. When the sun heats the ground, the water evaporates and the cycle begins again. The amount of water on Earth always stays the same as it is continually moving through this cycle.

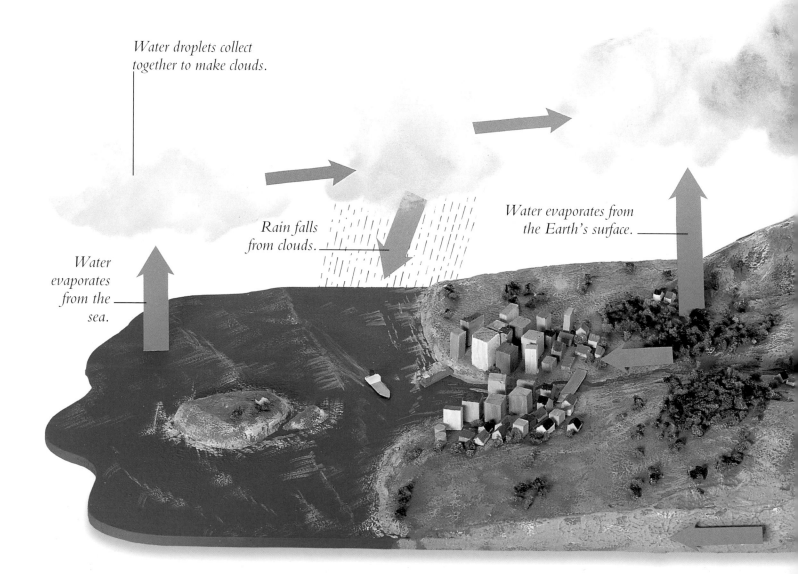

*Water droplets collect together to make clouds.*

*Rain falls from clouds.*

*Water evaporates from the Earth's surface.*

*Water evaporates from the sea.*

## RECORD EVAPORATION

**You will need:** a white saucer, a crayon, colored water

**1** Pour colored water into a saucer. With a crayon, draw a line on the saucer along the surface of the water.

**2** Now leave your saucer in a warm place for a day.

**Result:** A lot of the water evaporates and the water level drops. Leave your saucer in a cool place. Does the level fall farther in warm or cold conditions?

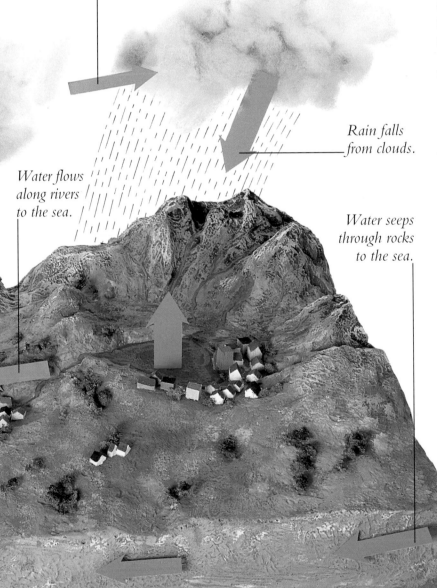

*Wind blows air from place to place, so water evaporating in one place falls as rain in another.*

*Rain falls from clouds.*

*Water flows along rivers to the sea.*

*Water seeps through rocks to the sea.*

## Water and heat

When water evaporates, it takes in heat, and when it condenses, it gives off heat. So as water in the water cycle is moved around the world, heat also moves. This changes the weather, because heat makes the air move and the movement of air makes the weather happen.

## WATCH CONDENSATION

**1** Breathe onto the surface of a cold mirror and watch what happens.

**Result:** When your warm breath meets the cold mirror, water vapor in your breath condenses to form small water droplets on the surface of the mirror.

# Clouds

On average, half the sky all over the world is covered with clouds at any one time. Clouds appear when moist air rises and cools down. As the water vapor in the air cools, it condenses on specks of dust in the air, forming tiny droplets of water or ice. These droplets are so small and light that they float in the air like steam coming from a kettle.

▷ *This model shows how warm air rises and cools, and how water vapor condenses to form a cloud.*

### 🌧 Air and humidity

There are three main reasons why air rises. Firstly, the ground may heat the air and make it rise. Secondly, air rises along weather **fronts** (see pages 32–33) and finally, air may be forced up over mountains. A cloud's height depends on how much moisture, or **humidity**, is in the air. Clouds are lower when there is more humidity.

*2 Warm air cools down.*

*3 Water vapor condenses to form clouds.*

*1 Warm ground heats the air, making it rise.*

## MEASURE HUMIDITY

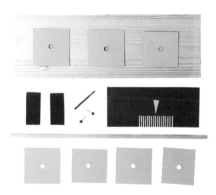

**You will need:** a 4 inch x 12 inch (10 cm x 30 cm) wood base, two small wooden rectangles, cardboard, two push pins, a thin dowel, a matchstick, blotting paper, glue, a pencil

**1** Glue the two small blocks, 1 inch (2 cm) apart at one end of the base. Glue the matchstick to the end of the dowel.

**2** Make a scale by drawing equal divisions on a piece of cardboard and adding a pointer, as shown left. Fold one end of the scale and glue it to the base so that it stands upright.

**3** Push a pin into each side of the dowel, a third of the way up. Slide blotting paper squares on to the end.

**4** Balance the dowel on the blocks and move the squares until the matchstick lines up with the pointer.

**5** Leave your humidity tester outside in a slatted box (see page 38) and see if, day by day, the pointer rises or falls.

**Result:** in humid conditions, the paper absorbs water and becomes heavier. This causes the needle to rise. In dry conditions, the needle falls. Are clouds lower in humid or dry weather?

▽ *Here the level of humidity has risen.*

## 🌧 Cloud spotting

There are three main cloud shapes: fluffy, cotton-wool clouds called cumulus (meaning heap); flat blankets of clouds called stratus (meaning layer); and thin, wispy clouds called cirrus (meaning curl of hair). Cirrus clouds are found only at high altitudes. Cumulus and stratus clouds can be found at different altitudes. Clouds that are a mixture of cumulus and stratus clouds are called stratocumulus.

## 🌧 All shapes and sizes

The name of a cloud can describe its shape, height, and whether it contains rain. The word 'nimbus' in the name cumulonimbus means it is a rain or snow cloud. The word 'alto–' in the cloud names altostratus and altocumulus means the clouds are at a height between 6,000 and 20,000 feet (2,000 and 5,000 meters). In the cloud name cirrostratus, the word 'cirro–' means the cloud is above 20,000 feet (5,000 meters).

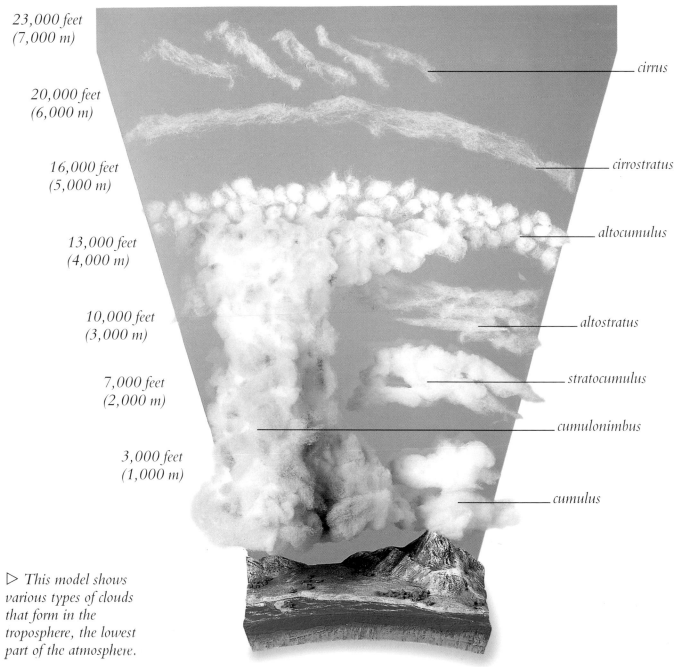

23,000 feet
(7,000 m)

20,000 feet
(6,000 m)

16,000 feet
(5,000 m)

13,000 feet
(4,000 m)

10,000 feet
(3,000 m)

7,000 feet
(2,000 m)

3,000 feet
(1,000 m)

cirrus

cirrostratus

altocumulus

altostratus

stratocumulus

cumulonimbus

cumulus

▷ *This model shows various types of clouds that form in the troposphere, the lowest part of the atmosphere.*

# Rain, snow, and hail

Water falling from clouds is called precipitation. Water may fall as rain, snow, or hail, depending on the air temperature and the type of clouds in the sky. When there are clouds in the sky, precipitation doesn't always happen. It only happens when clouds become too heavy to carry all the moisture in them. The amount of precipitation in one area can be measured using a rain gauge.

△ *Rainbows happen when sunlight shines through millions of raindrops in such a way that light is split into all its colors.*

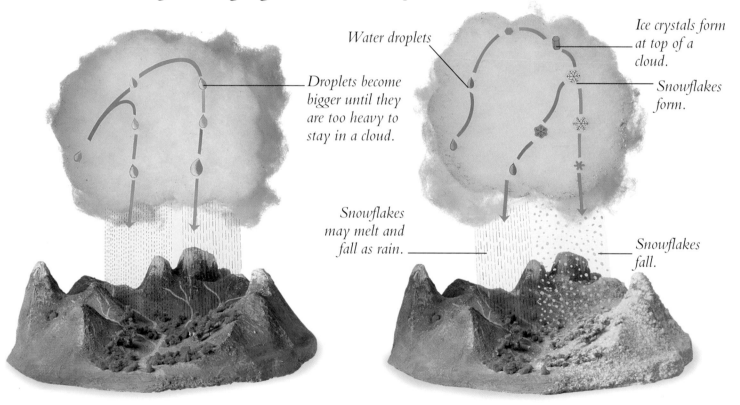

*Water droplets*

*Droplets become bigger until they are too heavy to stay in a cloud.*

*Ice crystals form at top of a cloud.*

*Snowflakes form.*

*Snowflakes may melt and fall as rain.*

*Snowflakes fall.*

△ *This cloud produces rain.*

△ *This cloud produces rain and snow.*

## Making rain
One way in which rain forms is by water droplets joining together. This happens in low, warm clouds. Inside these clouds, water droplets are blown about by the air. As the droplets bump into each other, they join together to make larger droplets. Eventually, they become too heavy to hang in the air and fall as rain. The longer the droplets stay in the cloud, the heavier the rain will be.

## Ice crystals and snowflakes
In cool areas, clouds are made up of ice crystals at the top and water droplets lower down. The ice crystals attract water droplets, which freeze on them. Many crystals stick together to make snowflakes which, when they are too heavy to hang in the air, fall out of the cloud. If the temperature rises above freezing (32 °F or 0 °C) as the snowflakes fall, they may melt and fall as rain.

## MAKE A RAIN GAUGE

**You will need:** a plastic bottle, colored tape, scissors, a ruler, a pencil

**1** Cut the top off the bottle where the curved top meets the straight sides.

**2** Turn the top upside down and fit it into the base. This will stop the water inside the bottle from evaporating.

**3** Cut thin strips of tape and use them to mark ¼-inch (5-mm) divisions along the straight part of the base. Pour water up to the lowest division.

**4** Place your rain gauge outside, away from any buildings and trees. Record the amount of rain each day for a week, and remember to pour out the water down to the lowest division each morning.

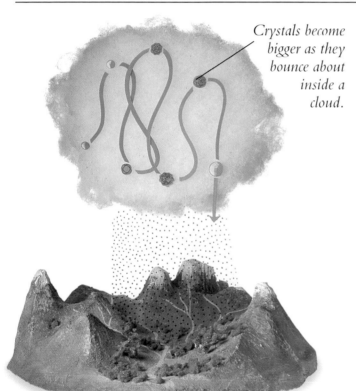

*Crystals become bigger as they bounce about inside a cloud.*

△ *This cloud produces hail.*

### 🌧 Balls of ice

Hail forms in thunderclouds when ice crystals are tossed up and down by strong currents of air. As the ice crystals are tossed up to the cold top of the cloud, the crystals attract water which freezes on them. Eventually, the crystals become too heavy to stay in the cloud and they fall to the ground as hail. Hailstones are often as big as marbles and may be bigger than tennis balls!

### 🌧 Mapping precipitation

Forecasters need to know about the precipitation in a particular place, to help them to predict the weather. They look at the various symbols that are marked on weather maps (see page 40).

▽ *These symbols are often used on weather maps to tell us about precipitation.*

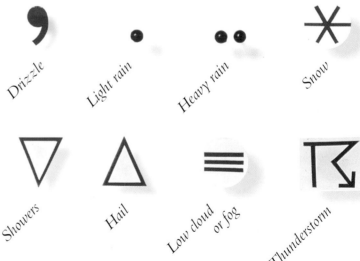

Drizzle  Light rain  Heavy rain  Snow

Showers  Hail  Low cloud or fog  Thunderstorm

### 🌧 Blizzards

Blizzards are snowstorms with very strong winds, low temperatures, and fine powdery snow. Wind-blown snow makes it impossible to see more than a short distance. Sometimes, people may experience *white-outs* in blizzards, when they cannot see at all and lose all sense of direction. The wind in a blizzard may also pile the snow into huge drifts, burying cars and sides of houses.

# Air masses and fronts

Air masses are enormous bodies of warm or cold air that lie above areas of land and sea. Air from these air masses is blown from one place to another by global winds. When a cold air mass meets a warm air mass, they mix very slowly along a line called a front. The weather near a front is unsettled and changeable, with clouds, rain, and storms.

▷ *This model shows the movement of a warm front being followed by a cold front. The fronts are moving from left to right.*

### ⚑ Why do air masses form?
In some parts of the world, such as the oceans or the middle of large **continents**, the Earth's surface is similar over huge areas. The huge air masses over these areas are hot or cold, and wet or dry, depending on the land or sea underneath. These air masses are named after the places where they form. They can be hot (tropical) or cold (polar) and may form over continents (continental) or the sea (maritime).

### ⚑ Air masses meet
The lines where air masses meet are called fronts because they are like the front lines of a battle zone. One air mass tries to make the other move out of the way. There are three main types of fronts: cold fronts, warm fronts, and occluded fronts.

### ⚑ Cold fronts
In a cold front, a cold air mass slides under a warm air mass, pushing the warm air upwards. Clouds and rain occur as the warm air rises and cools. A cold front usually follows a few hours after a warm front.

### ⚑ Occluded fronts
An occluded front happens when a cold front catches up with a warm front and they merge together. Occluded fronts often bring heavy rain.

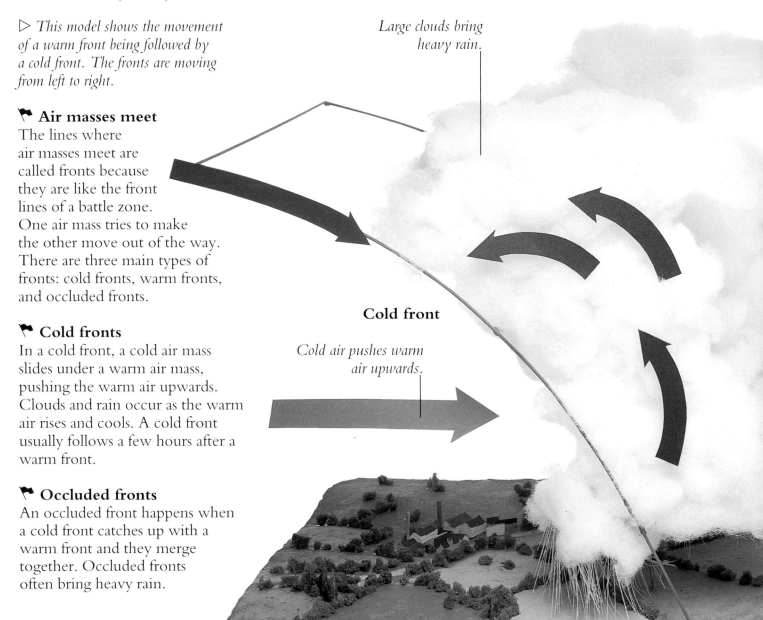

*Large clouds bring heavy rain.*

**Cold front**

*Cold air pushes warm air upwards.*

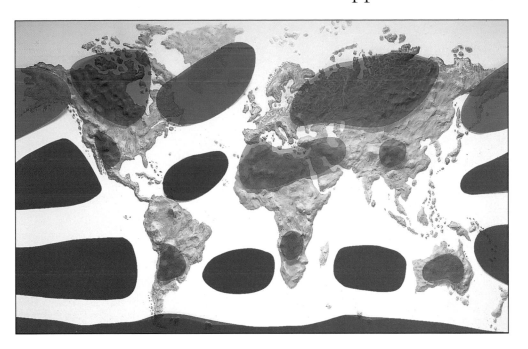

◁ *The main air masses around the world are shown on this map. The key below explains the colors shown on the map.*

**Continental polar:**
*Cold and dry*

**Continental tropical:**
*Hot and dry*

**Maritime polar:**
*Cold and wet*

**Maritime tropical:**
*Warm and wet*

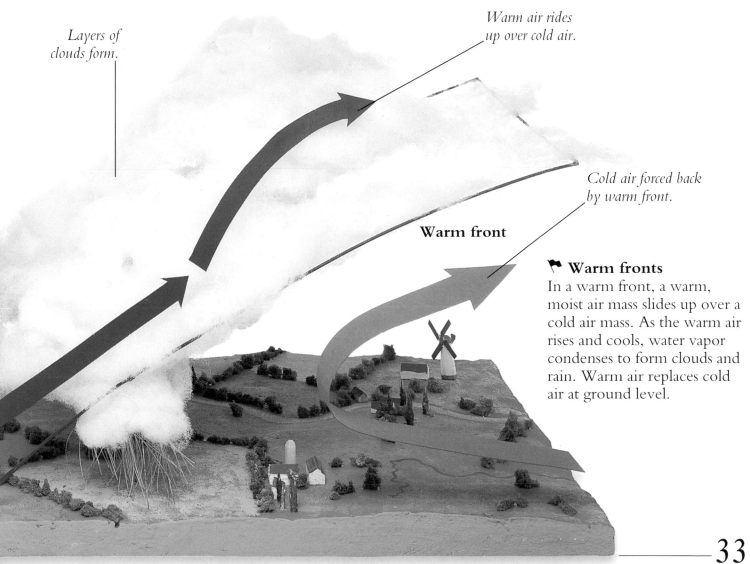

*Layers of clouds form.*

*Warm air rides up over cold air.*

*Cold air forced back by warm front.*

**Warm front**

⚑ **Warm fronts**
In a warm front, a warm, moist air mass slides up over a cold air mass. As the warm air rises and cools, water vapor condenses to form clouds and rain. Warm air replaces cold air at ground level.

# Storms

Storms are periods of bad weather that happen when huge clouds form and strong winds blow. Storms develop in different ways around the world. In temperate areas, they usually happen along fronts, where warm and cold air meet. In hot, tropical areas, storms develop because of large amounts of heat and moisture in the air.

△ *These impressive lightning flashes have enough energy to light up huge sections of the night sky.*

### ☔ Start of the storm

As many as 50,000 storms happen every day throughout the world. They begin when warm, moist air rises into cold air. Huge clouds build up as water vapor in the air condenses. The tops of these clouds may reach the very top of the troposphere, where the temperature is well below freezing point.

### ☔ Building up energy

Inside a storm cloud, currents of air move up and down very quickly. This makes droplets and ice crystals in the cloud rub against each other, giving them an electrical charge that can be either positive or negative. Both types of charge hold energy. After a while, positive charges build up toward the top of the cloud and negative charges build up toward the bottom.

### ☔ Flashes of lightning

As the positive and negative charges in a cloud become stronger, they move toward each other. Eventually, their built-up energy is released as a flash of lightning between the two charges. The air and the ground also carry charges, so lightning can jump from clouds to the air or to the ground. Lightning heats up the air, which then expands at great speed to make the sound we call thunder.

## MAKE LIGHTNING

**You will need:** a metal tray, a plastic sheet or cotton cloth, modeling clay, a screwdriver, a rubber glove, tape

**1** Tape the sheet or cloth to a surface.

**2** Adhere a ball of clay to the tray. Put on the glove and use the clay as a handle to rub the tray against the sheet or cloth for about two minutes.

**3** Make sure the room is dark. With an adult's help, hold the screwdriver in your gloved hand and bring it close to the edge of the tray. Do not touch the tray with your hands.

**Result:** The tray builds up a charge similar to that in a storm cloud. As the energy is released to the screwdriver, you should hear a crackle and see a spark of lightning.

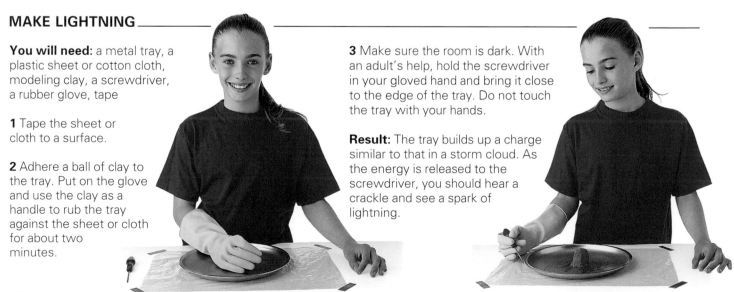

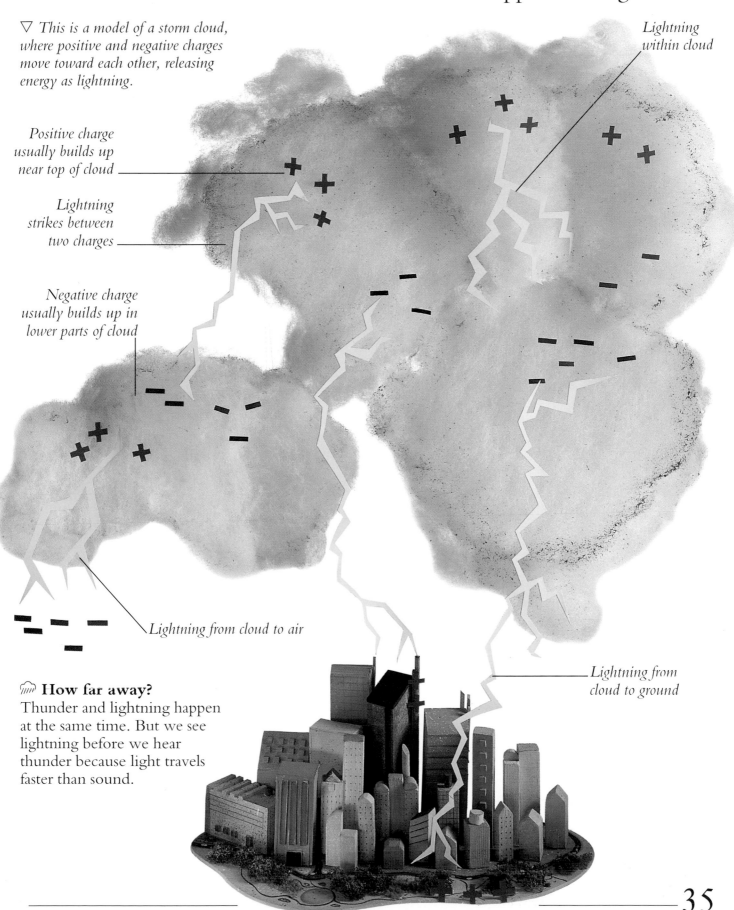

▽ *This is a model of a storm cloud, where positive and negative charges move toward each other, releasing energy as lightning.*

Lightning within cloud

Positive charge usually builds up near top of cloud ———

Lightning strikes between two charges ———

Negative charge usually builds up in lower parts of cloud

Lightning from cloud to air

Lightning from cloud to ground

〰 **How far away?**
Thunder and lightning happen at the same time. But we see lightning before we hear thunder because light travels faster than sound.

# Tornadoes and hurricanes

The most violent storms of all are tornadoes and hurricanes. Tornadoes happen over land, while hurricanes develop over warm, tropical seas. Tornadoes are spinning funnels of cloud that suck up everything in their paths. A full–blown hurricane consists of torrential rain and whirling winds. Hurricanes are much larger than tornadoes. They can be 300 miles (480 km) wide, while tornadoes are no more than about 1½ miles (2.4 km) wide.

△ *The winds at the center of this tornado can reach more than 200 mph (320 kph).*

### 🏳 🌦 Spiraling tornadoes

Water flows quickly down a drain because it speeds up as it spirals inwards. A similar whirling motion, known as a vortex, takes place within a tornado. Tornadoes happen where warm and cold air currents meet and are always accompanied by severe thunderstorms. They are most common in the Midwest.

### 🏳 🌦 In a spin

Air in a tornado cloud is set spinning into a vortex by winds in the top part of the cloud. As the winds get faster, the cloud becomes shaped like a funnel. At the bottom of the cloud, more air is sucked in and the funnel reaches down to the ground. Tornadoes are strong enough to lift animals, people, and even train cars.

## MAKE A VORTEX

**You will need:** a jug, two plastic bottles, a 20-inch (50-cm) piece of thick dowel (slightly thicker than neck of bottle), a piece of thin dowel, strong glue, scissors, modeling clay, tape

**1** Stick some tape around one of the bottles, about 2 inches (5 cm) above its base. Cut off the base, using the tape as a guide.

**2** Glue the necks of the bottles together. Then use tape and modeling clay to seal the joint.

**3** Stand the bottles on a table and push the thick dowel into the neck, as shown left. Use the jug to fill the top bottle halfway with water.

**4** With the thin dowel, stir the water around in one direction only. Now pull out the thick dowel and see what happens.

**Result:** The water in the top bottle spins around like the air in a tornado.

## The life of a hurricane

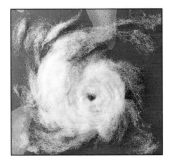

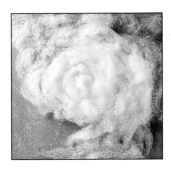

**1** A thunderstorm develops over the ocean.

**2** Huge clouds start to form a swirl.

**3** An "eye" forms. The storm is at its strongest.

**4** The hurricane passes over land and dies out.

### 🏴 🌧 Hurricane winds

Hurricanes form over warm, tropical seas near the equator. In a hurricane, strong winds circle around a calm area of low pressure called the eye. As the hurricane moves, it sucks in lots of warm, moist air toward the eye. The area just around the eye has the heaviest rain and strongest gales.

▽ *In this model of a hurricane, a section has been cut away so you can see how the winds spin.*

### 🏴 🌧 Moving faster

Near the center of the hurricane, air spirals upwards and water vapor condenses to form huge cumulonimbus clouds. The condensation gives out heat, making the air rise even faster, sucking in more winds. When a hurricane hits land, its supply of moisture is cut off and it starts to die down.

### 🏴 🌧 Tracking a hurricane

Hurricanes do not move in straight lines, but they do follow similar routes. They can be tracked by satellites so people living in a hurricane's path can be warned of any approaching danger.

*Air sinks slowly in eye of the storm.*

*Warm air spirals upwards around eye.*

*Rain falls from the thick clouds.*

*Direction of wind*

*Rings of thick cumulonimbus clouds*

*Hurricane moves in this direction.*

# Recording the weather

Weather forecasts predict how the weather might change. They are based on thousands of measurements of temperature, rainfall, and air pressure. With your own weather station, you can begin to make forecasts of your own.

### ◤ Setting up

You can use the measuring instruments you have made following directions that appeared earlier in this book, or you can buy items, such as a thermometer or a barometer, from a store. You may also want to use a box called a Stevenson screen to keep your instruments out of direct sunlight.

### ◤ Stevenson screens

A Stevenson screen is a raised box with slatted sides that keeps out sunlight but allows air to flow in. Its white surface reflects heat away from the instruments. If you don't have a Stevenson screen, put your instruments on a table and place a slatted wooden box over them.

▷ *Put your weather station in an open space, away from trees and buildings.*

### ◤ Keeping a weather record

To make weather forecasts, you need to take measurements at the same time every day, so you can compare them easily. Make a weather chart to record your measurements, as shown on the opposite page. Draw a row of columns, one for each weather feature you are measuring, such as wind speed or rainfall. Write the days when you take measurements down one side of the chart.

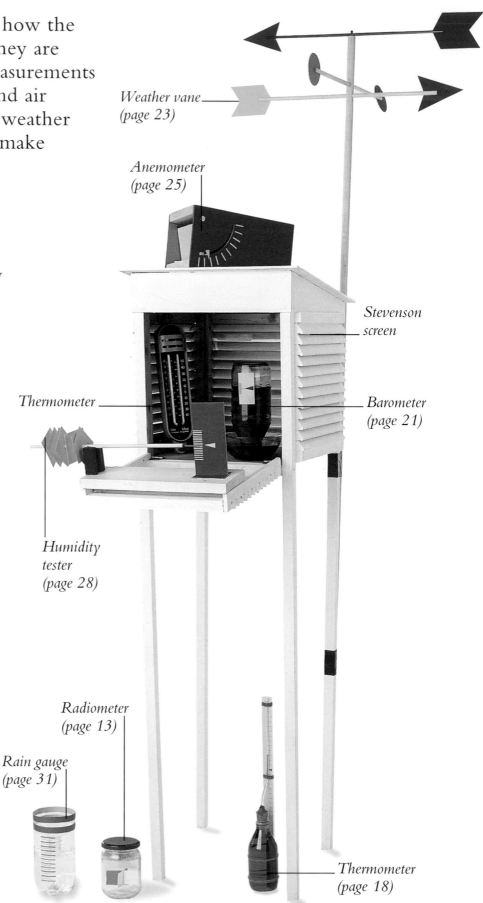

*Weather vane
(page 23)*

*Anemometer
(page 25)*

*Stevenson
screen*

*Thermometer*

*Barometer
(page 21)*

*Humidity
tester
(page 28)*

*Radiometer
(page 13)*

*Rain gauge
(page 31)*

*Thermometer
(page 18)*

## MEASURE CLOUD COVER

**You will need:** a mirror, narrow colored tape, a pen, paper

**1** With tape, divide a mirror into a grid of eight equal rectangles, as shown right.

**2** Lay the mirror on the ground outside and look at the clouds reflected in the mirror.

**3** The amount of sky covered by cloud is measured in oktas. Each okta means that one-eighth of the sky is covered by cloud. Add up the squares or parts of squares with cloud in them. This is the cloud cover in oktas.

▽ These symbols are used on maps to show different amounts of cloud cover.

○ No clouds

◐ $^4/_8$ (four oktas)

⊖ $^1/_8$ (one okta)

⊖ $^5/_8$ (five oktas)

◔ $^2/_8$ (two oktas)

◕ $^6/_8$ (six oktas)

◔ $^3/_8$ (three oktas)

◑ $^7/_8$ (seven oktas)

● Sky covered by cloud

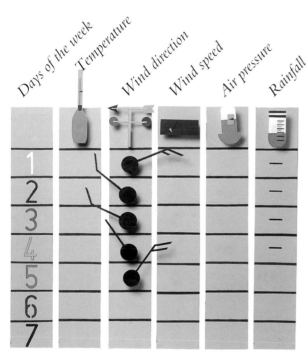

Days of the week | Temperature | Wind direction | Wind speed | Air pressure | Rainfall

▷ Use a notebook to record your measurements.

◁ This chart shows daily weather recordings. You can add columns for cloud cover and humidity.

### ✎ Looking at your data

After a while, you will be able to see the pattern of the weather in your area and start using your records to make predictions. Changes in air pressure are particularly important. When the air pressure is low, is the weather wet or dry? Which direction does the wind usually blow from? If the wind direction changes, does the weather change? Are there strong winds or light winds?

# Weather maps

When meteorologists have collected their weather information, or data, they display it on maps called **synoptic charts**. These charts show weather patterns over a large area. Forecasters use these charts to see how the weather is changing and to make predictions. Some synoptic charts have small groups of numbers and symbols, called station circles, to show the measurements taken at each weather station.

▷ *This synoptic chart gives us information about air pressure and weather fronts over Western Europe.*

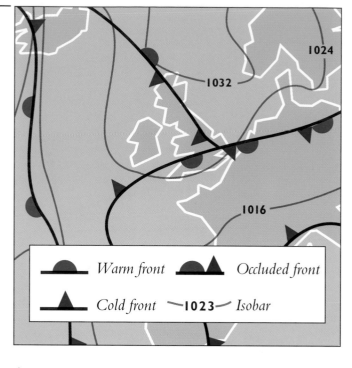

1024
1032
1016

| | Warm front | | Occluded front |
| Cold front | 1023 | Isobar |

## ✍ Isobars and fronts
On a synoptic chart, lines called **isobars** join places with the same air pressure. Lines with spikes and bumps show weather fronts. A cold front has spikes and a warm front has bumps. An occluded front, a mixture of these two fronts, is shown by a line with both spikes and bumps.

## ✍ Other maps
Synoptic charts are not the only kind of weather map. Television forecasters use simpler maps with picture symbols to show features, such as rainfall or sunshine. Maps are sometimes drawn over satellite pictures to show cloud cover and the movement of winds over a large area, such as a continent.

## ✍ Station circles
A station circle is a group of symbols that gives information about the weather at a weather station. Look at the example to see how this information is shown. When station circles are positioned on a map, the round symbol for cloud cover marks the actual position of the weather station.

▽ *This station circle shows the reading for a weather station.*

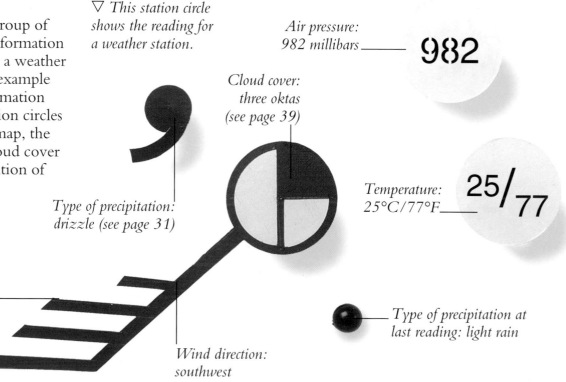

*Air pressure: 982 millibars* —— **982**

*Cloud cover: three oktas (see page 39)*

*Temperature: 25°C/77°F* —— **25/77**

*Type of precipitation: drizzle (see page 31)*

*Type of precipitation at last reading: light rain*

*Wind speed: strong gale (see page 25)*

*Wind direction: southwest*

## MAKE A WEATHER MAP

**Before you start:** Ask three friends who live near you to set up a weather station near their homes. You will need to make sure that the divisions on each instrument are the same at each weather station.

**You will need:** a map of your local area, pins, paper, and pens

**1** Use the map of your area to mark the main features, such as rivers and towns, on a piece of paper. Mark the position of each weather station on your map.

**2** Arrange with your friends to collect information from the weather stations at a particular time on a particular day.

**3** After collecting all the information, use paper shapes and pins to represent it on the map. Use the symbols shown on earlier pages in this book.

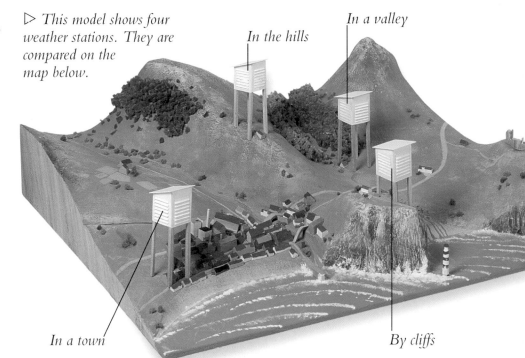

▷ *This model shows four weather stations. They are compared on the map below.*

*In the hills*

*In a valley*

*In a town*

*By cliffs*

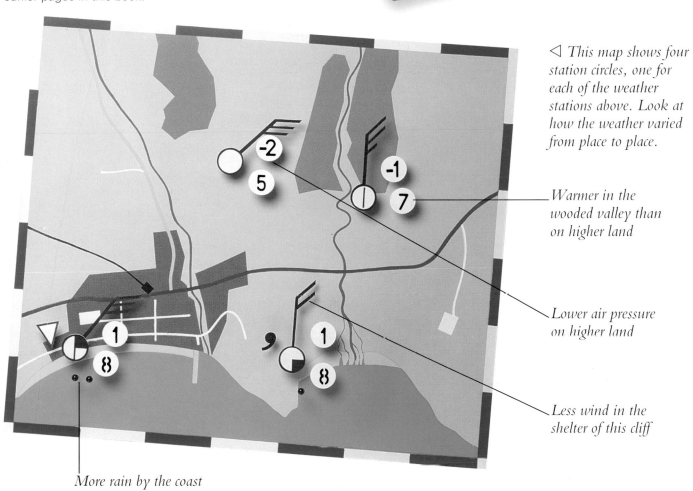

◁ *This map shows four station circles, one for each of the weather stations above. Look at how the weather varied from place to place.*

*Warmer in the wooded valley than on higher land*

*Lower air pressure on higher land*

*Less wind in the shelter of this cliff*

*More rain by the coast*

# Weather forecasting

Many years ago, people predicted the weather by watching changes in nature, such as the behavior of plants and animals. Pine cones, for example, open out in dry weather to let their seeds blow away. The cones close up when rain is on the way. Today, meteorologists collect data from weather stations at sea, on land, in the air, and out in space to predict the weather.

### 🔖 Gathering data

There are about 10,000 land weather stations around the world. At these stations, people make observations at least every three hours. At sea, ships and weather buoys take measurements and may send information to a central office via satellite. Above the Earth, aircraft and weather balloons carry instruments to measure temperature, wind speed, and air pressure.

*Satellite*

▽ *This model shows the main ways that forecasters gather information about the weather.*

*Aircraft*

*Weather station*

*Weather balloon*

*Ship at sea*

△ *This satellite picture shows a hurricane moving over Florida toward the Gulf of Mexico.*

### Weather satellites

Satellite pictures give details of the weather that cannot be seen from the ground. They show how fast clouds and fronts are moving and in what direction. There are two main types of satellites used by forecasters. Polar orbiting satellites are between 500 and 900 miles (800 and 1,400 km) above the Earth. They move around the Earth making observations over the whole planet. Geostationary satellites stay above one point on the Earth, about 22,300 miles (35,890 km) out in space. They collect information about just one area.

*Weather buoy*

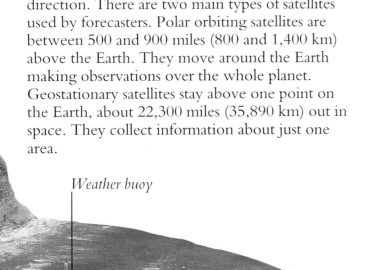

### Computer power

All the weather measurements for one area are fed into a huge computer at a central weather office. The computer uses the data to work out how the weather may change in a short period of time – say 30 minutes. It then repeats this process many times until it arrives at a forecast for up to one week or 10 days ahead. During its calculations, the computer uses past records so it can take into account how weather in that area usually changes.

△ *Forecasters put together colored maps on computers to make it easier to identify weather patterns.*

### People and computers

Although computers are very powerful, it is the meteorologists who ultimately forecast the weather. They look at computer predictions and satellite images and use their knowledge of local conditions to make forecasts. Their forecasts are presented on television, radio, and in newspapers.

### How accurate are the forecasts?

Even with the help of computers, accurate forecasts can only be made up to about a week ahead. This is because the atmosphere is always changing all over the world, and what happens in one area affects what happens everywhere else. Accurate forecasts of individual showers can only be made an hour or so ahead of time.

# Weather and the land

Weather and climate have an important effect on the shape of the land. Wind, rain, ice, and heat all help to break up the rocks in a process called **weathering**. Bits of weathered rock are picked up and carried away by rivers, **glaciers,** and the wind. This is called **erosion**. Eventually, the rocks are worn down and deposited in new places.

▷ *The wind and the rain have carved these desert rocks into remarkable shapes.*

## ⛰ Floods and landslides

When a lot of rain falls in a short time, the soil cannot soak up the water fast enough. Water collects on the surface and rivers burst their banks, causing floods. A flood can make large masses of soil and rock slide quickly downhill in mudflows or landslides. If a landslide happens on a steep slope, it can bury roads, buildings, and villages.

▷ *This model shows a landslide caused by heavy rain.*

## ⛰ Erosion in deserts

In some deserts, many rocky landscapes were shaped by water when the climate was wetter. Now, in dry climates, wind, heat, and gases from the atmosphere weather the rocks. Winds can easily blow away pieces of weathered rock because there are few plants to slow down the wind and hold the dry, light soil in place.

## ⛰ 🌧 Acid rain

Sometimes, rain contains chemicals that damage buildings and forests. This is called acid rain. It forms when polluting gases from cars and factories mix with water in the atmosphere. Acid rain has killed entire fish populations in a number of lakes. High concentrations can also harm forests and soil.

*Landslides often create huge steps along hillsides.*

## ⛰ Cracking ice

In cold, wet places, such as mountains in temperate areas, water seeps into cracks in rocks and freezes at night. Ice takes up more space than water, so it pushes against the rock, forcing the cracks wider apart. During the day, when it is warmer, the ice thaws and becomes water, only to freeze again if it gets colder. Eventually, bits of the rock may fall off. This causes piles of broken rocks called scree to gather at the foot of rocky cliffs.

▽ *This model shows a mountain slope that has been shaped by the action of water freezing and thawing.*

*Mountain tops shatter into jagged peaks.*

*Scree*

*Cracks in rock face*

*Large rocks roll to the foot of the slope.*

## TEST ICE POWER

**You will need:** an egg, a bowl, modeling clay, colored water, a freezer, a wooden skewer

**1** Tap the top of the egg gently on a table and pick away the shell to make a ½-inch (1-cm) hole.

**2** To empty the egg, poke a skewer into the hole and burst the yolk. Then shake the yolk and white out into a small bowl.

**3** Fill the egg up to the brim with colored water. Plug up the hole with a small piece of modeling clay. Now stand the egg in the freezer for about three hours.

**Result:** When water freezes, it expands with such force that the egg cracks. This is the same power that forces rocks to break off cliffs as they freeze and thaw.

# The changing climate

The Earth's climate has been changing for millions of years. We don't have much evidence of these changes, but we do know that the Earth has had many freezing **ice ages**. The last one ended about 10,000 years ago. Now, the Earth's climate may be warming up because people are polluting the atmosphere.

△ By looking at tree rings, you can investigate the climate of many years ago. Narrow rings mean a year of cool, dry weather. Wide rings mean warm, wet weather.

### ⛰ Looking at the past

People have kept accurate weather records for about 150 years. To look further back in time, geographers use natural records, such as **fossils** or tree rings. By looking at fossils, geographers can study the creatures that lived long ago. They work out the type of climate needed for the creatures to survive. In temperate areas, the size of growth rings in tree trunks also tells us about past climate.

### ⛰ Why does climate change?

Climate is affected by the Earth moving in space. If, for example, the Earth's path around the sun changes, our climate may warm up or cool down. Natural activity on the Earth's surface also affects our climate. Volcanoes sometimes form clouds of ash that stop some of the sun's energy reaching the Earth. This makes parts of the Earth cool down.

### 🌡 The greenhouse effect

Gases that occur naturally in the atmosphere, such as carbon dioxide and water vapor, trap heat and reflect it back to the Earth's surface. This is known as the greenhouse effect, because the gases act like the glass of a greenhouse – letting in sunlight but stopping heat from escaping. Cars, ships, factories, and burning forests release more of these gases into the atmosphere. This changes the natural balance of heat in the atmosphere and may be making the Earth warm up.

▽ *This model shows the many ways in which we pollute the atmosphere with greenhouse gases.*

*Sunlight heating up the Earth*

*Aircraft trails contain water vapor that reflects heat.*

*Fumes from ships*

## ‡ Global warming

At the moment, temperatures around the world seem to be rising by a part of a degree each year. This is called global warming. If temperatures keep rising, the middle of large continents, such as North America, may dry out during the next century, making it difficult to grow crops on the land. Water expands when it warms up, so sea levels may rise. This could flood coastal areas. Some countries are trying to reduce the amount of pollution so that global warming slows down.

△ *This volcano in Alaska sends clouds of ash into the sky, blotting out the sun for long periods of time.*

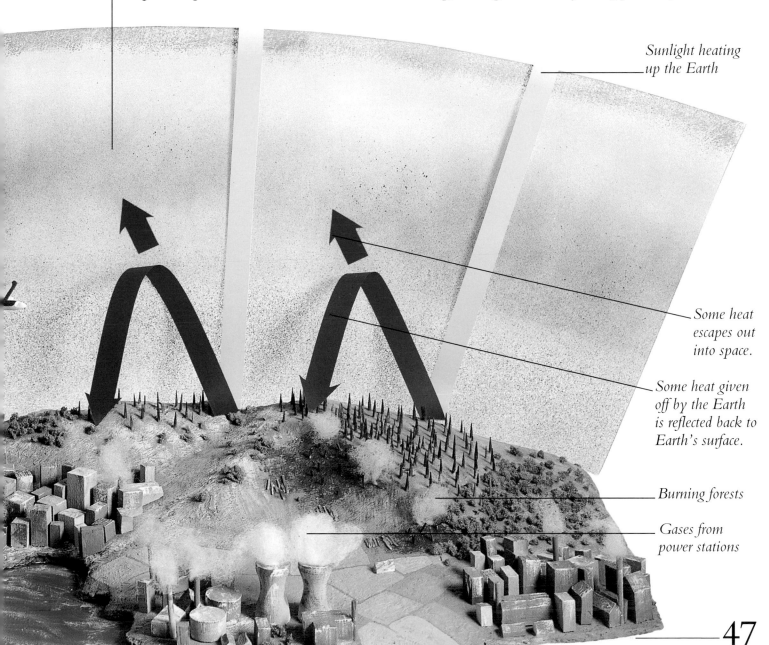

*Greenhouse gases in lower atmosphere trap Earth's heat.*

Sunlight heating up the Earth

Some heat escapes out into space.

Some heat given off by the Earth is reflected back to Earth's surface.

Burning forests

Gases from power stations

47

# Oceans

# Studying oceans

Geography helps us to understand what happened to the Earth in the past, how it is changing now, and what might happen to it in the future. Understanding oceans is an important part of geography because oceans cover over 70 percent of the Earth's surface. People who study oceans are called **oceanographers**. They try to understand how seawater moves around the world, how the oceans were formed, and what effects oceans have on coastlines.

### Exploring oceans

Studying the oceans is rather like studying outer space. Both places are remote and mysterious, and scientists need special equipment to survive there and to carry out experiments. The deepest parts of the Earth's surface lie beneath the oceans. We have only recently begun to explore these hidden places.

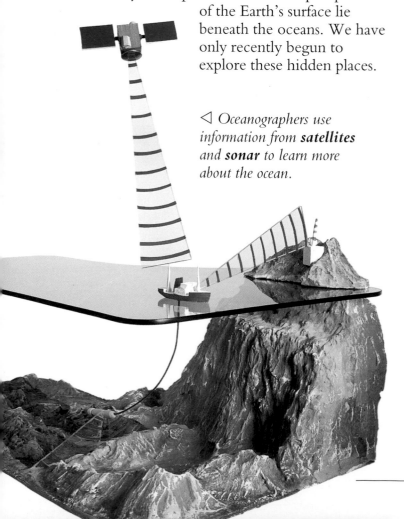

◁ *Oceanographers use information from **satellites** and **sonar** to learn more about the ocean.*

△ *Over millions of years, the Pacific Ocean has pounded the east coast of Australia and created these cliffs.*

### Life in the oceans

Life on Earth probably evolved in the oceans about 3½ million years ago. Today, an amazing variety of creatures lives in the sea, from the largest animal that ever lived, the blue whale, to microscopic organisms called **plankton**. The deepest parts of the ocean are more than 36,000 feet (11,000 m) below sea level, so it is difficult to study them. Oceanographers are still finding new forms of life in the oceans. Recently, they discovered giant tubeworms around underwater volcanoes.

### Oceans and people

Almost everyone depends on oceans to some degree. Oceans have an important effect on the world's weather. They are also an important source of food, and people use them for travel, trade, and sports. We also take oil and minerals from beneath the seabed and use the energy of the tides to create power. The way that we treat the oceans today will affect the Earth, the oceans, and the creatures that live in them in the future.

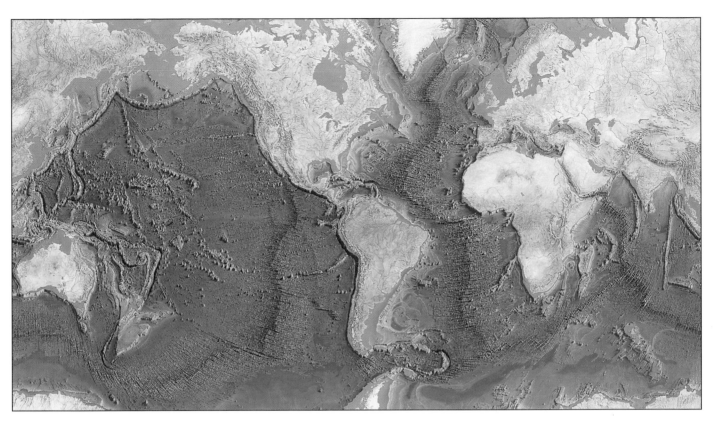

△ *There are mountain ranges under the sea, as well as on land. The long ridges running between the continents are mountain ranges many thousands of miles long.*

### Oceanography today

Studying the oceans brings together different subjects. Some oceanographers study the land at the edge of oceans and the rocks under the seabed. This area of study is called **geology**. Others concentrate on seawater itself—how hot or cold it is, how much salt it contains, and how **ocean currents** move around the globe. Marine biologists study sea creatures and try to understand how they interact with their environment.

Throughout this book, we have used symbols to show where information relates to particular topics. The symbols are:

| | | | |
|---|---|---|---|
| geology | 🏔 | tides, waves, currents | 🌀 |
| temperature | 🌡 | seawater | 〰 |
| marine life | 🐟 | energy | ⛽ |
| human | 👫 | mapmaking | 📖 |

### Make it Work!

The Make it Work! way of looking at geography is to carry out experiments that will help you understand how geography shapes the world we live in. By studying the models, you will discover more about the oceans.

▽ *Some experiments in this book will help you understand how water in the oceans moves around the world.*

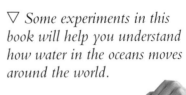

# The world's oceans

There are three main oceans on Earth: the Pacific, Atlantic, and Indian. There are also two smaller ones: the Arctic and the Southern, or Antarctic. They flow into each other, so you could say that there is really only one vast ocean. Each ocean contains smaller areas of water called seas, bays, or gulfs, which are all partly enclosed by land.

## ☦ Temperature of the oceans

The temperature in the oceans and seas varies from one place to another, and from the surface to the ocean floor. The waters of the Arctic and Southern oceans are icy cold. However, tropical seas, such as the Caribbean, are much warmer. All the water in the oceans constantly flows around the Earth. Cold water, which is heavier than warm water, sinks at the North and South poles, then flows along the ocean floor toward the equator. At the equator, the water becomes warmer and rises. Then it flows back to the poles.

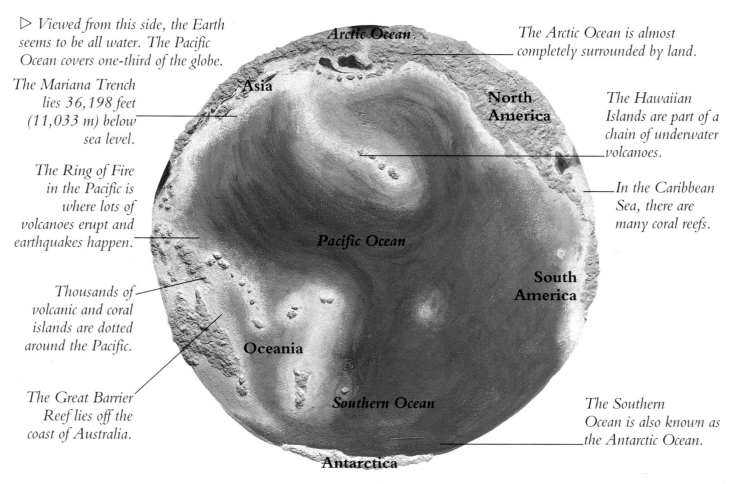

▷ *Viewed from this side, the Earth seems to be all water. The Pacific Ocean covers one-third of the globe.*

*The Mariana Trench lies 36,198 feet (11,033 m) below sea level.*

*The Ring of Fire in the Pacific is where lots of volcanoes erupt and earthquakes happen.*

*Thousands of volcanic and coral islands are dotted around the Pacific.*

*The Great Barrier Reef lies off the coast of Australia.*

*The Arctic Ocean is almost completely surrounded by land.*

*The Hawaiian Islands are part of a chain of underwater volcanoes.*

*In the Caribbean Sea, there are many coral reefs.*

*The Southern Ocean is also known as the Antarctic Ocean.*

Arctic Ocean

Asia

North America

Pacific Ocean

South America

Oceania

Southern Ocean

Antarctica

## The Pacific Ocean

This is the largest ocean in the world. It is also the deepest, with an average depth of 12,900 feet (3,940 m). There are many deep valleys, or **ocean trenches**, around the edge of the Pacific, along the east coast of Asia and the west coast of South America. The Mariana Trench, off the coast of the Philippines, is the deepest place on Earth.

## The Southern Ocean

This ocean is located around the continent of Antarctica. The waters of the Pacific, Atlantic, and Indian oceans all mingle in the Southern Ocean, just above Antarctica. More than half of the Southern Ocean freezes over in winter. In summer, some of the ice melts, breaks up, and drifts out to nearby oceans as huge icebergs.

*◁ Two percent of all the water in the Arctic Ocean is frozen in huge icebergs like this.*

## The Arctic Ocean

The Arctic is the world's smallest and shallowest ocean. It is unusual compared to other oceans because it is almost completely surrounded by land—Asia, North America, Greenland, and Europe. It is also covered by a thick layer of ice for six months of the year. Beneath every ocean are huge dips in the Earth's crust called **ocean basins**. The Arctic Ocean has four basins.

*▷ This view of the world shows the Atlantic and Indian oceans, with the Arctic Ocean at the top and the Southern Ocean at the bottom.*

*Cold water flows south into the Atlantic Ocean.*

*The Mediterranean Sea flows into the Atlantic.*

*The Atlantic, Indian, and Pacific oceans meet around the Southern Ocean.*

*The Arctic Ocean is, on average, about 3,905 feet (1,205 m) deep.*

*The Red Sea is about 220 miles (350 km) at its widest point, and it is widening slightly every year.*

*The Java Trench is 23,376 feet (7,125 m) deep.*

*The Indian Ocean is the world's third largest ocean.*

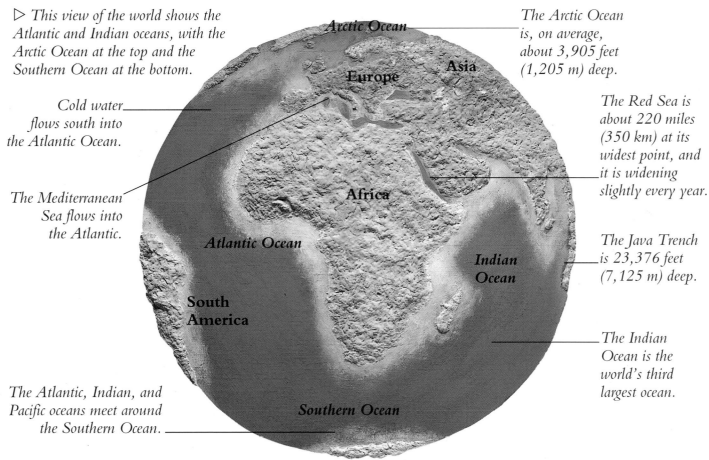

Arctic Ocean
Europe
Asia
Africa
Atlantic Ocean
Indian Ocean
South America
Southern Ocean

## The Atlantic Ocean

This is the world's second largest ocean. It covers about one-fifth of the Earth's surface. The Atlantic has the greatest number of shallow seas. These include the Gulf of Mexico, the Caribbean Sea, and the Mediterranean Sea. The Atlantic is also less salty than other oceans because a lot of fresh water flows into it from rivers on the surrounding continents.

## The Indian Ocean

Along the floor of the ocean runs a long chain of underwater volcanic mountains called a **mid-ocean ridge**. The ridge in the Indian Ocean connects with those in the Pacific and the Atlantic (see picture page 51). The deepest point in the Indian Ocean is the Java Trench. There are also many **coral reefs**, including the Maldive and Seychelle islands, dotted around this ocean.

# Birth of an ocean

When the Earth formed some 4½ billion years ago, there were no oceans. Most scientists say that rain collected in dips on the Earth's surface to make oceans. Over millions of years, the shape of the land and the ocean basins has changed. They are still changing because heat from inside the Earth makes the outer crust move.

### Rocks on the move

The Earth is made up of three main layers: the crust, the **mantle**, and the core. The crust is the outermost layer of the Earth. The mantle is made up of hot rocks. As the rocks melt and combine with gases, they form **magma** and rise up near the crust. When magma erupts through cracks in the crust, either on land or underwater, it creates volcanoes. When it cools, it turns into solid rock. Where magma rises through a mid-ocean ridge, it makes new ocean floor.

### How the oceans formed

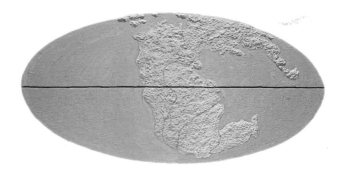

**1** About 200 million years ago, there was one main land mass surrounded by one vast ocean.

### Ridges and trenches

As magma erupts through the ocean floor, it is forced upward, forming mountain ranges, long mid-ocean ridges. Over millions of years, the old ocean floor is pushed slowly outward, away from the ridge. When part of the ocean floor is pushed into the edge of another, one edge gets forced down under the other, sometimes creating a deep trench.

▽ *This model shows how hot rocks in the Earth's mantle force their way through the crust, creating new ocean floor.*

*Magma rises through a mid-ocean ridge, cools, and makes new seabed.*

underwater volcano

Earth's crust

*New ocean floor pushes old ocean floor slowly over millions of years.*

**2** By 200 million years ago, the land had begun to separate and water filled in the spaces.

**3** By about 60 million years ago, the positions of the land and oceans were similar to those of today.

*volcanoes erupting on land*

*a continent*

*Magma also rises underneath the continents.*

*An ocean trench forms where ocean floor is forced under the edge of another piece of land.*

## 🏔 Moving continents

The Earth's crust is broken up into about 30 pieces, like the cracked shell of a hard-boiled egg. These pieces are called plates. The plates drift on top of the Earth's mantle, moving a few centimeters a year. Over millions of years, these small movements can tear continents apart, leaving huge ocean basins. Where the **Earth's plates** meet, mid-ocean ridges and trenches form.

## 🏔 Plate movement

Plates may move apart, move together, or slide past each other. At ocean ridges, plates move apart, whereas at trenches they push together. Often, volcanoes erupt and earthquakes happen along the edges of plates, where the Earth's crust is unstable, or weak.

### MAGMA EXPERIMENT

Ask an adult to help you.

**You will need:** bowl, cooking oil, red food coloring, sterno candle, stand, matches, eyedropper

**1** Pour the oil into the bowl. Place the bowl on the stand, with the candle underneath. Now light the candle and warm the oil.

**2** Using the eyedropper, squeeze a few drops of food coloring onto the bottom of the bowl, above the flame.

**Result:** The food coloring warms and rises. When it reaches the surface, it spreads out, cools, and sinks back down. This is similar to how magma behaves.

# The ocean floor

The landscape under the oceans is even more varied than on dry land. Mountain ranges are longer, valleys are wider and deeper, and slopes are steeper. One reason for this is that rivers wash enormous amounts of **sediment** into the sea. Another is that magma constantly erupts along mid-ocean ridges, forming new ocean floor.

## The continental shelf

From the edges of the continents, the land slopes gently downward. The sea is not very deep here, perhaps only about 430 feet (130 m) deep. This shallow ledge of ocean floor is called the **continental shelf**.

## The continental slope and rise

At the edge of the continental shelf, a steep slope drops about 2¼ miles (3.6 km) to the ocean floor. This is the continental slope. In many places, sediment is washed down to the bottom of the slope, forming a ridge called a continental rise.

## The deep-ocean floor

Between 14,000 and 18,000 feet (4,300 and 5,500 m) below the surface of the sea are vast, flat areas of ocean floor called **abyssal plains**. These plains are covered in thick layers of sediment. In some places, deep-ocean currents flowing across abyssal plains form large mud waves in the sediment.

▽ *If you could drain all the water out of an ocean, you would see some of these features. This model shows a section of ocean floor thousands of miles across.*

*edge of a continent*

*continental shelf*

*continental rise*

*abyssal plain*

*continental slope*

*thick sediment on the ocean floor*

*mid-ocean ridge*

◁ *This image was made using sonar signals (see pages 88 and 89). It shows part of the mid-ocean ridge in the Pacific. The deepest parts are dark blue, and the shallowest are pink.*

### 🐚 Seamounts

Sometimes, magma forces its way through an abyssal plain. When this happens, underwater volcanic mountains called **seamounts** form. Some seamounts are flat-topped. These are called **guyots**. Their tops are probably worn away by waves over thousands of years. Most seamounts are found in groups or chains. When they rise above the sea surface, seamounts become islands. The Hawaiian Islands are a chain of seamounts.

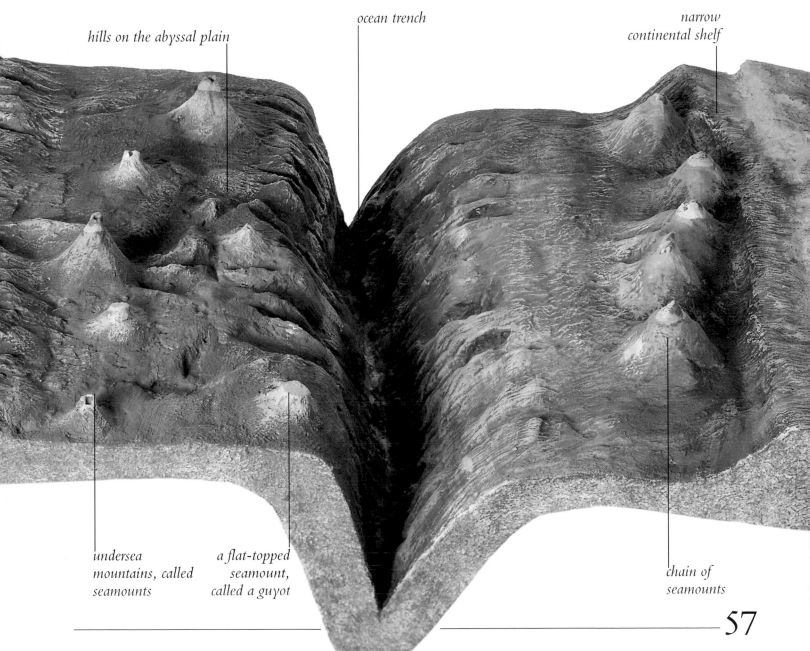

hills on the abyssal plain

ocean trench

narrow continental shelf

undersea mountains, called seamounts

a flat-topped seamount, called a guyot

chain of seamounts

# Seawater

Seawater undergoes many changes from the surface to the ocean floor. Surface water is warm because it is penetrated by sunlight, whereas water near the seabed is cold and dark. The weight of all the water pressing down on the seabed also means that the pressure is much greater there. Seawater contains dissolved minerals and salt, but the amounts vary from ocean to ocean.

▷ *This model shows the depth to which people can dive using special equipment.*

### ≋ ♦♦ Water pressure

As you go deeper under the sea, more water presses down on you. At the surface there is hardly any pressure. But people cannot dive to the bottom of the ocean because the pressure would crush them as easily as you can crush an egg on land. Instead, people descend in small submarines called **submersibles**. These vehicles are made to withstand the enormous pressure of the watery depths.

### ≋ Why is the sea blue?

Although water is colorless, the sea often appears blue-green. This is because blue and green light (two of the colors you see in a rainbow) reach deeper below the surface than the other colors. Tiny particles in water also scatter blue and green light, spreading it through the water. The sea also reflects the color of the sky, making it seem blue or gray, depending on the weather.

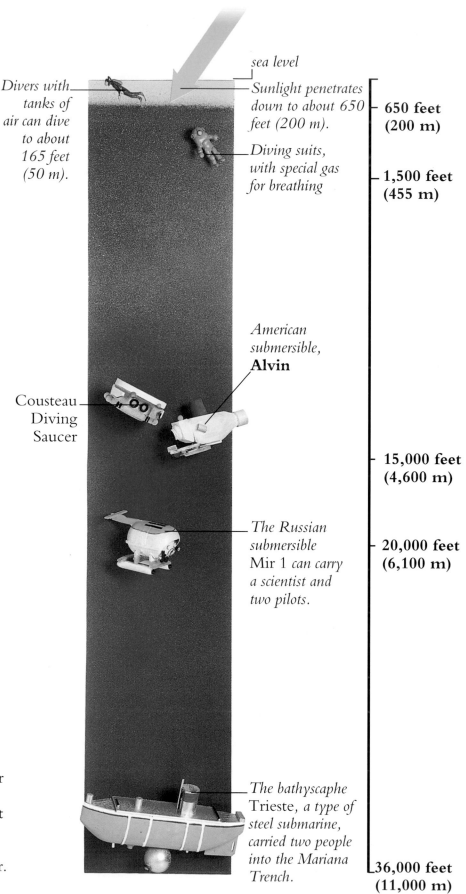

*Divers with tanks of air can dive to about 165 feet (50 m).*

*sea level*

*Sunlight penetrates down to about 650 feet (200 m).*

*Diving suits, with special gas for breathing*

*American submersible,* **Alvin**

Cousteau Diving Saucer

*The Russian submersible* Mir 1 *can carry a scientist and two pilots.*

*The bathyscaphe* Trieste, *a type of steel submarine, carried two people into the Mariana Trench.*

**650 feet (200 m)**

**1,500 feet (455 m)**

**15,000 feet (4,600 m)**

**20,000 feet (6,100 m)**

**36,000 feet (11,000 m)**

## WATER PRESSURE TEST

**You will need:** long plastic tube, balloon, tank or bucket of water

**1** Attach the balloon to the tube.

**2** Blow up the balloon. You should find that the balloon is easy to blow up.

**3** Now place the balloon in the tank, near the surface of the water. Blow up your balloon again.

**Result:** It should be more difficult than in step 2 because of the pressure of the water pressing on the balloon.

**4** Place the balloon at the bottom of the tank and blow up the balloon again.

**Result:** It will be a lot more difficult this time, because the pressure at the bottom of the tank is greater than at the surface.

### Water temperature

The temperature of the surface of an ocean varies from one part to another. In warm, shallow waters, it may reach 86 °F (30 °C). In the cold polar oceans, temperatures drop to 28 °F (-2 °C). Surface temperatures also change with the seasons, but the temperature at the ocean floor tends to stay the same all year, at about 34 to 39 °F (1 to 4 °C).

### Why is the sea salty?

Some of the salts and minerals in seawater are washed off the land by rivers. Other salts come from gases released by volcanoes on land. The gases mix with rain, which falls on the sea. Still more salts escape from cracks in the ocean floor.

### Why does seawater rise and fall?

All these salts and minerals in seawater make it dense. Density means how heavy something is for its size. Water that is dense and cold, sinks. Water that is less dense and warm, rises. This means that the density of seawater affects the way water moves through the oceans (see pages 62 and 63). To measure water density, we use a hydrometer.

## MAKE A HYDROMETER

**You will need:** glass, straw, modeling clay, tape, water, salt

**1** Attach a blob of clay to one end of the straw. Your straw is a hydrometer, and with it you will be able to test the density of water.

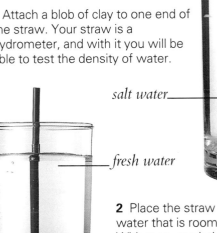

*salt water*

*fresh water*

**2** Place the straw in a glass of water that is room temperature. With tape, mark the straw where it meets the surface of the water. Now add salt to the water.

**Result:** The straw floats higher because salt water is denser than fresh water. The salt in the water pushes up against the straw and helps hold it nearer the surface.

# Frozen oceans

During winter, huge areas of the Arctic and Southern oceans freeze. In the Southern Ocean, the ice spreads out across the sea from the edge of the ice-covered continent of Antarctica. In the Arctic, however, there is no land, only a thick sheet of ice on top of the ocean. In summer, half of the ice melts, and the waters warm up slightly. Then, the Arctic becomes a rich feeding ground for whales and other wildlife.

△ *In the summer, humpback whales migrate to the Arctic Ocean to feed in the plankton-rich waters.*

## ⚇ Why the Arctic Ocean is frozen

For six months of the year, the Arctic Ocean is plunged into freezing darkness. This is because the North Pole is tilted away from the sun. The waters of the Arctic receive less heat than waters at, or near, the equator because they are not heated directly by the sun. The dazzling ice sheet also reflects back 95 percent of the heat from the sun, which helps keep temperatures extremely cold.

▷ *This model shows winter in the Arctic Ocean, when sea ice covers an area one-and-a-half times the size of Canada.*

## ≋ ⚇ Icebergs

Icebergs are large chunks of ice that break off the ends of **glaciers** at the edge of the sea. The biggest ones, which are found in the Southern Ocean, tower up to 400 feet (120 m) above the water and are many miles long. Icebergs float because when water freezes, it takes up more space, which makes it lighter, or less dense, than water.

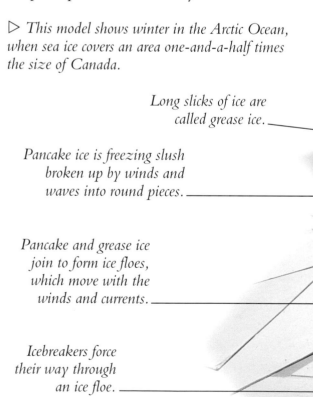

*Long slicks of ice are called grease ice.*

*Pancake ice is freezing slush broken up by winds and waves into round pieces.*

*Pancake and grease ice join to form ice floes, which move with the winds and currents.*

*Icebreakers force their way through an ice floe.*

## ♨ When seawater freezes

Fresh water freezes at 32 °F (0 °C), but seawater freezes at a slightly lower temperature. It is the salts in the water that make seawater freeze at a lower temperature.

## ↻♨ Sinking seawater

When ice forms, most of the salt in the water is left behind in the sea, so icebergs are made of fresh water. This means that the surface of the sea underneath an iceberg is saltier than usual. The extra-salty water is denser than normal seawater, so it sinks. Sinking cold water helps to push water around the world's oceans and is an important driving force behind the world's ocean currents.

## FLOATING ICEBERG TEST

**You will need:** water, plastic bag, tank or sink

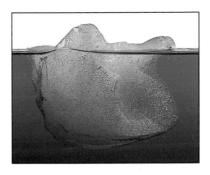

**1** Pour some water into the plastic bag. Tie the bag tightly and place it in a freezer overnight.

**2** Remove the iceberg from the bag and float it in a tank of water.

**Result:** Although 85 to 90 percent of the iceberg will lie below the water level, the iceberg will still float. This is because ice is less dense than water.

*Most Arctic icebergs break off the ends of glaciers in Greenland.*

*Whales migrate south at the start of the Arctic winter.*

*Small icebergs, called bergy bits, are about the size of an average house.*

*Only 10 to 15 percent of an iceberg is above water.*

*Icebergs are eventually carried into the Atlantic Ocean by ocean currents.*

# Ocean currents

Ocean currents are "rivers" of water that flow on, or near, the surface of the ocean or deep underwater. They are caused by the wind, the spin of the Earth, and differences in the density of water. Ocean currents may be warm or cold, depending on where they have come from.

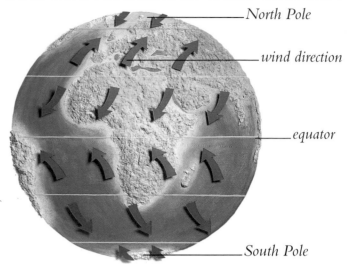

△ *The world's winds blow in six main bands, pulling the surface of the oceans along with them.*

### ℝ Surface currents

Currents in the top 1,500 feet (455 m) of the ocean are called surface currents. They travel about 6 miles (10 km) a day and are driven mainly by the wind. Because of the Earth's spin, the world's winds and surface currents veer sideways. This is called the **Coriolis effect**. The winds, along with the shapes of the continents, make surface currents flow in five large loops, called **gyres**. The gyres south of the equator flow into each other above Antarctica because there is no land to stop them.

▽ *This map shows warm surface currents in red and cold ones in blue. The thickest lines show the strongest currents.*

### ℝ Currents and climate

The equator receives more of the sun's heat than the poles. Ocean currents and winds help spread this heat around the Earth. Warm surface currents flow away from the equator toward the poles, carrying heat with them. This circulation of heat prevents places near the equator from becoming hotter and hotter, and stops the poles from becoming even colder.

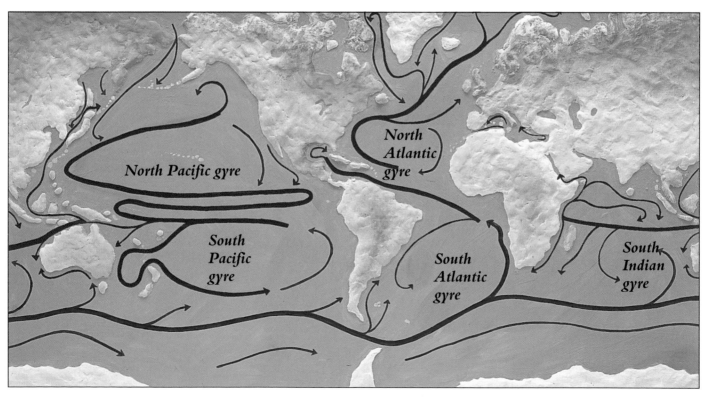

### ℞ Deep-ocean currents

Currents in the deep ocean were discovered only recently. They move more slowly than surface currents—less than 350 feet (105 m) a day. Deep-ocean currents begin in the Arctic and Southern oceans. Cold, extra-salty water sinks to the ocean floor. From the poles, cold water flows along the seabed toward the equator, where it warms up. As cold currents warm up, they become lighter, or less dense, and rise to the surface. Then they flow back to the poles again as warm surface currents.

### ℞ Currents and marine life

All living things need oxygen to survive. Ocean currents are very important to marine life because they carry oxygen from the surface to the deep ocean. Water at the ocean surface takes in oxygen from the air. When this water sinks in polar regions, it carries oxygen down with it. Deep-ocean currents traveling along the ocean floor bring oxygen to the creatures that live there. Without ocean currents sinking and rising, there would be no oxygen, and therefore, no life on the ocean floor.

## WARM AND COLD CURRENTS TEST

**You will need:** water, tank, plastic bottle, ice cubes, tape, jug, stones or fishing weights, salt, food coloring

**1** Cut the top off an empty plastic bottle. Put tape around the cut edge. Next, put some weights or stones in the bottle.

**2** Place the bottle at one end of the tank. Fill the tank with warm water. Now fill the bottle with ice cubes.

**3** Fill the jug with ice-cold water, some salt, and food coloring. Gently pour some of the colored water down the outside of the plastic bottle and wait.

**Result:** The cold, salty water sinks to the bottom of the tank. It does not mix with the warmer, less dense water above it.

Slowly, the cold water travels to the end of the tank, always staying below the layer of warm water. Eventually, the cold water warms up and mixes with the water above it. It starts to rise, just as cold deep-ocean currents do when they reach warm water at the equator.

63

# Waves

Waves can be anything from gentle ripples to huge storm waves crashing against coasts. Since early times, sailors have noticed that when it is windy at sea, the height of the waves is affected. Today we know that wind speed is the most important force in driving ocean waves.

## ℃ Wind and waves

Most waves are caused by the wind pulling and pushing the surface of the ocean. The size and power of waves depends on the speed of the wind, how long it has been blowing, and how far it has blown. Other types of waves are started by erupting seamounts, earthquakes, and tides.

△ *These surfers are being carried quickly toward the shore by a steep, powerful wave.*

## ℃ Water in waves

The top of a wave is called the crest, and the bottom is the trough. The distance from one crest to the next is called the wavelength. As waves travel over deep water, they make the water at the surface move in circles. Big waves make water deeper down move in circles too. These circles of moving water get smaller and smaller.

When a wave reaches the shore, the water in the wave starts to move in oval shapes instead of circles. The crest gets higher and steeper, and the distance between waves becomes shorter. The wave slows down, making the crest topple over and break on the shore.

## WATCHING WAVE ACTION

**You will need:** long tank, gravel, tape, paddle

**1** Put a layer of gravel on the bottom of the tank. Half fill the tank with water. Mark the water line with tape. Make gentle, steady waves at one end of the tank.

**Result:** You will see that the distance from the top (crest) of the wave to the water line is the same as the distance from the dip (trough) to the water line.

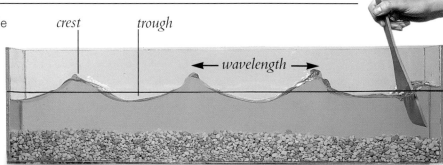

## DEEP WAVE EXPERIMENT

**You will need:**
long tank, waterproof glue, 5 pieces of cork, 5 washers, string, gravel, paddle

**1** Cut five different lengths of string. Glue a piece of cork to each end and tie a washer to the other end. Pour gravel into the tank. Fill the tank with water. Arrange the strings as shown. Make gentle waves near the surface. Only the corks at the top will move. The corks at the bottom stay still because the water is not moving there.

**2** Now lower your paddle and make slow, steady waves.

**Result:** The waves will be bigger than before, and the corks at the bottom of the tank will move. This is because large waves make the water circulate farther down. Strong winds blowing over the ocean make big waves in this way.

### ℛ Passing waves

Waves pass through the water. They do not take water with them as they move. You can see this if you watch a bottle on the water. As the waves pass by, the bottle bobs up and down but stays more or less in the same place. The bottle will move slowly over time because it is carried by surface ocean currents.

▽ *The green arrows show how water moves when a wave passes through it.*

### ℛ Tsunamis

These destructive waves are caused by erupting seamounts, undersea earthquakes, or by hurricanes, cyclones, or other large storms at sea. Tsunamis typically travel 500 to 600 miles (800 to 970 km) per hour beneath the surface of the open ocean. When the small waves reach shallow water, they are forced to slow way down, causing the waves to suddenly rise up and slam down on the land. Such huge waves have caused terrible damage to coasts, killing people and destroying buildings and crops.

*water moving in circles*  *water moving in ovals*  *waves closer together near the shore*  *crashing wave*  *sloping shore*

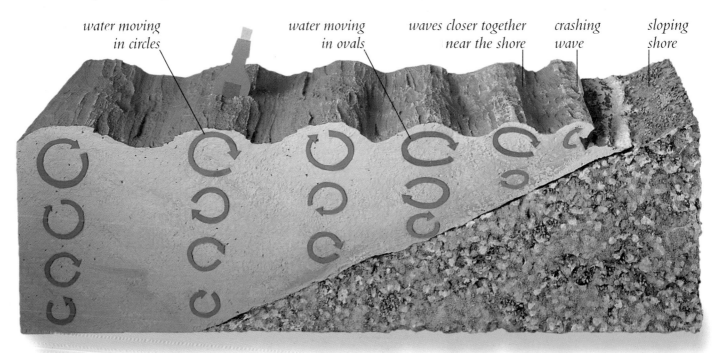

# Tides

Every day, the level of the sea rises and falls. This is called the **tide**. At high tide the sea rises, and at low tide it falls. There are usually two high and two low tides each day. They are caused mainly by the pull of the moon and the sun on the Earth.

## ☾ The moon's pull

The moon gives off a pulling force, called **gravity**. This force pulls the oceans outward on the side of the Earth nearest the moon. As the Earth spins, these bulges of water move across the ocean like an enormous wave, making the tides rise and fall.

*moon*

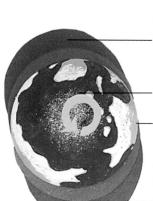

◁ *This model shows how the moon's gravity causes tides on Earth.*

*Oceans are pulled toward the moon, making high tide.*

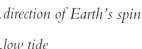

*direction of Earth's spin*

*low tide*

*Earth's spin throws oceans outward.*

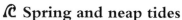

## ☾ Spring and neap tides

The sun also pulls the Earth's oceans, but its pull is weaker because it is much farther away. Twice a month, when the sun, moon, and Earth are in a line, the pull of the sun and the pull of the moon combine. This makes higher and lower tides than usual, called **spring tides**. When the sun, moon, and Earth form a right angle, the sun's pull works against the moon's pull, making less extreme tides called **neap tides**.

66

▽ *These models show how the pull of the moon and sun produce two spring tides and two neap tides each month.*

▷ *key*

*effect of moon's gravity on oceans*

*effect of sun's gravity on oceans*

*sun*

**new moon: spring tide**
*The moon and sun pull together in a straight line.*

**first quarter: neap tide**
*The moon and sun pull against each other because they are at right angles.*

**full moon: spring tide**
*The moon and sun pull in a straight line.*

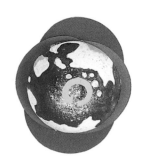

**third quarter: neap tide**
*The moon and sun are at right angles again and pull against each other.*

## ℞ Tidal range

Along the shore, the difference between **sea levels** at high and low tide is called the tidal range. The average tidal range for an ocean coast is about 10 feet (3 m). Seas that are almost completely surrounded by land, such as the Mediterranean Sea, have smaller tidal ranges.

## ℞ 🐟 Surviving the tides

Tides affect the marine life that lives on or near the shore. Creatures that can survive out of water for long periods at low tide, live high up the shore. Creatures that need to be in water more of the time, live on the lower shore. When creatures are exposed by low tides, they need to avoid drying out and must hide from predators. Periwinkles, for example, stay in their shells to stay moist. This also protects them from birds.

△ *This is a beach in Scotland at low tide. You can see the tidal zones and some of the plants that live there.*

▽ *This model shows the different areas of the shoreline, called tidal zones, and some of the creatures and plants that live in each zone.*

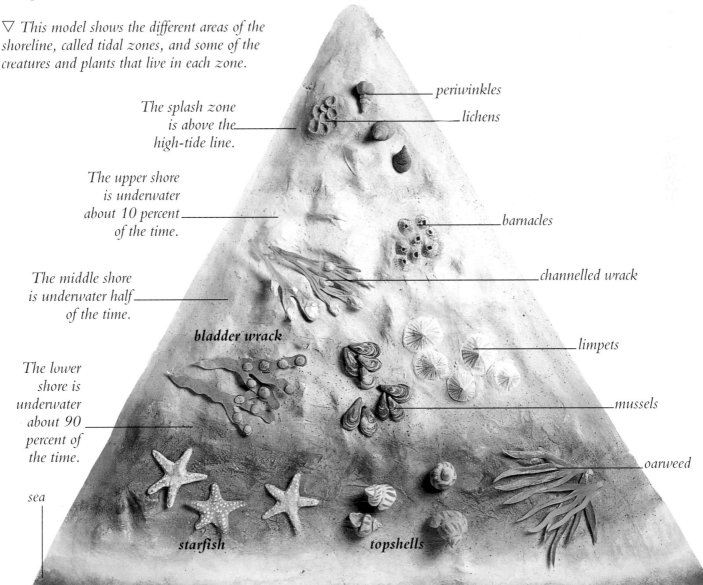

The splash zone is above the high-tide line.

periwinkles

lichens

The upper shore is underwater about 10 percent of the time.

barnacles

channelled wrack

The middle shore is underwater half of the time.

**bladder wrack**

limpets

The lower shore is underwater about 90 percent of the time.

mussels

oarweed

sea

**starfish**

**topshells**

# Changing sea levels

For millions of years, sea levels have risen and fallen. These variations have been caused by changes in climate or by movements deep inside the Earth that alter the shape of the ocean floor. As sea levels change, so do coastlines. Two features that show how sea levels have changed over time are **fjords** and **raised beaches**.

### 🏔🌡 Rising and falling
As the temperature of the Earth rises and falls, sea levels also rise and fall. During the last 100 years, the Earth has warmed up slightly, and sea levels have risen about 5 inches (12 cm). This is because some of the ice at the poles has melted and because water expands when it is heated. Sea levels also change when forces inside the Earth make the outer crust move up and down, for example, when earthquakes happen.

### 🏔🌡 Flooded valleys
The last great climate change occurred more than 10,000 years ago when the Earth experienced an **ice age**. At this time, glaciers carved out long valleys in areas such as Norway and Alaska. When the Earth warmed up, some glaciers melted. The level of the sea rose and flooded the valleys, forming long stretches of water called fjords.

▷ *This is a model of a fjord. The valley, formed by a glacier, now lies below the water.*

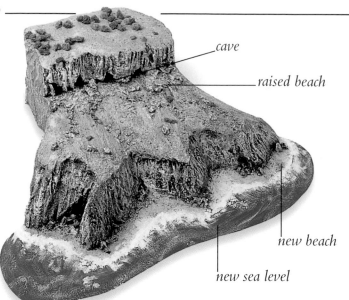

cave

raised beach

new beach

new sea level

△ *This model shows a raised beach. Cliffs and caves that were formed by the sea (see pages 70 and 71) now lie above sea level.*

### 🏔 Raised beaches
When the land rises, or the sea level falls, old shorelines are sometimes left stranded. These shores form platforms, called raised beaches, which lie above the new level of the sea.

shallow mouth of valley

sea level today

valley floor that was once above sea level

## Rising sea levels

Today, sea levels are rising, and by the year 2100 they may have risen 15 inches (40 cm). Even such a small rise may cause floods in cities near coasts, such as New York and London. In countries such as Bangladesh, which lies close to sea level, many people could lose their homes and farms to the sea.

▽ *The Thames Barrier was built across the River Thames in England to stop London from being flooded by spring tides and storm waves from the North Sea.*

## Sea barriers

As sea levels rise, more people are having to build barriers to protect themselves and their cities from high tides and storm waves. In 1953, almost 2,000 people in the Netherlands and 300 people in Britain were killed when huge waves from the North Sea swept across low areas of land.

In the Netherlands, permanent sea walls have been built to prevent another disaster. In London, a mechanical barrier lies across the River Thames. It is raised during spring tides when there is a danger of flooding and when there are storm waves.

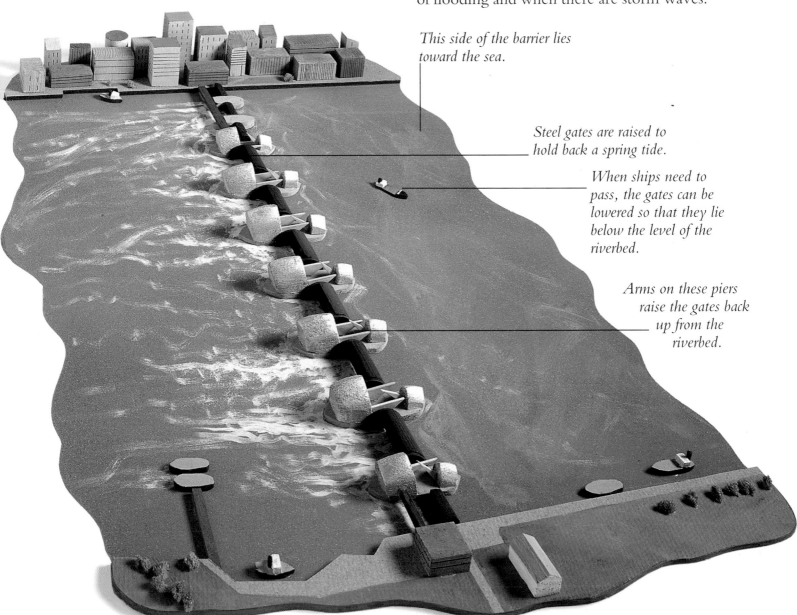

*This side of the barrier lies toward the sea.*

*Steel gates are raised to hold back a spring tide.*

*When ships need to pass, the gates can be lowered so that they lie below the level of the riverbed.*

*Arms on these piers raise the gates back up from the riverbed.*

# Coasts

The place where ocean meets land is called the coast. Coastlines are always changing shape. Wind and waves wear away some coasts and build up others. Coasts that are being worn away by waves are called eroding coasts. Powerful waves eat into the land, forming steep cliffs and deep caves.

## Hard and soft rocks

The shape of an eroding coast depends partly on the type of rock the land is made of. Soft rocks, such as limestone, wear away more easily than hard rocks, such as granite. Headlands are rocky outcrops jutting out from the coast. They are usually made of hard rock. Bays, which are carved into the coast, are made of softer rocks.

▽ *This model shows some features of an eroded coast.*

## Pebble and water power

The main way in which the sea wears away the land is by hurling sand and pebbles against it. This makes pieces of the land break off. The force of the waves crashing against rocks also helps break rocks into smaller pieces.

## Air power

As waves pound against the coast, they force air into cracks in the rocks. When the waves pull back, the forced air spreads out quickly and explodes out of the cracks, weakening the rock.

## Changing coastlines

When waves approach a shallow shore, they slow down gradually and travel along the coast. But when a wave meets a headland in deep water, it still has a great deal of energy, or power. This power erodes headlands more quickly than sheltered bays. Over time, waves will wear away a headland, leaving a straight coastline.

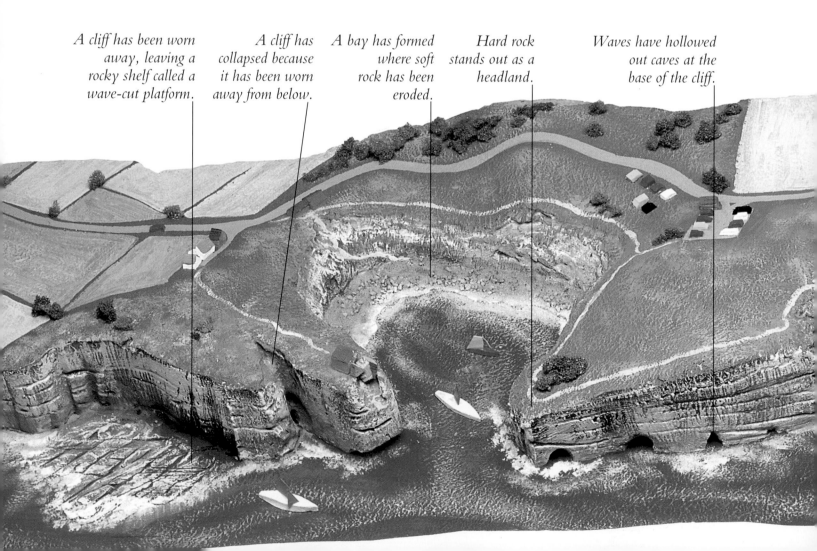

*A cliff has been worn away, leaving a rocky shelf called a wave-cut platform.*

*A cliff has collapsed because it has been worn away from below.*

*A bay has formed where soft rock has been eroded.*

*Hard rock stands out as a headland.*

*Waves have hollowed out caves at the base of the cliff.*

## 🏔 ℞ How caves form

When the sea crashes against rocky cliffs, cracks appear in natural joints in the rock. Eventually, due to constant wave erosion, the cracks become bigger and bigger until a large hole, or cave appears. Waves constantly pushing and compressing the air in a cave may punch a hole through the roof of the cave. This is called a blowhole.

## 🏔 ℞ Arches and stacks

In some places, two caves form on opposite sides of a headland. If they grow large enough, they may meet in the middle to form an arch. The sea continues to widen the arch until the roof, or lintel, falls, leaving behind a pillar of rock called a stack.

△ *Living at the edge of an eroding coast can be dangerous. As a coast becomes unstable, large sections may fall into the sea in landslides.*

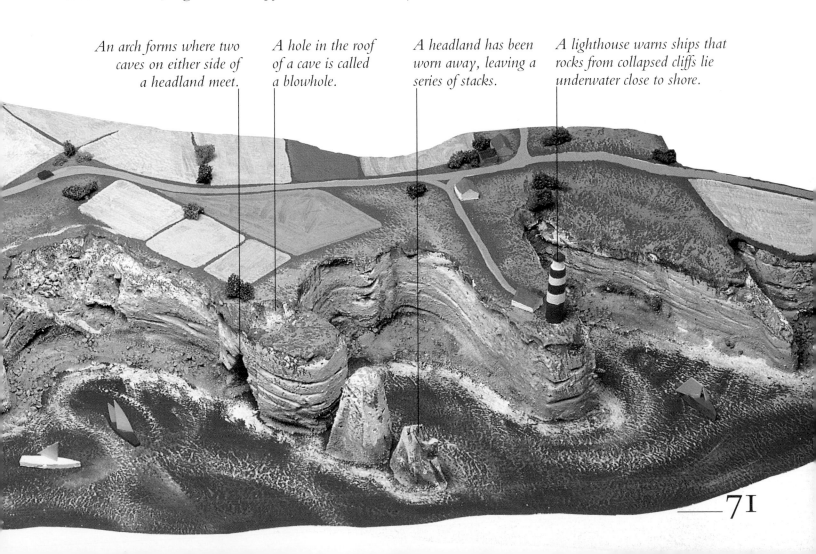

*An arch forms where two caves on either side of a headland meet.*

*A hole in the roof of a cave is called a blowhole.*

*A headland has been worn away, leaving a series of stacks.*

*A lighthouse warns ships that rocks from collapsed cliffs lie underwater close to shore.*

# Coasts

## 🏔 ℝ New land from waves

When coasts are eroded, the sea carries away loose rocky material, such as sand and pebbles. Some of this sediment is swept out to sea, but some is carried along the coast and deposited in sheltered bays. Over time, the deposited sediment forms new land, such as a beach. Sand and mud are also carried into the sea by rivers. This sediment settles around the mouths of rivers to form mud flats and salt marshes.

## ℝ 🏔 Longshore drift and spits

In some places, waves hit the coast at an angle. They travel across the beach and then fall down in a straight line. The waves follow a zigzag path, dragging sediment with them along the coast. The sideways movement of waves is called longshore drift. Where this happens, sea walls called groynes are built along the beach to stop longshore drift. When a coastline curves or changes direction, longshore drift may wash sand and pebbles out to sea, forming a ridge called a spit. Spits often curve because waves push them back toward the coast.

▽ *This model shows some of the features of a growing coast, where waves drop sediment to build up new land.*

△ *Salt marshes make good feeding and breeding grounds for birds. This salt marsh is on the Atchafalaya Delta in Louisiana. It is fed by the waters of the Gulf of Mexico.*

## 🏔 Tombolos and lagoons

When a spit forms between an island and the coast, linking the two, it makes a tombolo. In other places, spits extend from one headland to another and seal off bays from the sea, creating **lagoons**. Over a long period of time, plants start to grow in the lagoon and eventually it turns into dry land.

*Two headlands are joined by a spit, creating a lagoon.*

*Waves have pushed the tip of this spit into a hook shape.*

*Fine sediment has been deposited in a bay, forming a beach.*

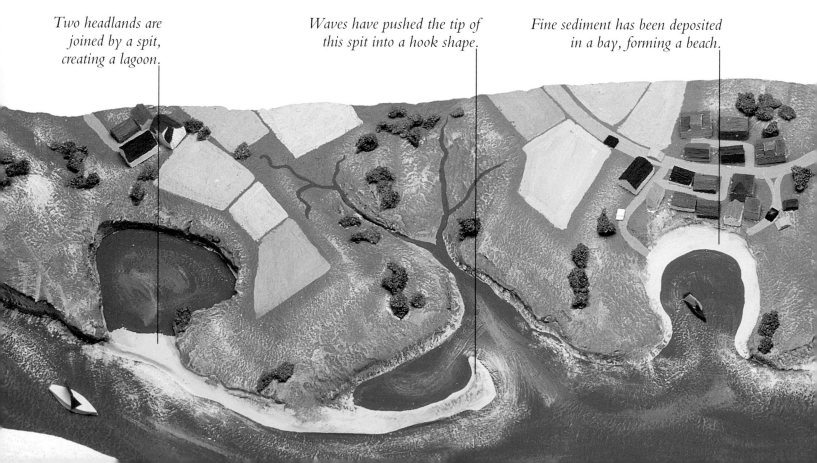

### ⛰ Bars and barrier islands

Bars are ridges of sediment that build up parallel to gently sloping shores. Unlike spits, bars are not joined to the coast, and they are made of material from the seabed, not the coast. If a bar breaks the sea surface, plants grow and the bar becomes a barrier island. Miami Beach, Florida, is an example of a barrier island.

### ⛰ Mudflats and salt marshes

Behind spits and bars, or at the mouth of a river, seawater is shallow and protected from waves. Over time, mud and sand drop out of the water and create mud flats. Plants that can survive in salt water grow on the mud. The plants help form a more solid structure called a salt marsh.

### ⛰ Sand dunes

Sand dunes may form behind salt marshes or mud flats. The wind blows loose sand inland and it piles up into small hills called dunes. Plants such as certain grasses grow on the dunes. Their spreading roots help bind the sand and stop it from being blown away.

## LONGSHORE DRIFT EXPERIMENT

**You will need:** large tray, water, sand, paddle, 3 long pieces of wood

**1** Make a narrow beach along one side of the tray. Pour water in the other side of the tray.

**2** Paddle from one corner of the tray toward the sand.

**Result:** All the sand will drift across the tray. This is what happens when waves break at an angle along beaches.

**3** Arrange the sand as before and wedge the wood in the sand as shown. Paddle again.

**Result:** This time, the wood stops the sand from drifting across the tray, just as groynes do on a beach.

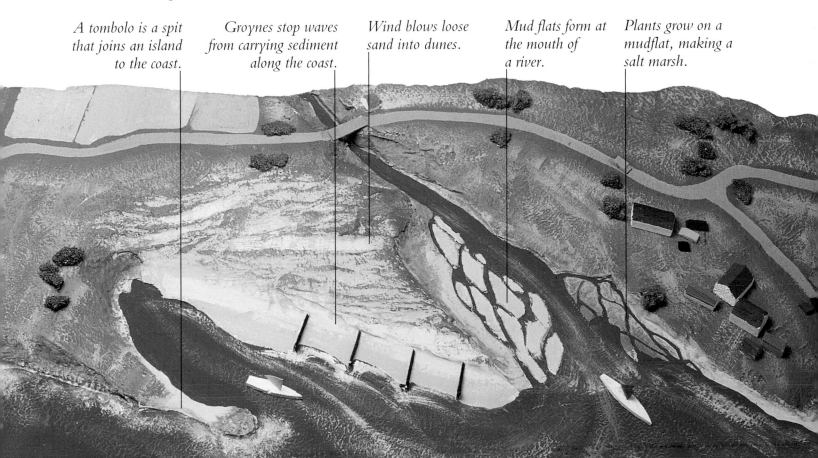

*A tombolo is a spit that joins an island to the coast.*

*Groynes stop waves from carrying sediment along the coast.*

*Wind blows loose sand into dunes.*

*Mud flats form at the mouth of a river.*

*Plants grow on a mudflat, making a salt marsh.*

# Coral reefs

Coasts are also shaped by tiny marine animals called polyps. They live in warm, shallow waters and create brilliantly colored structures called coral reefs. Polyps are soft creatures with hard outer cases called coral. When polyps die, they leave the coral behind. Over time, millions of corals build up to form walls called reefs. A coral reef may start off as a fringing reef. As it grows, it may become a barrier reef, and later, an atoll.

△ This is part of the Great Barrier Reef. Polyps only live at the top of the reef. The rest of the coral is dead.

### ▶ ⛰ Fringing and barrier reefs

A fringing reef is a flat reef of living coral joined to a coast, like the reefs around the Hawaiian Islands. Barrier reefs are long, coral ridges separated from the coast by lagoons. The Great Barrier Reef, off the coast of Australia, stretches for about 1,250 miles (2,010 km) and is the largest structure ever made by living creatures. It is so big that astronauts could see it from the moon.

### ▶ ⛰ Atolls

An atoll is a ring- or horseshoe-shaped wall of coral built up from a sunken bank or crater with a shallow lagoon in the middle. As soil lodges on the reef, plants grow there, and the reef becomes a coral island. The Maldive and Seychelle islands are atolls in the Indian Ocean.

## How coral atolls form

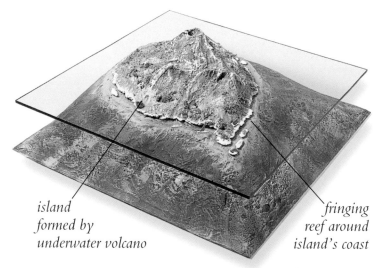

island formed by underwater volcano

fringing reef around island's coast

lagoon

island sinking below sea level

reef that grows upward

### 1 Fringing reef

When seamounts, or underwater volcanoes, erupt above sea level, they form volcanic islands. Polyps are attracted to the warm, mineral-rich waters around the shores of these islands. Over time, a small wall of coral forms at the edge of the coast.

### 2 Barrier reef

After hundreds or thousands of years, the island may sink, or the sea level may rise. The coral wall continues to grow upward because polyps need light to survive. The coral forms a barrier reef, creating a lagoon between the reef and the island.

## MAKE A VOLCANIC ISLAND

**You will need:** plastic bottle, tubing, scissors, baking soda, chicken wire, newspaper strips, flour-and-water paste, paint, jug, vinegar, red food coloring, large square board

**1** Cut the bottle in half. Carefully cut three holes so that the tubes fit in securely.

**2** Fill the bottle up to the first tube with baking soda. Place the bottle on the board. Make a volcano shape around it with the wire. Cover with newspaper strips dipped in the paste.

**3** Make sure the ends of the tubes poke through the frame. Leave a large hole in the top, above the bottle. Let your volcano dry, then paint it.

**4** Pour some vinegar into a jug—about the same amount as the baking soda. Add red food coloring.

**5** Slowly pour the vinegar into the hole at the top and stand back!

**Result:** The volcano erupts and lava (the soda) pours out. In real life, the lava cools and becomes a volcanic island. In warm waters, coral reefs will grow around the island.

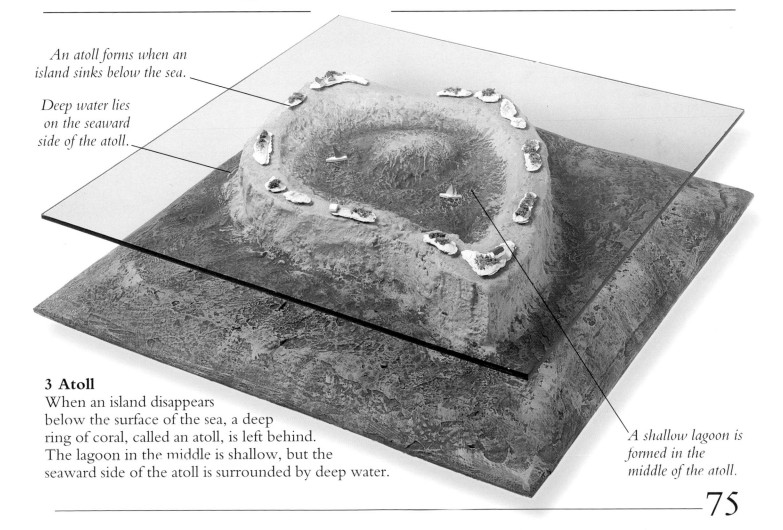

*An atoll forms when an island sinks below the sea.*

*Deep water lies on the seaward side of the atoll.*

### 3 Atoll
When an island disappears below the surface of the sea, a deep ring of coral, called an atoll, is left behind. The lagoon in the middle is shallow, but the seaward side of the atoll is surrounded by deep water.

*A shallow lagoon is formed in the middle of the atoll.*

# Black smokers

One of the most exciting discoveries in oceanography happened in 1977. Scientists found hot water gushing up through cracks in the ocean floor called **deep-sea vents**. The water contains dissolved minerals. When the hot water cools, the minerals become solids and form tall chimneys. Colored water escapes from the chimneys, so these vents are often called black smokers or white smokers.

△ *Deep-sea vents in the Pacific Ocean are rich in giant crabs and other marine life.*

### Birth of a deep-sea vent

Vents occur along the mid-ocean ridges. Seawater seeps down through cracks in the crust toward the hot rocks below. As the rocks heat the water to extreme temperatures, water dissolves minerals out of the surrounding rocks. The hot water then shoots back up through the crust. Cold seawater from above cools the hot water. The dissolved minerals harden and form chimneys.

### Pacific and Atlantic vents

The first vents to be discovered were in the eastern Pacific, off the coast of South America. Oceanographers think that these sites may be between 100 and 1,000 years old. Vent communities have also been discovered along the Mid-Atlantic Ridge. These sites are thought to be much older, and have been smoking for tens of thousands of years.

## MAKE A BLACK SMOKER

**You will need:** tall tank, water, gravel, fish-tank thermometer, small plastic bottle, small fishing weights, food coloring, two lengths of narrow tubing, modeling clay, wooden skewer, waterproof tape

**1** Fill the tank with cold water. Tape the thermometer to the inside of the tank. Put gravel on the bottom.

**2** Put some weights into the bottle to make it heavy. With an adult's help, fill the bottle with very hot water and food coloring.

**3** Feed both tubes into the bottle so that they reach the bottom. Mold the clay around the tubes to seal the top of the bottle. Plug one tube with the skewer.

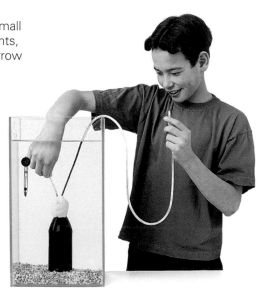

**4** Record the temperature, then place your bottle (chimney) and the plugged tube into the tank. Remove the skewer and blow gently through the other tube until a layer of hot, colored water sits on top of the cold water. Record the temperature again.

**Result:** The hot, colored water will make the temperature in the tank rise slightly. Real black smokers make the temperature of surrounding waters very hot.

## ❂ Pacific vents

In the Pacific, many large and unusual animals, such as giant tubeworms, giant crabs, and clams, live in the warm water that surrounds deep-sea vents. About 95 percent of these animals have never been seen anywhere else on Earth. Unlike other animals in the ocean or on land, most vent creatures do not eat plants or other animals (see page 78). Instead, they feed on microbes that feed off the minerals which pour out of the vents.

## ♟♙ ❂ New discoveries

Deep-sea vents have only recently been discovered, so there are still many mysteries waiting to be solved. For instance, how many deep-sea vents are there in all the world's oceans? Why do vent creatures grow so big, and how quickly do they do this? Do creatures travel from vent to vent, and if so, how?

▽ *This model shows a submersible investigating the creatures living around vents in the Pacific Ocean.*

*Smoke rises several hundred feet above the seabed.*

*The Russian Mir 1 submersible has been used to study vents.*

*Chimneys are, on average, 50 to 65 feet (15 to 20 m) tall.*

*Giant tubeworms grow up to 12 feet (3.7 m) long.*

*Giant white clams are the size of a dinner plate.*

# Marine life

All ocean life can be divided into three groups: plankton, animals that swim freely in the sea, and creatures that live on or near the ocean floor. Plant life is only found near the surface, where there is sunlight, but animals are found at all depths.

▷ *This model shows some of the creatures that live in the world's oceans.*

▽ *Key to the model.*

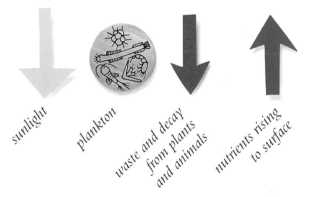

sunlight

plankton

waste and decay from plants and animals

nutrients rising to surface

## 🐟 Plankton

Plankton is the main food supply in the oceans. There are two types of plankton: plantlike organisms called phytoplankton, and animals called zooplankton. Like plants on land, phytoplankton need light to make food and survive. They are eaten by zooplankton and some larger animals. Zooplankton include tiny baby fish and shrimplike krill. They swim for some food but mostly are carried by ocean currents.

## 🐟 Food chains

In the ocean, as on land, most creatures either eat plants or other animals. Each plant or animal is like a link in a chain. A series of five or six animals feeding on each other is called a **food chain**. Animals from one food chain may feed on animals in other food chains. If there is a change in one link in a food chain, then this may affect creatures in the other chains.

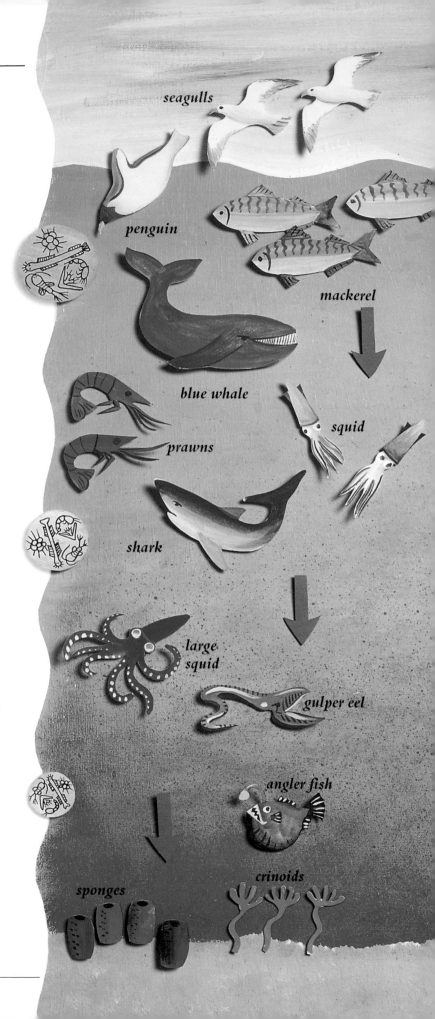

seagulls

penguin

mackerel

blue whale

squid

prawns

shark

large squid

gulper eel

angler fish

crinoids

sponges

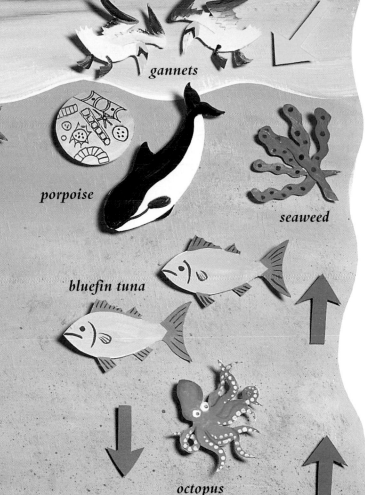

ocean
zones

sea level

sunlit
zone

twilight
zone

abyssal
zone

dark
zone

ocean trench

*gannets*

*porpoise*

*seaweed*

*bluefin tuna*

*octopus*

*rat-tail*

*hatchet fish*

*brittlestar*

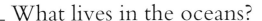
### ✦ 🐟 The sunlit zone

The part of the ocean that receives the most light and heat is called the sunlit zone. Phytoplankton and all ocean plants live here. Many animals also live in this zone because they need the warm temperatures to survive and because there is a large food supply.

### 🐟 Twilight and sunless zones

Below the sunlit zone, the sea is cold and dark, and there are no plants. Animals feed on each other or on animal and plant remains that float down from above. Many fish, such as the hatchet fish, glow in the dark to attract prey or to find mates. Food is more scarce. Fish, such as the gulper eel, have huge mouths and stretchy stomachs so they can eat as much as possible when they find a meal.

### 🐟 The abyssal zone

In the darkness of the ocean deep, many fish are blind. They feel their way around the seabed. Some animals in this zone, such as sponges, are fixed to the seabed. Others crawl or burrow in the sediment. Animals feed on each other or on remains falling from above. In the cold temperatures, fish such as the angler fish grow slowly and live much longer than those on the surface.

### 🌀 🐟 Upwelling

In some areas, winds cause surface waters near the coast to move offshore, allowing colder, deeper waters rich in minerals and dissolved plant and animal remains to rise to the surface. This is called **upwelling**. The nutrients carried by the upwelling provide food for marine life near the surface, which is why these areas have great numbers of fish.

79

# Deep-sea sediments

A constant rain of particles falls, like snow, onto the ocean floor. These particles come from soil and rocks on land, from erupting seamounts, from the remains of sea creatures, and even from space. The particles have built up layers of sediment that are millions of years old. By studying sediments, scientists can find out what happened on Earth in the past.

## 🔺 Turbidity currents

Rivers wash enormous amounts of sediment onto the continental shelf. Every few thousand years, this sediment may be dislodged, perhaps by an earthquake or other disturbance. Then sediment flows quickly across the shelf and down the continental slope. Currents of moving sediment are called **turbidity currents**. They have the power to cut huge valleys, called submarine canyons, in the continental slope. When a turbidity current reaches the abyssal plain, it fans out and slows down.

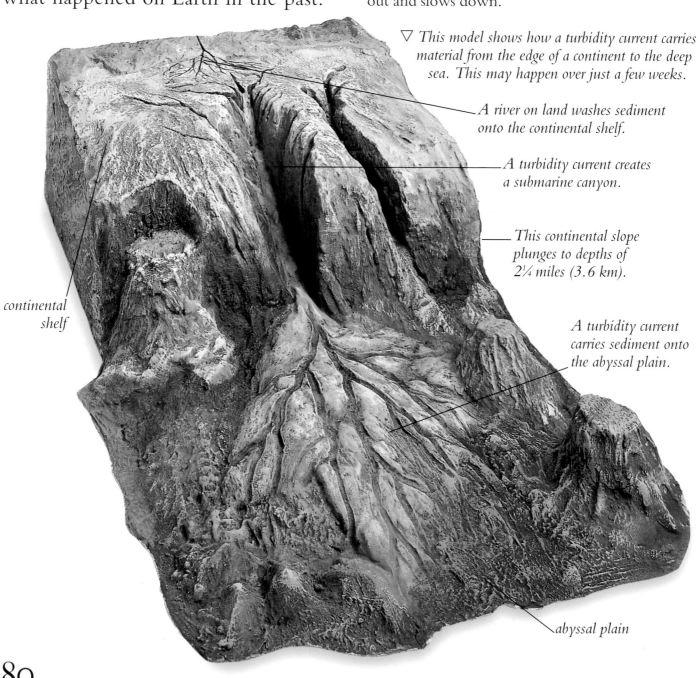

▽ *This model shows how a turbidity current carries material from the edge of a continent to the deep sea. This may happen over just a few weeks.*

*A river on land washes sediment onto the continental shelf.*

*A turbidity current creates a submarine canyon.*

*This continental slope plunges to depths of 2¼ miles (3.6 km).*

*A turbidity current carries sediment onto the abyssal plain.*

*continental shelf*

*abyssal plain*

## ⛰ From sediments to rock

In the deep ocean, sediments washed off the land mix with other kinds of sediments, such as plant remains, animal skeletons, and bits of shell and coral. As layers of sediment build up, particles are pressed together, and the water is squeezed out. Over millions of years, soft sediments are turned into hard sedimentary rocks.

## ⛰ 👫 Deep-sea cores

Most sediments in the deep ocean build up over a long time. It takes 1,000 years to lay down one-third inch (1 cm) of sediment. Oceanographers use special drills to dig into the seabed and take samples, called deep-sea cores, of sedimentary rocks. These cores tell us about climate changes and ocean currents millions of years ago.

Oceanographers also study the sediments in cores to find out how the Earth has changed over time. Sediments show that about 20,000 years ago, the Earth was experiencing an ice age. Gradually, the Earth warmed up and as this happened, the type of sediments deposited on the ocean floor changed.

▷ *This is a model of a deep-sea core 31 inches (80 cm) deep. The sediments were laid down between 7,000 and 20,000 years ago.*

▽ *Key to the sediments on the model*

volcanic dust and ash

dust carried in air

shells and coral

sea plants

rocks and soil

sand from land

bony animal remains

7,000 years ago

*All the sediment in this part of the core was dropped by a turbidity current. It was laid down in just a few weeks, 7,000 years ago.*

*Larger, heavier pieces of sediment, such as sand and gravel, sank to the bottom of the turbidity current.*

7,000 years ago

*This layer of sediment took 6,000 years to form.*

13,000 years ago

*This layer formed over 7,000 years, during an ice age.*

20,000 years ago

81

# Ocean resources

The world's oceans contain many **resources**. The sea supplies us with food, such as fish and salt, and we make medicine from plankton and coral. We mine beneath the seabed for minerals, such as oil and gas, and make electricity using the power of the tides. We also use sand and gravel sediments in industry.

### ⚓ 🏭 Where do oil and gas come from?

Oil comes from plants and the bodies of creatures trapped in sedimentary rock millions of years ago. This rock lies deep within the Earth's crust, under the continents and the seabed. Heat and pressure around the rock slowly turn the remains into drops of oil. As this happens, natural gas forms. Most oil and gas is spread through rocks in tiny amounts. But in some places, large amounts collect between layers of very hard rock. At sea, oil rigs drill into the seabed to find these reserves.

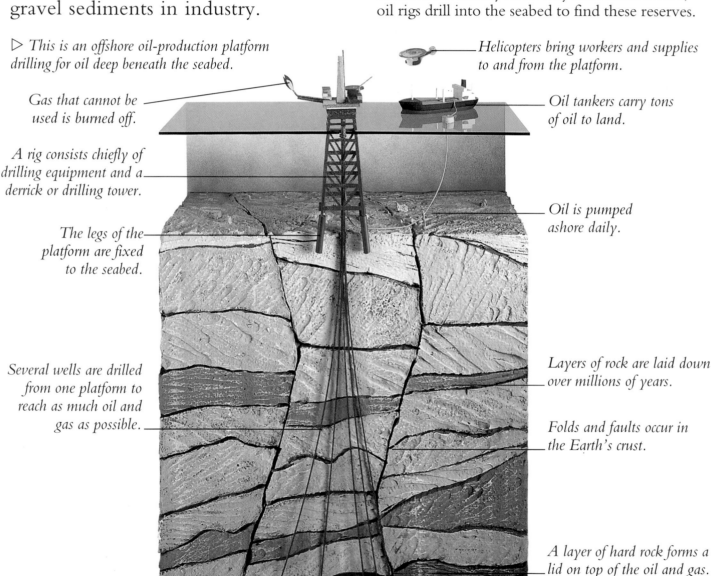

▷ *This is an offshore oil-production platform drilling for oil deep beneath the seabed.*

*Gas that cannot be used is burned off.*

*A rig consists chiefly of drilling equipment and a derrick or drilling tower.*

*The legs of the platform are fixed to the seabed.*

*Several wells are drilled from one platform to reach as much oil and gas as possible.*

*Most oil and gas wells are thousands of feet under the sea.*

*Helicopters bring workers and supplies to and from the platform.*

*Oil tankers carry tons of oil to land.*

*Oil is pumped ashore daily.*

*Layers of rock are laid down over millions of years.*

*Folds and faults occur in the Earth's crust.*

*A layer of hard rock forms a lid on top of the oil and gas.*

*Oil and gas is trapped between layers of hard rock.*

*Hard rock stops oil and gas from seeping downward.*

△ *Most of the world's salt is produced in hot countries, such as Sri Lanka. Shallow pools of seawater are left in the sun. When the water evaporates, salt is left behind.*

## Oil and gas reserves

Most of the known oil and gas deposits on land have already been used up. Oil companies are exploring the oceans more widely in their search for new deposits. In the late 1990's, about two-fifths of the world's oil and gas came from under the oceans. Once oil and gas are pumped to shore, they are refined and used as sources of energy. From oil, we make petroleum, which we use to power cars and engines, to generate electricity, and to make plastics. We use both gas and oil for heating and lighting in homes and in industry.

## Other resources

After oil and gas, the most important ocean resources are gravel and sand. These are mined from continental shelves. Many of the world's countries use these sediments for building on land. Salt is another important resource. It accounts for two-thirds of all the minerals in seawater. The oceans contain other minerals, but researchers haven't found an economical way to extract them yet.

## The energy crisis

One problem facing the world is the shortage of energy sources. Oil and gas take millions of years to form. Scientists believe that if we continue to extract the reserves we know about at the current rate, they will be used up in 100 years. We need to find new reserves and new sources of energy to create power.

## New sources of power

We already know how to produce electricity using the ebb and flow of the tides, but scientists are still trying to find a way to use wave power. They know that when the wind blows over the ocean, energy is transferred to the water, creating waves. If the power of the waves could be harnessed, it would create a never-ending supply of energy.

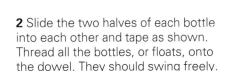

## TEST WAVE ENERGY

**You will need:** craft knife, 3 plastic bottles, tape, shallow tank, dowel as long as the width of the tank, modeling clay, 2 clothes pins, water, large paddle

**1** Ask an adult to help you cut the top off the bottles and cut the bottles in half lengthwise. Make a hole in the end of each bottle half as shown.

**2** Slide the two halves of each bottle into each other and tape as shown. Thread all the bottles, or floats, onto the dowel. They should swing freely.

**3** Attach the ends of the dowel to the tank with clay. The floats should not touch the bottom of the tank. Support the dowel with clothes pins . Now, fill the tank halfway with water.

**4** Move the paddle toward the floats.

**Result:** The barrier will swing gently, and water will ripple more on one side of it than the other because the floats take up some of the energy of the water. If used on a large scale at sea, this energy could be used to turn an engine, which could then produce electricity.

# Ports and settlement

For thousands of years, people have lived by the sea so that they can fish and earn a living. Today, 60 percent of the world's population lives on or near the coast. Many people live in large cities that have grown up around ports used for fishing or trading. Ports are places where ships can load and unload close to sailable waters. Most of the world's trade is carried out from large ports, such as New York, Rotterdam, and Yokohama.

△ *This is a small coastal village in Vietnam. Most of the people who live here earn their living through fishing.*

### 👬 🐟 Fishing for a living

Nowadays, most fishing is done from large fishing ports by a relatively small number of people who use ships called trawlers. Modern trawlers have huge nets and electronic equipment to help locate the catch. Modern trawlers catch millions of tons of fish every year. However, most of the world's fishermen live in small coastal towns and villages. They catch far fewer fish because they use simple hooks and lines, or baskets and nets.

▽ *These cities are also the world's busiest ports. They handle most of the ocean-going trade around the world.*

### 👬 World ports

Most of the world's trade is handled by large ports at the edges of the oceans. Ports are often at points where rivers meet the sea because goods can be easily transported inland by river to other towns. Rotterdam, in the Netherlands, is near the mouth of the river Rhine and is the world's busiest port. Other ports are in natural bays along coasts, where ships can shelter from the open sea. The port of San Francisco is in the world's largest natural bay.

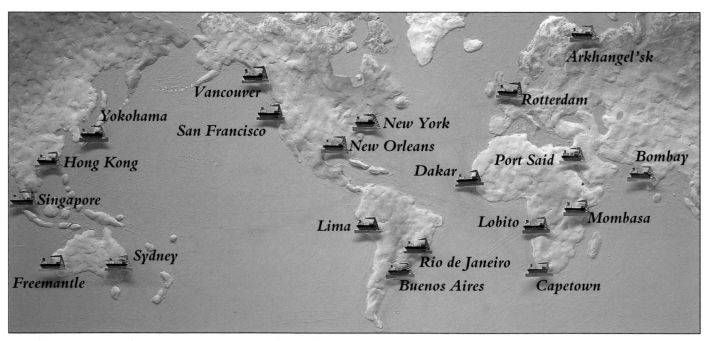

## 𝕚 An ideal port

San Francisco port is one of the busiest ports in the world. It was developed in the 1850's on the western shores of San Francisco Bay. It is an ideal place for a port for several reasons. Firstly, the bay is wide and deep, so it can take many ships. The bay is also on the shores of the Pacific Ocean, which makes it ideally placed for trade with South America, Hawaii, Australia, Japan, and other parts of Asia. Lastly, when the port was first established, ships heading north to hunt whales needed a clear route to the Arctic Ocean. San Francisco provided a convenient place to start from or to stop off.

▷ You can see on this map how San Francisco Bay is sheltered from the Pacific Ocean.

*San Pablo Bay*

*Oakland Bridge*

*The port of San Francisco grew on the east side of the city.*

Golden Gate Bridge crosses the entrance to the bay.

This red area is the city of San Francisco.

*Pacific Ocean*

*San Francisco Bay*

◁ This model shows the main port area of San Francisco today.

This area is the oldest part of the port and the city.

Some of the shore once lay under the sea, but it was drained to extend the port.

Oakland Bridge leads to the newer port of Oakland.

Huge ocean-going carriers, such as container ships and RoRo (Roll-on/Roll-off) cargo ships, load and unload all along these piers.

Goods arriving at the port are carried by rail to the rest of the United States.

Grain and steel are stored in large terminals before being shipped abroad.

# Exploring oceans

Oceans have always been difficult places to explore because of the lack of air, the bitter cold, and the extreme pressure. The first pieces of equipment invented to help divers stay underwater were diving bells, but they did not hold much air. Today, submersibles are built to withstand pressure and supply enough oxygen for oceanographers to explore the ocean floor for up to eight hours.

## ♁ Breathing underwater

In the past, the biggest problem exploring the ocean floor was how to breathe underwater. In 1690, Edmund Halley invented the diving bell. A large wooden bell was lowered to the seabed by rope from a ship at the surface. Air trapped inside the bell and in barrels close by, supplied divers on the ocean floor. It wasn't until 250 years later, in the 1940's, that two Frenchmen, Jacques Cousteau and Emile Gagnan, invented equipment that allowed divers to carry their own air. This invention was called **scuba**.

▽ *This is a model of **Alvin** investigating giant tubeworms near a deep-sea vent.*

*Pressure in the cabin is the same as at sea level.*

*still camera*

*video camera*

*spotlights*

*Side thrusters push Alvin backward and forward.*

*The porthole allows the crew to view the deep-ocean floor.*

*The basket holds samples of rocks and sediment.*

## DIVING BELL EXPERIMENT

**You will need:** clear plastic bottle, craft knife, plastic tubing, modeling clay, tall tank, water, gravel

**1** Ask an adult to cut the bottom off the bottle. Feed the tube into the bottle. Seal the top with clay. Then cover the bottom edge with clay. Place gravel in the tank and fill with water.

**2** Cover your end of the tube so that no air escapes. Hold the bell upright and push it down so that it touches the gravel. The water level may rise a little inside the bell, but the air in the bell will stop it from filling up.

**3** Modern diving bells have an air supply to drive the water out of the bell. To remove the water from your bell, blow into the tube. If it were a full-size diving bell, divers could now work on the seabed, on the area covered by the bell.

### ♟ Submersibles

People cannot dive below about 165 feet (50 m) because of the immense pressure in the ocean. **Submersibles**, such as *Alvin*, carry people down to depths of over 15,000 feet (4,600 m), although the submersible *Mir 1* can go down farther. Using these special underwater craft, oceanographers observe the deep sea and deep-seabed close-up.

*A mechanical arm collects samples of rocks, seawater, and tubeworms.*

### ♟ Undersea robots

Undersea robots are called ROV's, which stands for Remote Operated Vehicles. These are sent down to collect information when conditions are too dangerous for divers. ROV's are attached by cables to a research ship or submersible so that they can be controlled automatically from a distance. ROV's take photographs and collect rock and sediment samples from the ocean floor. They can also stay underwater much longer than people—for months at a time if necessary.

### ♟ Taking measurements

Satellites in space are also used to explore the oceans. They take measurements of the ocean surface. They record the temperature of the ocean surface and provide important information about ocean currents and sea ice. To monitor the oceans depths, oceanographers place other instruments in the seawater. Such instruments include cameras, echo-sounders for mapping the ocean floor (see pages 88 and 89), and machines that measure water density, temperature, and depth.

# Mapping the seabed

In the past, the only way of finding out the depth of the ocean was to lower a weighted rope from the side of a ship and measure the rope. Now, sound waves beamed underwater are used to build "sound pictures" of the seabed. Satellites in space can also tell us about the shape of the seabed.

## 👥 📓 Mapping with sound

Since the 1920's, the invention of sonar has made it much easier to map the seabed. A ship sails in a line, towing a device that sends pulses of sound straight down into the water. Oceanographers time how long it takes for the sound echoes to bounce back from the seabed. They know how far sound travels in a certain time, so they can work out the distance to the seabed. Using the same method, people on research ships beam signals to fixed points on land to find out where they are.

△ *Ocean depth was first measured using weighted ropes called plumb lines. Such measurements were used to make the first depth maps.*

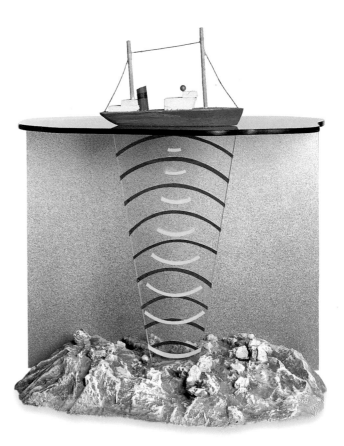

△ *Today, sound waves are used to measure depth. The waves are beamed to the seabed (yellow waves), then they bounce back to a research ship (red waves).*

## 👥 📓 Using plumb lines

In the 1800's, people first began to understand what the ocean floor might be like. Between 1872 and 1876, a British ship called HMS *Challenger*, took 492 deep-sea measurements around the world using plumb lines. Oceanographers marked each depth measurement on a chart before moving to a new position.

## 📓 SEASAT

In 1978, the first sea satellite, SEASAT, was launched. It measured the distance between itself and the sea surface. Peaks and valleys on the surface were found to match those on the seabed. For example, the surface of the sea can be dozens of feet higher above mid-ocean ridges or continental shelves than above ocean trenches or abyssal plains.

### ✎ Faster mapping

A special underwater sonar system called **GLORIA** is towed along the seabed to provide detailed pictures of features such as submarine canyons. It beams two wide fans of sound, building up sound pictures of a much wider area of the bed than ordinary sonar. GLORIA is towed in a straight line up and down sections of an ocean. It is important for a research ship to know exactly where it is, so that it does not map the same area twice. Research ships use satellites in orbit and fixed points on land to determine their position at sea.

*A satellite beams information about the ship's position.*

*A research ship tows GLORIA above the seabed.*

*A ship uses sonar to determine its position from a fixed point on land.*

▷ *This model shows how the seabed is mapped today.*

*GLORIA maps a section of the seabed.*

*area being mapped*

*Sound waves fan out on either side of GLORIA.*

*seabed*

### ✎ Making maps

Maps of the seabed are called **bathymetric maps**. They show the depth of the seabed according to information collected by sonar. First, mapmakers plot the depth of the ocean floor as a series of points. Then they join points that are at the same depth, creating a series of lines. Undersea maps are like contour maps of dry land, in which lines join points that are at the same height above sea level.

▷ *This is a map of the seabed in the model above. The deepest parts are dark green, and the shallower areas are pale.*

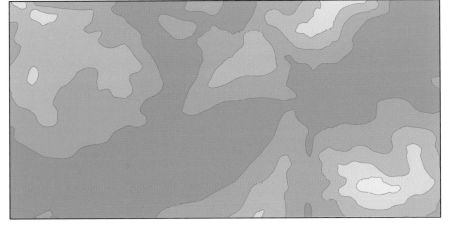

# Oceans under threat

People use oceans for trade, travel, tourism, and recreation. We also take food and resources from the oceans. All these activities can have harmful effects on the oceans and the creatures that live in them. Overfishing and pollution are the most common problems. The oceans link all the countries of the world. And because seawater circulates around the globe, what we do in one part of the ocean can affect another.

▷ *This model shows some of the ways that people interact with the oceans and some of the harmful effects they can have.*

### ⁂ ▶ Overfishing

In parts of the world, fishing trawlers with huge nets sometimes take too many of the same species of fish from a small area. This means that some ocean waters are overfished. As a result, there are not enough fish left to breed in these areas. This affects other fish in the food chain, and it affects people because there eventually may not be enough fish left to eat. In some places of the world, limits have been set for the number of fish that can be caught at one time.

### ⁂ ▶ Threats to marine life

Some species of marine creatures are now rare because too many have been killed for food or sport. Tropical islands and coasts with coral reefs also attract large numbers of tourists every year. Although this helps people develop an understanding of marine life, when corals and shellfish are destroyed by heavy boat anchors and by divers hunting for souvenirs, people are disrupting the natural life cycles of marine life.

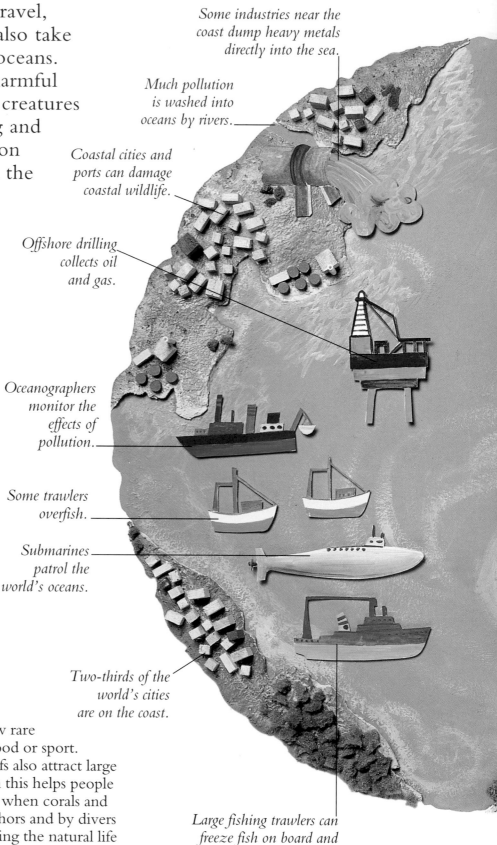

*Some industries near the coast dump heavy metals directly into the sea.*

*Much pollution is washed into oceans by rivers.*

*Coastal cities and ports can damage coastal wildlife.*

*Offshore drilling collects oil and gas.*

*Oceanographers monitor the effects of pollution.*

*Some trawlers overfish.*

*Submarines patrol the world's oceans.*

*Two-thirds of the world's cities are on the coast.*

*Large fishing trawlers can freeze fish on board and stay at sea for months.*

*Tourists watch whales migrating to the North Pole.*

*Oil spilling out of a supertanker damages marine life and coasts.*

*Container ships carry goods vast distances across the ocean.*

*Sea walls protect coastal cities from high tides and storm waves.*

*Coral reefs and other marine life are threatened by careless tourists.*

*Small coastal fishing boats sometimes damage coral reefs.*

## 👥 Pollution

One of the biggest threats to the oceans is contamination from industry. Most pollution happens in coastal areas. Heavy industries in coastal cities and ports discharge chemicals and sewage into rivers. The rivers wash the pollutants into the sea. Once they settle on a continental shelf, pollutants form part of the sediment. We do not know a great deal about the long-term effects of pollution. However, we do know that the North and Black seas in Europe have been polluted so much that the marine life is poisoned and may never recover.

△ *In 1993, this oil tanker ran aground off the coast of Scotland. It spilled thousands of tons of crude oil, which severely affected local marine life.*

## 👥 Possible solutions

All countries of the world need to work together to share ocean resources fairly and to make laws that will prevent overfishing and pollution. It is often difficult to agree on the best way of doing this. It is also hard to make people obey laws when the oceans are so vast and difficult to patrol. The work of oceanographers is vital if we are to understand how best to manage the world's oceans now and in the future.

# Rivers

# Being a geographer

Geography helps us to understand what happened to the Earth in the past, how it is changing now, and what might happen to it in the future. To try to make sense of our world, geographers study features of the Earth, such as rivers, rocks, oceans and the weather. This is called physical geography.

### What is geography?

Geography is a science of the Earth. It is not only about the physical features that shape our world, but also about the human ones. Geographers look at how people use land for things like settlement, farming, shopping and transport. This is called human geography. They also gather information by studying maps, aerial and satellite photographs and computer databases. In this way, geographers can suggest how best to use the land now and in the future.

▷ *A map and a compass are just some of the tools that geographers use.*

## Geography of rivers

Rivers are an important and powerful force in shaping the land. They carve out **river valleys**, slopes and cliffs by a process called **erosion**. They also carry away rocks, sand and mud, and leave them in other places where they fill in lakes, or build up rich farming land. In this book we will look at rivers and some of the features that you might find along them, such as waterfalls, caves and **meanders**.

### Key to geography symbols

Geographers have to cover a range of topics in their studies. We have introduced symbols where the text refers mainly to important themes. They will help as you read through the book.

 **statistics**        energy

physical       rock types, or **geology**

weather       human

###  Parts of the river

A river can be roughly divided into three main parts. The first part starts from the source of the river and is called the **upper river**. This is often in the mountains where there are steep valleys, rushing water and narrow streams.

The second part is the **middle river**. Here, the valley is wider and deeper, and so is the river. The river carries more sand, gravel and mud, or **sediment**, than it did in the upper river.

The last stage is the **lower river**. The river winds slowly over a broad, flat plain, dropping some of the sediment it is carrying. Eventually, the river flows into the sea or a lake.

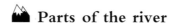

granite
(hard rock)

sandstone
(soft rock)

slate
(hard rock)

### Geographers' tools

Geographers use maps to study changes in the landscape, to look at human settlement, or simply to find their way from place to place. A compass shows which direction to take. A small hammer and brush are useful for breaking off and dusting small pieces of rock to identify. They are also useful if you are looking for **fossils** hidden in rocks. Take photographs or make sketches of the features and things you see, so that you can record them accurately.

### ⛰ Reading rocks

The shape of the land also depends on the rocks under the ground. Some are soft and easily worn away by the wind, rivers or rain. Other rocks are hard and stand out as mountains or hills. Geologists are people who study rocks. Geographers must also study rocks and soil to understand the forces that shape the land.

△ *Geographers often study rock samples from an area.*

### Make it Work!

The Make it Work! way of looking at geography is to carry out experiments and make things that help you understand how geographical processes work. By studying the models and following the step-by-step instructions for the experiments, you will be able to see how rivers work.

You may need to use sharp tools for some of the experiments in the book. Always be careful and ask an adult to help you.

▷ *By studying rivers, geographers can help prevent damage to people and property from flooding.*

△ *Photographs are a useful way of recording how places change over time.*

# Rivers of the world

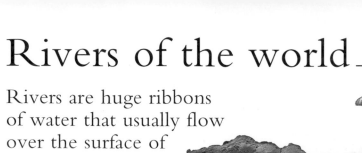

Rivers are huge ribbons of water that usually flow over the surface of the land. All rivers flow in a shallow trench or channel they have cut in the ground. On average, about 5,600 cubic miles of water flow down the world's rivers each year—enough water to cover all dry land in a layer 12 inches deep. Each year, rivers carry away about 22 billion tons of rocks, soil and sand from the land and dump it into the sea or into lakes.

## 👫 Rivers past and present

Some of the world's largest cities have grown along the banks, or at the mouths of important rivers. Shanghai sprang up on the Yangtze River in China; New York, in the U.S., is at the mouth of the Hudson River and is an important port; and Cairo, the largest city in Africa, has stood on the banks of the Nile for over a thousand years.

People all over the world live near rivers because they need them for water, farming, industry and transport. Although rivers are useful to people, they can be dangerous. When rivers flood, they can cause damage to crops and property and great loss of life—especially to people who live on **deltas**.

▷ *These symbols are used to locate some of the world's largest cities, deltas and waterfalls.*

delta    city    waterfall

**North America**

*Lake Superior is the largest freshwater lake in the world.*

*St. Louis*

*New Orleans*

*The Mississippi flows for 2,340 mi. into the Gulf of Mexico.*

*Manaus*

*Angel Falls is the world's highest waterfall at 3,212 ft.*

*The source of the Amazon River is in the Andes Mountains in Peru.*

*One-fifth of the fresh water in all the Earth's rivers flows in the Amazon.*

**South America**

*The banks of the Amazon Delta are farther apart than London and Paris.*

△ *This map shows the world's largest rivers and some of the cities that are found along them.*

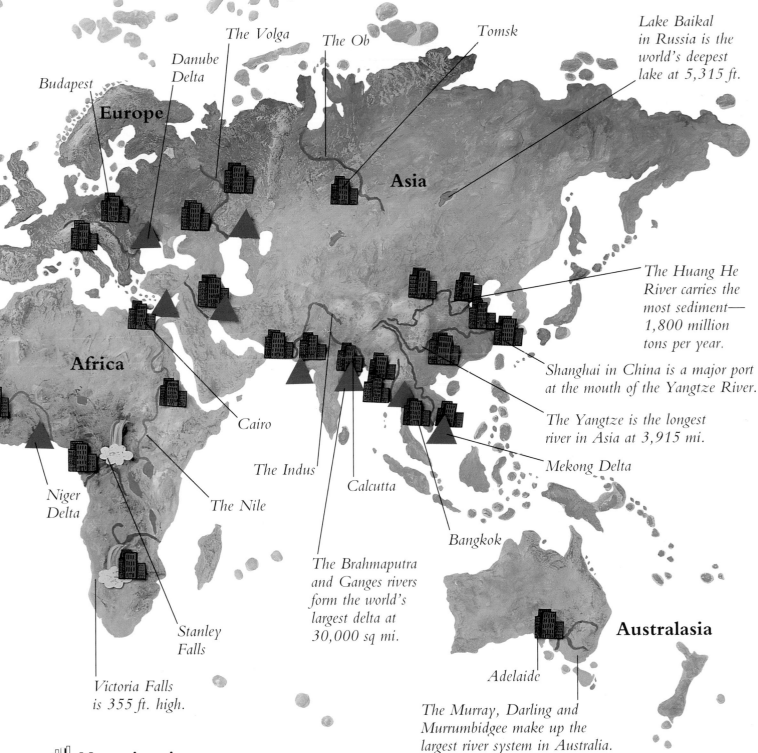

The Volga

Danube
Delta

The Ob

Tomsk

Lake Baikal
in Russia is the
world's deepest
lake at 5,315 ft.

Budapest

**Europe**

**Asia**

The Huang He
River carries the
most sediment—
1,800 million
tons per year.

**Africa**

Shanghai in China is a major port
at the mouth of the Yangtze River.

Cairo

The Yangtze is the longest
river in Asia at 3,915 mi.

Mekong Delta

The Indus

Calcutta

Niger
Delta

Stanley
Falls

The Nile

Bangkok

The Brahmaputra
and Ganges rivers
form the world's
largest delta at
30,000 sq mi.

**Australasia**

Victoria Falls
is 355 ft. high.

Adelaide

The Murray, Darling and
Murrumbidgee make up the
largest river system in Australia.

## Measuring rivers

Rivers are not only bodies of water—they also
carry huge quantities of sediment that help
to shape the landscape. To measure a river's
power to eat into the land and carry it away,
geographers calculate the amount of water in
the river, and the speed at which it flows.

Geographers work out how much rain falls
into rivers, and how much soaks into the soil.
A lot of the rain that falls on the land eventually
finds its way into rivers, so it is important to
know how much rain falls, and how much
water the soil can hold.

# The water cycle

The water cycle is the never-ending movement of water between the land, the sea and the **atmosphere**. Rivers contain less than 1 per cent of all the fresh water on Earth, yet they form a vital part of this cycle.

*▽ This model shows how water is recycled between the Earth and the Earth's atmosphere.*

*melting glacier*

☼ **How water is recycled**

The sun heats the water in rivers, lakes, oceans and plants. The water evaporates, which means that it changes into **water vapor**. Water vapor rises because it weighs less than cold air. High in the sky, the vapor cools and changes back into drops of liquid water. This is called condensation. The drops gather together to make clouds and eventually fall as rain, hail or snow. The cycle then starts all over again.

*water falls from clouds as rain, hail or snow*

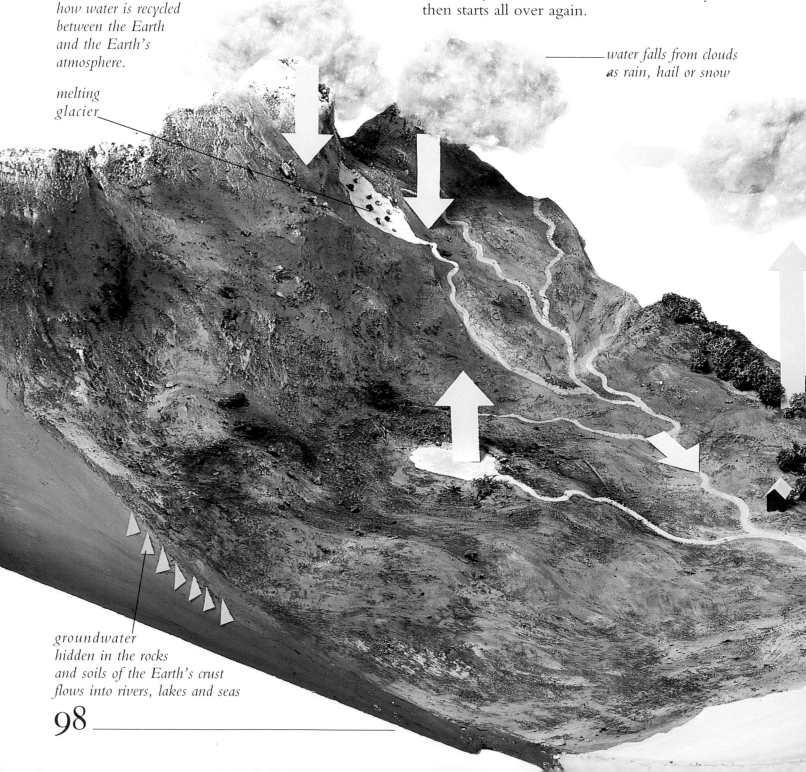

*groundwater hidden in the rocks and soils of the Earth's crust flows into rivers, lakes and seas*

△ *Rainfall is often heaviest in the mountains where the air temperature is cooler. This causes the water vapor to condense and fall as rain, hail or snow.*

### ⛰ Forms of water

Water exists in three forms: liquid water in rivers, lakes or the sea; water vapor, which is invisible gas in the air; and solid water, or ice, which is in glaciers and frozen rivers, lakes, ponds or seas.

### ☀ A freshwater supply

The Earth's water is constantly recycled, so the amount of water on Earth always stays the same. However, 97 per cent of all the Earth's water is salty and makes up the oceans and seas. Most of the fresh water is frozen in ice sheets and glaciers at the North and South Poles and in mountains, so we cannot use it. But when water evaporates from the sea, the salt is left behind. This means that the water vapor in the atmosphere, which condenses and falls as rain, is fresh water.

### CREATE A WATER CYCLE

**You will need** sheet of glass, 12 bricks, hardboard, plastic tray, boiling water (kettle)

*clouds made of millions of droplets of water or ice suspended in the sky*

*water condenses and forms clouds*

*water evaporates from land and sea*

**1** Position the bricks, glass, tray and hardboard as shown. The bricks represent mountains, the tray is the sea, the glass is the atmosphere and the hardboard is land.

**2** Ask an adult to boil some water in a kettle and pour it into the tray. (We added food coloring to show what happens more clearly.)

**Result:** steam rises from the hot water. This shows how the heat of the sun makes water evaporate and form rain clouds over land or sea. When the steam hits the cold glass, the water condenses and droplets form (rain). The water falls onto the hardboard and runs down the slope (river) toward the tray (sea).

# Sources of rivers

The beginning of a river is called its source. Many of the world's biggest rivers begin in natural hollows in the land. Water trickles in from the surrounding soil to form a tiny flow of water called a seep. Even huge rivers, such as the Nile in Egypt or the Amazon in South America, start from small sources like this. Other rivers flow from a marsh or a lake, or from the end of a slowly melting glacier in the mountains.

△ In marshes such as this one in Ireland, the soil is water-logged and covered with plants that hold a lot of water in their roots, leaves and stems.

**DRAINAGE TEST**

**You will need** sphagnum or garden moss, slate, bricks (some broken), sand or soil, plastic tray, hardboard, watering can, bradawl, watch or stopwatch, plastic window box

**1** Make a hole at the bottom of one side of the tray with the bradawl. Fill the tray with moss. Position the tray, bricks, window box and hardboard as shown above. The hole in the tray should sit just over the hardboard, at the end close to the window box.

**2** Fill the watering can, then pour the water evenly over the moss. Time how long it takes for the water to filter through the moss and trickle down the board. You should find that the moss, which is found in marshy areas or peat bogs, holds water very well.

**3** Repeat the experiment with soil or sand in the tray. You will notice that the water carries some of the sand with it. This shows how the river wears away **sedimentary rock**, which does not hold water as well as sphagnum moss, and carries it farther downstream.

## Water drainage

Some rocks such as chalk and limestone, have pores, cracks and joints in them that let water drain easily. These are **permeable** rocks. Rocks that do not let water pass through them are impermeable. The size of the particles in rocks and the way they are arranged affect how permeable they are.

## ⛰ Springs, glaciers and marshes

Sometimes water collects underground. It runs over impermeable rocks until it finds a way out and surfaces as a spring. Many rivers begin as mountain springs.

Glaciers are "rivers of ice." They form when snow is squashed into ice that is so thick and heavy that it slides slowly downhill. The tip of a glacier is called a snout or a lip. When the snout melts, it may become the source of a river.

In marshes and other wetland areas, the soil is often made of peat. Peaty soil is made of plants that have partly rotted down. They hold a lot of water that may eventually be released to supply a river.

△ *The Indus, Ganges and Mekong are three of Asia's largest rivers. Their sources are high in the Himalayan mountains, in glaciers like this one.*

**4** See what happens in a limestone region by arranging some broken bricks in the tray, as above. The gaps between the bricks represent the natural joints found in rock. Now pour on the water. The water does not pass through the bricks, but it drains well through the cracks.

**5** Finally, place a piece of slate on top of the bricks. Pour water onto the slate and measure the time it takes for it to run off. The slate does not absorb any water as it is impermeable, so the water runs off very quickly. This is what happens in an area of hard, impermeable rock.

*mica schist (impermeable)*

*limestone (permeable)*

*slate (impermeable)*

*granite (impermeable)*

*red sandstone (permeable)*

*pumice (permeable)*

# Drainage patterns

From its source, a river flows downhill. This is because of the Earth's gravity which pulls everything down towards the ground. Small trickles of water join up and form a stream. The amount of water in the stream increases steadily as more streams, called **tributaries**, join it. Eventually, the stream becomes big enough to be called a river.

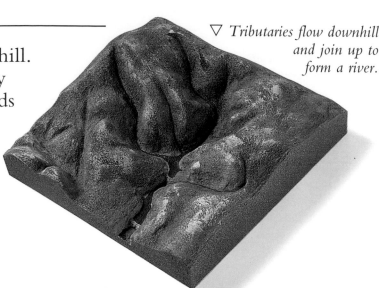

▽ *Tributaries flow downhill and join up to form a river.*

## MAKE A DRAINAGE PATTERN

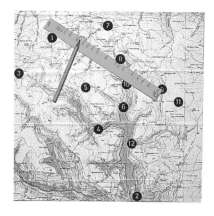

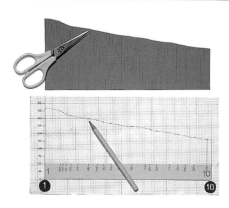

**You will need** contour map with rivers, scissors, ruler, strips of paper, pen, graph paper, plasticine, stickers

**1** Select a river and six tributaries.

**2** Number the stickers. Place the first one at the source of a tributary and the second where the tributary joins the main river. Cut a strip of paper the same length as the tributary. Copy the sticker numbers onto each end of the strip. Do this for all the tributaries and the river.

**3** Match each strip to its tributary. Copy the **contour lines** and the height every 50 yds. on the strip.

**4** Plot a scale on graph paper from the lowest to the highest point (0=sea level). Place each strip on the graph. Plot the height to create a profile.

### ▲ Supplying the river

A **drainage basin** is all the land that supplies a river and its tributaries with water (see page 107). If you could look down on a river from above, you would see that it branches. This is called a **drainage pattern**. The shape of the pattern depends on rocks, soil, climate and the changes made to the river. Radial drainage occurs when streams flow down from a central high point, such as a mountain top. Other rivers, such as the Amazon, form a pattern like the branches of a tree. This is called dendritic drainage.

*radial drainage*

*dendritic drainage*

Rivers and their tributaries can form many other types of drainage patterns.

Parallel drainage occurs when streams flow in valleys that are parallel to one another. This might be because movements in the Earth, millions of years ago, made the rocks "fold" into parallel lines.

Trellis drainage is common where massive layers of sedimentary rock have "slipped." Streams flow in channels that are parallel to each other, and tributaries join the streams at right angles.

*parallel drainage*

*trellis drainage*

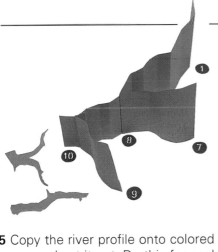

**5** Copy the river profile onto colored paper and cut it out. Do this for each tributary and the main river.

**6** Fix each profile to the river and its tributaries with plasticine. Does the pattern on your map match any of the drainage patterns shown here?

▷ *This is the drainage pattern of the landscape model at the top of the opposite page.*

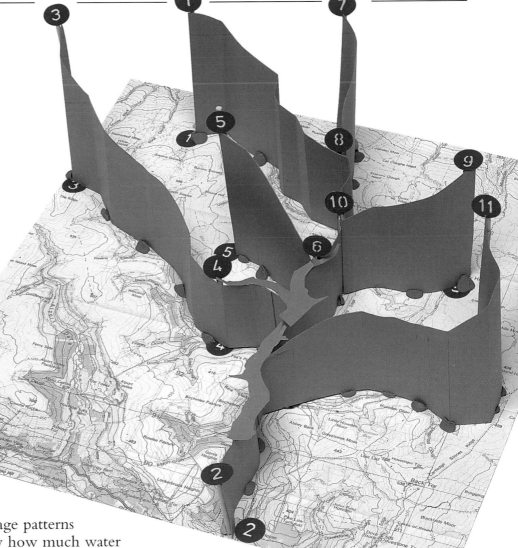

📊 **Comparing rivers**

By measuring river profiles, drainage patterns and rainfall, geographers can study how much water flows down a river. This helps them to predict when most water will flow in the river and also to compare rivers from different areas (see page 108).

# Underground rivers

As water seeps underground, it can eat into soft, permeable rock such as limestone, forming caves and river channels. Rainwater is slightly acidic and, over time, dissolves away the rock. The water seeps into the natural cracks and joints in limestone and enlarges the gaps by slowly dissolving the rock.

*1 talc (fingernail)*  *2 gypsum (fingernail)*  *3 calcite (copper coin)*

 **Underground water**

Rivers can also form under the ground in places where rocks are so full of water they cannot hold any more. The top of a layer of water-logged rock is called the **water table**. If the water table reaches above ground level, a spring appears. Underground pockets of water held in rocks are called **aquifers**.

 **Mohs scale**

About 180 years ago, a German geologist called Friedrich Mohs worked out a way of arranging minerals in order of hardness. He invented a scale from 1–10, called Mohs scale. The softest mineral, talc, is 1 on the scale and the hardest, diamond, is 10. Each mineral will scratch those below it on the scale, and will be scratched by those above it.

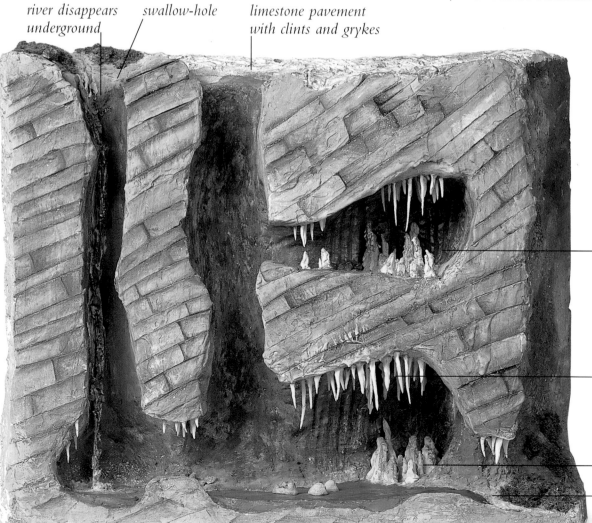

*river disappears underground*

*swallow-hole*

*limestone pavement with clints and grykes*

◁ *Underground caves are mostly caused by water eroding rock—either in coastal areas, or in limestone regions.*

*cave hollowed out by water*

***stalactites** grow about 10 in. in 500 years*

***stalagmites***

*river reappears where water table reaches ground level*

*4 fluorite*

*5 apatite (penknife)*

*6 orthoclase (window glass)*

◁ *Mohs scale is based on these 10 minerals. Here, some of them are compared to everyday objects of equal hardness.*

*7 quartz (steel knife)*

*8 topaz (sandpaper)*

*9 corundum*

*10 diamond*

△ *If the roof of a cave collapses, a larger cave called a cavern is formed. This is Carlsbad Caverns in N.M.*

## Limestone regions

As water flows over an area of limestone rock, it enlarges the natural cracks and joints, forming a limestone pavement. The grooves are called grykes and the blocks between them are called clints. When the water disappears underground, a hole called a swallow-hole forms. These holes can eventually grow into large potholes.

Many underground caves are found in places where the rock is mostly limestone. As water drips down from the roofs in limestone caves, it dissolves the minerals in the rocks. At the same time, the dripping water evaporates, leaving the minerals behind. These build up, over hundreds of years, into stalactites, which hang down from the roof, and stalagmites, which grow up from the ground. Sometimes they meet in the middle and form a pillar.

## Rocks and minerals

Rocks are usually made from mixtures of building blocks called minerals. Gold, copper and diamond are all minerals, and so is talc, which is used to make talcum powder. Other minerals have more unusual names such as corundum or apatite. Chalk and limestone are made of calcite, and granite is made of the minerals quartz, feldspar and mica.

Chalk is a **porous** rock. This means that it has many small air spaces, or pores, which hold water like a sponge. Chalk is also permeable: it lets water drain through the gaps in it.

## MAKE A STALACTITE

**You will need** paper clips, two glasses, washing soda crystals, string, saucer, distilled water

**1** Half-fill both glasses with distilled water and gradually pour in as many soda crystals as the water will dissolve.

**2** Dip a length of string in the solution. Run it between both glasses, securing with paper clips. Place a saucer between the glasses and leave for three or four days.

**Result:** the solution travels along the string as if it were the roof of a cave. When the solution reaches the lowest point, it drips onto the saucer. The water evaporates, leaving soda deposits that form a hanging soda stalactite. In a few more days, a soda stalagmite will also grow in the saucer.

# The upper river

The way rivers shape the land depends on how fast they flow and the kinds of rocks they flow over. In its upper course in the mountains, the river carves out a narrow, steep-sided valley that is usually in the shape of the letter V. The riverbed has a steep slope, or gradient, and the water cuts down into the land because the force of the water breaks up the rocks beneath it. Loose pebbles, stones and bits of grit bounce along the river bottom, rubbing against the rocks and wearing them away even more.

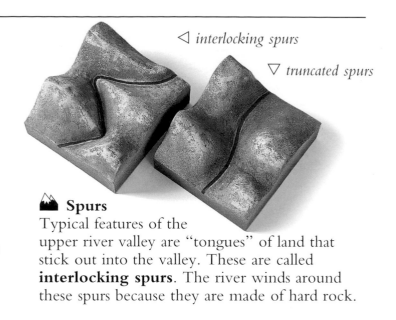

◁ *interlocking spurs*

▽ *truncated spurs*

### 🏔 Spurs

Typical features of the upper river valley are "tongues" of land that stick out into the valley. These are called **interlocking spurs**. The river winds around these spurs because they are made of hard rock.

Eventually the river may wear away the tips of the spurs, so that they become blunted instead of pointed. These are called truncated spurs.

△ *Braided rivers, like this one in Bhutan, occur in many places, although they are more common where the sediment is coarse and slopes are steep.*

### 🏔 Braided rivers

Braided rivers look rather like a braid in a person's hair. They appear in places where valley slopes are steep, or in dry areas where there is a lot of sand and gravel. The river threads its way around bars of gravel, sand and other coarse sediment. In the upper river, braiding usually occurs where a river works loose a lot of material that it cannot carry away.

▽ *In its upper course, the river takes up most of the narrow valley floor, winding around obstacles and eroding the steep valley sides.*

*boulders carried down by the river in times of flood when the river has great power*

*very little flat land for people to build homes, farms or roads*

*braided channels wind around bars of coarse material*

## ⛰ Land shapes

The upper river often runs through deep, narrow valleys with interlocking or truncated spurs. Wide, flat-topped mountains or hills lie between the valleys. The river is too shallow for transporting goods or people easily. It is also difficult to build roads or railroads across the river, although this has been done in the European Alps and the Andes of South America.

## 👫 Uses of the upper river

The steep valley sides make it difficult to grow crops, although animals can graze on them. **Dams** and **reservoirs** are often built on the upper river because it is easy to block the water here and distribute it to people downstream (see pages 114-115).

*V-shaped valley with steep sides*

*tributaries*

*rivers often begin in the mountains where there is a lot of rain*

*waterfall*

*drainage basin*

*broad hilltop forms a dividing line between two drainage basins*

*drainage basin*

*the river cuts downwards through hard rock to make a steep-sided gorge*

# The upper river

### 📊 Looking at rivers in profile

Geographers look at profiles of rivers to compare the way they flow at different points along their length. Rivers always move from higher areas down to lower ones. They usually begin with a fairly steep fall, then slope more gently as they continue their journey down, before flattening out as they finally reach the sea.

▷ *This is a profile of the Amazon River which is 4,000 miles long. Each marker on the base represents 100 miles. Geographers compare rivers from different areas by making profiles like this.*

### 📊 The mighty Amazon

The Amazon has an unusual profile. From its source in the Andes, it plunges down the mountainsides, dropping 5,470 yards in its first 620 miles. Then it runs almost level, dropping only 4 inches every 1.8 miles, as it winds across South America. It is so powerful that it carries sediment 60 miles out to sea and pours five times more water into the sea than any other river.

## RIVER LOAD EXPERIMENT

**You will need** bowl, wooden spoon, jug of water, coarse sand

**1** Place all the sand in the bowl and then pour in the water.

**2** Stir the water quickly with the wooden spoon, without touching the sand. You will see that the moving water picks up the sand particles, or sediment, and moves them around.

**3** Remove the spoon and let the water settle. The large particles of sand should sink first (they are heavier). As the water slows, the smaller particles settle. Only moving water will carry any particles.

## MAKE A SEDIMENT MEASURE

**You will need** two long strips and six small strips of wood, plasticine, three jars with screw-top lids, acrylic paint, glue, plastic tubing, three funnels, three rubber bands, piece of muslin

**1** Make two holes in the jar lid. Push the neck of the funnel into one hole and a short length of plastic tubing into the other. Secure them both with plasticine.

**2** Use a rubber band to fix a small piece of muslin over the plastic tube, on the inside of the lid. Then screw the lid on the jar. The funnel lets the water and sediment in; the tube lets the water out. Make two more sediment measures in the same way.

**3** Measure the width of your jars. Then make a ladder from the pieces of wood, as shown and paint. The rungs and rails must be wide enough apart for you to wedge in the jars at different levels along the ladder.

**4** Rest your sediment measure upright in a shallow stream in the opposite direction to the flow of the river (one jar should rest on the riverbed). After an hour, remove the measure and unscrew the lids. Compare the type of sediment and the amount collected in each of the jars.

**Result:** the jar at the bottom should contain coarse sediment that moves by jumping along the riverbed. A river's **load** is heaviest near the riverbed. The top jar should contain finer particles of sediment. This is because the water nearer the top of the river travels faster than the water at the bottom and carries lighter particles.

## ⛰ The power of a river

The power of a river is so great that it can erode the land and change its shape. But this depends on the type of channel it flows along and the type of material, or load, it picks up and carries to the sea. It also depends on how much water the river contains, how fast it is moving and how steeply the land slopes down to sea level.

▽ *The measure can tell us how much, and what type of sediment is in the river.*

## ⛰ Eroding the land

The water in rivers has some important effects on the shape of the land. First, as it flows through the river channel, water can dissolve minerals in the rocks so that they disappear and are carried away. Second, water can push into cracks and crevices, breaking off bits of rock and mud along the riverbank.

Third, rivers wear away the land by a process called abrasion. This is when the river's load scratches and scrapes against rocks and soil in the channel. Fourthly, the load itself is broken down into smaller particles. This process is called attrition. The effect of abrasion and attrition is to wear away the riverbed and riverbanks, making them wider and deeper.

## ⛰ Moving the load

Most of a river's load is moved during short periods of heavy flooding. The river carries its load in three ways. Particles of stones, gravel and coarse sand, called the bedload, move along the riverbed by rolling, tumbling or bouncing downstream in small jerks and jumps. As one particle lands, it bumps into another, making it hop along the riverbed. This jumping movement is called saltation.

Other tiny particles of fine sand and **silt** hang or float in the water. These are called the suspended load. Some materials dissolve in the water. This is the dissolved, or solution load.

# Waterfalls and rapids

Waterfalls and rapids are often found along the upper river. A waterfall occurs where a river falls steeply over a band of hard rock, often making a deep pool as it hits softer rock below. **Rapids** are stretches of fast-flowing water tumbling over a rocky, shallow riverbed.

### A thousand-year process

If a river flows over hard and then soft rock, it wears away the softer rock first, leaving a small step of hard rock sticking up into the river. Over thousands of years, the soft rock is worn away until eventually the river falls from a great height.

▽ *Eventually the hard rock is eroded and a new waterfall forms farther upstream.*

△ *The soft rock below the hard rock is worn away over time to form a waterfall.*

*water falls over a vertical layer of hard rock*

*plunge pool*

## MAKE A WATERFALL

**You will need** glass tank or water container, six bricks, three small tiles, small stones (shingle), large stones, plasticine, slate or large tile, jug, water

**1** Set up the bricks and tank as shown. Balance the slate on the bricks in the tank. Use the remaining bricks to support the slate at the other end.

**2** Put a layer of shingle in the glass tank. For rapids, lay the small tiles at an angle to the shingle, facing the waterfall. Secure with large stones and plasticine.

**3** Make raised banks on the sides of the slate using plasticine, shingle and stones. Pour water onto the slate.

**Result:** the water runs over the waterfall, making a plunge pool as it swirls around and shifts the shingle. The water should froth as it hits the tiles, or rapids.

**Waterfalls of the world**

Not all waterfalls and rapids are created by rivers alone. Some are made when movements in the Earth's crust push up a cliff or rock; others are formed by glaciers. Some waterfalls form on cliffs near the coast, or even under the sea, where the seabed is pushed up to make underwater steps. In fact, the world's biggest waterfall is under the sea between Greenland and Iceland—the water falls an amazing 2 miles. The highest waterfall on the Earth's surface is Angel Falls in Venezuela which is 3,212 feet high.

 **Plunge pools**

Plunge pools are found in soft rock at the bottom of some waterfalls. They are deep pools, carved out by boulders and stones that are whirled around by the huge force of the falling water.

**Rapids and cataracts**

Cataracts are series of rapids that form where bands of hard rock are tilted at an angle to the river. The rocks break up the flow, but are not big enough to form a waterfall. White, frothy water appears on top of cataracts in shallow areas.

△ *The water over rapids and cataracts foams and splashes to make patches of "white water." This canoeist faces the challenge of the rapids in a deep gorge in Austria.*

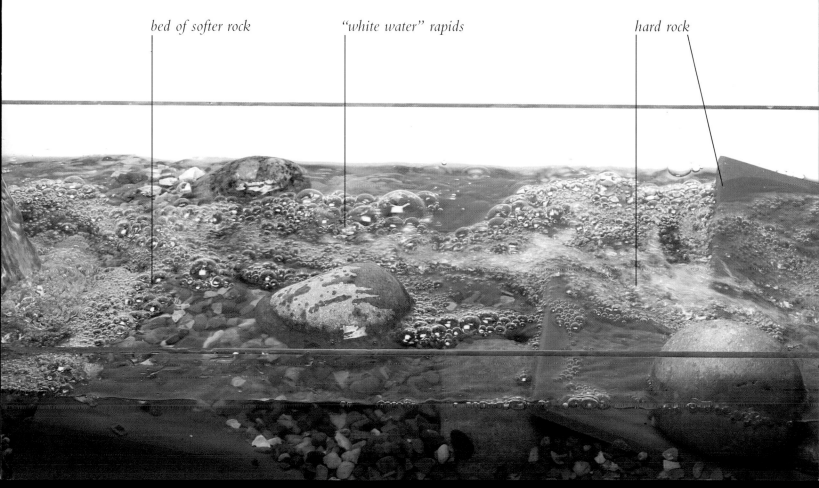

*bed of softer rock*       *"white water" rapids*       *hard rock*

# Energy from the river

Flowing water is an endless source of energy. People have used water energy for thousands of years by placing water wheels in rivers. The water provides the wheels with the energy to turn the millstones that grind grain. In many countries, water wheels are used to lift water from the river to **irrigate** crops.

▷ *These ancient water wheels on the Orontes River in Syria are still used to irrigate nearby fields.*

## MAKE A WATER WHEEL

  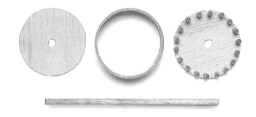

**You will need:** length of rain gutter, four gutter stops, piece of drainpipe, bricks, balsa wood, soft wood (pine), bradawl, washer, matchsticks, jug, water, hand drill, glue, 1/6 in. dowel, craft knife (ask an adult to help you when cutting)

**1** The wheel: cut two balsa circles, 4 in. across. Make a 1/5 in. hole in the center of each. For paddles, cut 18 balsa rectangles, 2 x 1/3 in.

**2** Glue the paddles to one circle as shown. Glue a piece of drainpipe, 2 in. long x 3 in. in diameter, in the middle of the paddles. Glue on the final circle.

**3** The cogs: cut a 1 in. length of drainpipe. Cut two balsa circles, 2 in. across. Make a 1/5 in. hole in each. Glue to each side of the drainpipe. Cut 18 pieces of dowel 1/3 in. long.

**4** Glue the dowel pieces around one of the circles, as shown above. Make a second cog following steps 3 and 4.

**5** The water-wheel support: cut one piece of pine 10 x 3 in. Cut two more, 6 x 3 in. and make two 1/5 in. holes at the top center of each. The support must be wide and tall enough to surround the gutter.

 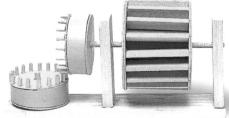 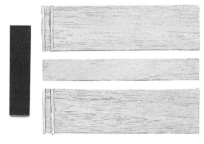

**6** Glue the pieces together as shown above. Then, cut an 8 in. length of dowel. Glue a cog to the end of it. Slide the dowel through the hole in the upright, the water-wheel and the second upright.

**7** Place the second cog on the base so that its teeth mesh with the water-wheel cog. Mark position on base.

**8** Remove the cog and drill a small hole over the mark. Cut a 1 in. length of dowel and push it into the hole in the base. Put a washer over the dowel, as shown above left.

**9** Replace the second cog so that it rests on the washer. The teeth of both cogs should mesh together comfortably.

**10** Cut four lengths of balsa wood: one 5 x 3/4 in.; one 5/8 x 3 in.; two 5 x 1 1/2 in. Glue four matchsticks across the two large pieces (1/10 in. apart) as shown above.

**11** Glue the pieces together to make a long, narrow, open-ended box. Slide the shortest piece of wood (sluice gate) between the matchsticks.

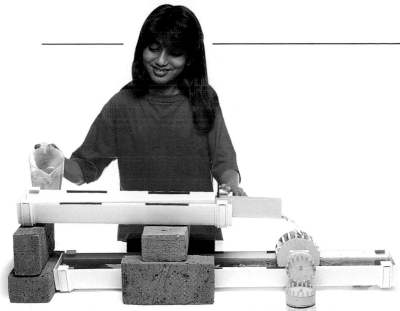

### ✿ Under or over—which is best?

In an undershot water wheel, water pushes the paddles around from below. In an overshot wheel, the water falls onto the wheel from above. The overshot wheel is more efficient, because the weight of water held in the paddles gives the wheel more pushing power.

Most water wheels are located on the upper river. This is because the gradient of the river bed is steeper, so the fast-flowing water provides more power, and because the narrow channel makes the wheel more stable in the river.

### ✿ Modern water power

Nowadays, water is used all over the world to generate electricity by turning gigantic water wheels called turbines (see pages 114–115). Modern turbines weigh thousands of tons and are designed to make as much use of the energy from the moving water as possible. They are much more efficient than the original water wheels.

**12** Cut a long piece of rain gutter and slide it through the support for the water wheel. Seal off the ends of the rain gutter with gutter stops.

**13** Cut a second length of rain gutter and seal with gutter stops. Rest it on top of the first rain gutter using the bricks as supports. Cut a gap in one gutter stop, small enough for the trough to slide in. Finally, pour water into the top rain gutter and let it flow onto the water wheel. By raising and lowering the sluice gate you can control the flow of water.

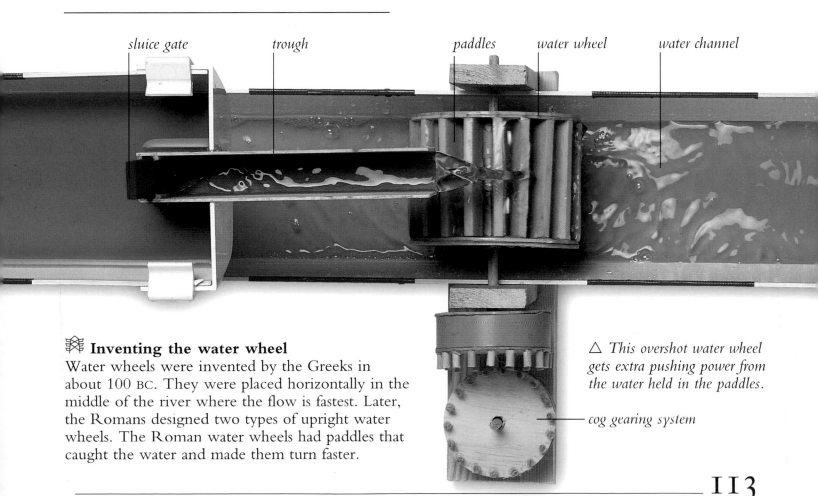

*sluice gate*     *trough*     *paddles*     *water wheel*     *water channel*

### ✿ Inventing the water wheel

Water wheels were invented by the Greeks in about 100 BC. They were placed horizontally in the middle of the river where the flow is fastest. Later, the Romans designed two types of upright water wheels. The Roman water wheels had paddles that caught the water and made them turn faster.

△ *This overshot water wheel gets extra pushing power from the water held in the paddles.*

— *cog gearing system*

# Dams and reservoirs

A dam is a very strong, thick wall built across a river valley to hold back the water. The lake that forms behind the dam is called a reservoir. Large amounts of water can be stored safely in the reservoir and gradually released downstream.

△ *The Hoover Dam in the U.S. blocks the Colorado River, creating Lake Mead.*

*an arched wall makes a very strong dam*

▽ *Dams are often built across the upper river in narrow V-shaped valleys.*

*reservoirs may be used for recreation, such as sailing*

## 👫 Dams

Large dams are usually either gravity dams or arch dams. A gravity dam is triangular in shape and is held in place by its weight. An arch dam gets its strength from the shape of its arch. Dams are wider and stronger at the bottom than at the top. This is because the water presses down more at the base of the dam.

## ❋ Reservoirs

Water from the reservoir behind the dam drives turbines that make electricity. In the powerhouse at the bottom of the dam, the fast-flowing water pushes huge turbines. They in turn drive generators that make electricity.

*cables carry electricity away from power stations to homes and factories*

114

## TEST A DAM

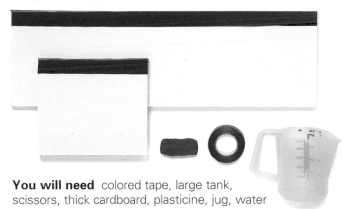

**You will need** colored tape, large tank, scissors, thick cardboard, plasticine, jug, water

**1** Cut a rectangle of cardboard slightly wider than the tank. Place it in the tank. The cardboard should curve in the middle.

**2** Seal the sides and bottom of the cardboard to the tank with plasticine, so that it is watertight. Next, to measure the water level, cut thin strips of tape and stick them at regular intervals along one side of the tank.

**3** Pour water slowly and steadily into the tank. Take regular readings of the water level. At what point does the cardboard give way under pressure from the water?

### ⚡ Hydroelectric power

A power station that uses energy from water to make electricity is called a **hydroelectric power** station. Such stations are often built on the upper river where the valley is narrow and easy to dam, and there is plenty of rainfall. In mountainous countries, such as Switzerland, nearly all the electricity is generated by hydroelectric power.

**4** Make a curved dam with a rectangle of cardboard that is twice the width of the tank. Now, repeat the experiment.

**Result:** the second dam will hold much more water than the first because the dam gets its strength from its greater curved shape.

*roads are sometimes built across the tops of dams*

*water tower*

### ⚡ Power stations

Dam walls are high so that the water falls a long way and provides a huge force to drive the turbines that generate electricity. Water is a never-ending source of energy and hydroelectric power stations do not pollute the environment in the way that power stations running on coal or oil do. But changing the natural flow of water in a river can cause a lack of water downstream for people, farms, plants or animals.

# Lakes and basins

Lakes are large hollows, or basins, in the surface of the land. They appear at different places along the length of a river; sometimes they are the source of a river, at other times they are the place where rivers end up. Lakes can be formed by natural forces such as glaciation, movements in the Earth, or even by beavers blocking rivers with twigs and branches. People also create lakes by building dams across rivers.

▷ *Water collects in a natural hollow in the land to form a lake. The water comes from rivers, rainfall, melting snows or rainwater that seeps through soil and rock.*

## ⛰ Disappearing lakes

Lakes can be almost any size, shape or depth. Some are regular features of the landscape, while others appear only at certain times of the year, perhaps when there are very heavy rains. Lake Eyre in Australia dries up completely in some years and often remains dry for two or three years at a time. The one thing that all lakes have in common is that they do not last forever. The water eventually evaporates, or is drained by rivers, or fills in with plants and soil. Given time, most lakes will turn back into dry land.

*river tributaries*

*main river*

*mud, sand and pebbles carried by the river settle on the edges of the lake*

*beach shows where lake once reached a higher level*

*natural hollow*

*water seeps through soil and rock until it reaches the water table (the top of a layer of water-filled rock)*

### Rift valley lakes

*rift valley lake*

Forces inside the Earth can cause a block of land to slip downward, making a steep-sided valley called a rift valley. Lake Tanganyika in Africa and Lake Baikal are rift valley lakes. These lakes are long, narrow and very deep—the bottom is often below sea level.

### Barrier lakes

When glaciers melt, they leave behind rocks, mud and other material. Water collects in hollows, and the rocks and mud stop it from seeping away. Hundreds of small lakes called barrier lakes can form this way. The lake plateau of Finland has many barrier lakes. It is known as "the land of 40,000 lakes."

△ *This is an erosion lake in Washington state.*

### How are they formed?

Most lakes are found in hollows that were scooped out by glaciers and ice sheets during the ice ages thousands of years ago. Other lakes formed when rivers were blocked by material left behind by ice sheets or volcanoes. In North America, the huge weight of one ice sheet made the land sink into a basin. After the ice melted, the basin filled with water to form the Great Lakes.

Some of the world's biggest lakes, such as Lake Baikal in Russia, were formed by powerful movements inside the Earth. Earth movements also push volcanoes up from the land. Sometimes the top of a volcano collapses and fills with water to form a crater lake.

### Erosion lakes

At the start of a mountain glacier, the ice may erode a bowl-shaped hollow in the rock. When the ice melts, the hollow fills up with water to form a round lake, known as an erosion lake. The English Lake District was formed in this way.

*barrier lakes*

*erosion lake*

# River canyons

In parts of the world that have long dry seasons, some rivers carve deep valleys called **canyons**. The rivers get their water from mountains far away, or from underground. When rain falls on canyons, it is usually in short, heavy bursts. There is little soil and few plants to soak up the water, so it rushes over the land, carrying loose rocks with it. Two of the world's most spectacular canyons are the Grand Canyon in Arizona and the Nile Canyon in Egypt.

### The world's largest canyon

The Grand Canyon is almost 277 mi. long, up to 18 mi. wide and 1 mi. deep. It takes a whole day to walk to the bottom. The Grand Canyon formed over the past six million years as the land rose and the river cut downwards into it. Layers of hard and soft rock have worn away at different rates. Today, the hard rock stands out as cliffs, while the soft rock has formed slopes.

## How the Grand Canyon was formed

**1** About 2 billion years ago, powerful forces inside the Earth caused layers of sediments and volcanic lava to fold. Slowly, these layers were pushed into a mountain range 5-6 mi. high.

**2** Gradually the mountains were worn away and more sediments built up as seas flooded the land. The land tipped up to form new mountains, but by 600 million years ago, all that remained was a hilly plain.

▷ *The walls of the Grand Canyon have been carved out by wind, rain and the Colorado River.*

*limestone, sandstone and shales*

*steep-sided valley, or canyon*

## EROSION TEST

**3** Pour water slowly into the center of the tank and watch what happens.

**Result:** the water quickly forms a deep pit or canyon in the dry sand. This is roughly how canyons are formed, although the real process takes millions of years!

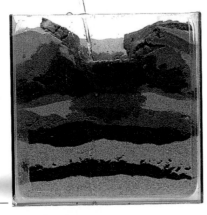

**You will need**
several colors of sand, glass tank, jug of water

**1** Pour the dry sand into the tank, using layers of different colors to represent beds of sedimentary rock.

**2** Add the final layer and make sure it is level.

**3** Seas and rivers covered the land again, depositing more sediments up to 1½ mi. thick. This lasted until 65 million years ago.

**4** Over millions of years the layers of rock were worn away. The Colorado River started to drain westward over the area.

**5** In the past few million years, the land has risen and the river has cut down into the layers of ancient rocks to form a canyon.

### 🏔 Earth history

Walking down the Grand Canyon is like stepping back in time. The limestone rocks found at the top are the most recent. They formed below the sea 250 million years ago. Fossils of reptiles and insects that were alive millions of years before people existed have been found in these rocks.

The rocks halfway down the canyon are 400 million years old; some contain fish remains. Lower down, in rocks 500 million years old, there are only shellfish and worm fossils. Right at the bottom of the canyon, the rocks are 2 billion years old. Life may have existed on Earth then, but no traces of living things have been found.

*cliffs collapse as softer rocks are worn away*

*the Colorado River may be up to 30 million years old*

*muddy river carries soil and small pieces of rock (this shows it is eroding the surface of the land)*

# The middle river

As a river gets farther from its source, more tributaries join it. The amount of water and material in the river increases. The land slopes more gently and the river starts to cut sideways into the land, rather than downward. The riverbed is no longer littered with pebbles and boulders. Instead, the water carries sand, mud and small stones, and the bed becomes lined with a smooth layer of mud and silt.

### Cutting a smooth course

At this stage, the river carries its load suspended in the water. It also begins to swing from side to side, cutting into some banks and drifting away from others. There are no obstacles such as rapids, so the river's course becomes smoother and more regular.

△ *This is the middle section of the Mekong River in Cambodia. The river carries a lot of mud and silt.*

▷ *This is a river in its middle course, flowing through tropical rain forest. The river winds its way across a flat valley floor and thick rain forest grows to the river's edge.*

## MAKE A FLOW METER

**You will need:** strip of wood, dowel, funnel, balsa wood, plasticine, tape, thumbtack, glue, drill, paints, protractor, craft knife (ask an adult for help)

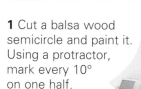

**1** Cut a balsa wood semicircle and paint it. Using a protractor, mark every 10° on one half.

**2** Glue the semicircle, or dial, to your wood strip, about a third of the way down.

**3** Drill a small hole in the dowel, about a third of the way along. Paint this third—this is your needle.

**4** With the thumbtack, attach the needle to the wood strip, just below the dial. Make sure it can swing freely.

**5** Make a stopper in the end of the funnel with plasticine. Tape or glue the funnel to the unpainted end of the needle. Paint the rest of your flow meter.

**6** Place the meter upright in the middle of a shallow stream (the funnel should face upstream). The flow of the river will make the needle move across the dial. The farther the needle moves toward the horizontal, the faster the flow. Test the flow closer to the river bank. Is there a difference?

120

## 👥 Transport and trade

In many parts of the world, people rely on the middle river for food, transport and trade. In the rain forest, people also rely on the trees and vegetation that grow to the river's edge. Rain forests contain valuable trees such as teak, mahogany and rosewood. Sometimes, areas of the forest are cleared by cutting down the trees. Logs are floated downriver and loaded onto ships where the river meets the sea. Once the trees and vegetation are cleared away, the thin soil is easily washed away by heavy rain. Then the land cannot be used for growing crops or more trees.

## 🏔 Speed of flow

Along the middle river, the channel is deep and lined with smooth mud and silt. There is less friction between the river and the riverbed because there are no boulders or stones to slow down the flow of the river. The water flows fastest in the center of the river channel near the surface, where there is least friction.

*floodwaters leave mud and silt on the riverbank*

*village built on higher land near river*

*meandering river*

*river drops material on inside bend to make a beach*

*trees cut down for timber cause more soil to be washed into the river*

*sawmill pollutes the river*

# The middle river

## ⛰ The changing course

The path of the middle river is always changing as it cuts sideways into the land and starts to deposit its load. Loops, called meanders, and **oxbow lakes** are typical features of this part of the river. During a storm, meanders stop river water flowing easily. This causes water to build up in places, and may lead to flooding.

## ⛰ How meanders form

Rivers twist and turn naturally as they flow over the land creating meanders. These tend to form in places where there are wide, strong riverbanks. Large rivers, such as the Mississippi in the U.S., have meanders that are many miles across.

△ *This photograph shows an oxbow lake along the Manu River in the rain forest of Peru.*

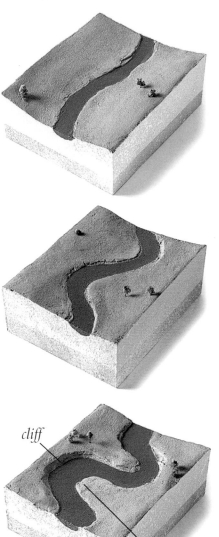

*cliff*

*bar*

**1** As the river travels along more gently sloping land, it starts to curve across the valley floor. When rivers swing from side to side, they flow more slowly than when they flow in a straight line.

**2** Over time, the meander becomes bigger. As the river slowly cuts away the bank on the outside curve, it leaves the material it is carrying on the inside curve. These ridges of sand and gravel are called bars.

**3** A wide swing forms along the path of the river. Gradually, a cliff starts to form on the outside bend where the river has cut into the banks.

## ⛰ From meanders to oxbow lakes

Oxbow lakes begin as meanders. As the river continues to wear away the bank on the outside bend of the meander, the river channel becomes more U-shaped. Eventually, the river cuts through the neck of the meander to make a new channel.

*oxbow lake*

**1** The river has formed a meander so wide that it is almost a circle. There is only a narrow strip of land separating the sections of the river channels.

**2** The river has cut through the "neck" of the meander and formed a new, straighter channel.

**3** As the river continues along its new path, it leaves behind a horseshoe-shaped lake called an oxbow lake. Over time, plants and vegetation will grow over this lake.

## ⛰ River terraces

When the surface of the land is pushed up by movements under the Earth, rivers cut down into the land. This also happens with a drop in the level of the lake or sea into which a river flows. A step-like strip is left behind on the sides of the valley, at a higher level than the new river channel. This is a river terrace. Terraces can also form if rainfall increases. The river becomes more powerful and cuts into the land.

**1** As the river meanders along the valley floor, the land may rise or the water level may drop. Then the river starts to cut down into the land.

*old valley floor*        *river terrace*

**2** The river forms a new valley at a lower level. The old valley floor forms a river terrace on the valley sides. Over time, many terraces may form.

---

**THE GRADIENT TEST**

**You will need** three bricks, small plastic window box, sheet of hardboard, jug, plasticine, plastic cup, water

**1** Arrange the bricks, hardboard and window box as shown above. Pour water down the steep slope and watch.

**Result:** over a steep gradient, you will see that water takes the most direct path to the window box (sea).

**2** Reduce the height of the bricks to make a shallow slope. Make a small hole near the bottom of the plastic cup and place it at the top of the board. Make a narrow channel with the plasticine and press it around the hole and onto the board. Pour the water into the cup and watch.

**Result:** over a shallow gradient, water begins to meander and travels more slowly on its journey to the sea.

# The middle river

## 🚶 Living along the middle river

In **developed countries**, such as those of Europe or North America, the middle river is used in all sorts of ways. Towns and cities have grown up in places where it is easy to cross the river. A flat valley floor is ideal for building roads and railroads, while the river is an efficient way to carry people and goods from place to place.

## 🏔 Soil fertility

The success of farming along the middle river often depends on the soil. Some types of soil are more suitable for growing crops than others. To test soil, farmers find out its pH (potential hydrogen) value. This is measured on a scale from 0–14. Neutral is 7, anything less than 7 is acidic, and anything greater is alkaline. Some crops grow better in slightly acid soil, whereas others prefer more alkaline soil.

## TEST SOIL pH

**You will need** a pH testing kit from your local garden center, jug, glass, distilled water, pipette, soil

**1** Place some soil in a glass and add some distilled water. Stir and leave the mixture to settle.

**2** Take a sample from the glass with a pipette and add to your testing kit. Open the capsule that comes with the testing kit and add it to the water and soil mixture in the kit. Replace the lid on the testing kit and shake well for about a minute.

**3** Match the color of the mixture to the pH value on the kit.

**Result:** the redder the color, the more acid the soil; the blacker the color, the more alkaline the soil. Neutral is pH 7.0.

## 🚶 Early settlements

Thousands of years ago, when people first lived in towns and cities, they chose sites near rivers for their settlements. They needed water for drinking, as well as for farming and transport. The first great civilizations all developed along rivers—the Nile in Egypt, the Huang He River in China, the Tigris-Euphrates in Iraq and the Indus in Pakistan. These river valleys all had something in common: a fertile **floodplain** with rich fields for farming and fresh water to supply a growing population.

## 🚶 River transport

Until a hundred and fifty years ago, there were no railroads, and many roads were simply muddy tracks. The safest way to transport heavy goods was by barge and boat along rivers. In many parts of the world today, rivers are still important highways for moving goods. To keep river channels deep enough for large boats to use, dredgers clear away the silt and mud.

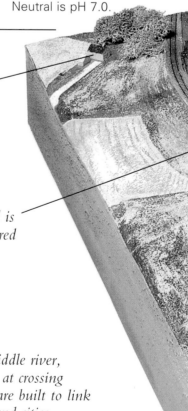

*farming on valley floor and sides*

*fertile marshland is drained and cleared for farming*

▷ *Along the middle river, towns spring up at crossing points. Bridges are built to link different towns and cities.*

## 🏔 The middle river valley

The model below shows some of the features you might see on rivers such as the Rhine or the Danube in Europe, or the St Lawrence in Canada. The river winds its way across a flat valley floor, dropping some of its load to form bars on the inside curves of meanders. Dams and lakes farther upstream control the flow of the river. The river and its valley are vital for settlements, farming and transport.

△ The town of Cochem grew at a bridging point along the middle course of the Moselle River in Germany.

river is used for sailing, fishing and water-skiing

river has worn away most of the valley sides to make a flat valley bottom

river is used to transport raw materials and goods to and from factories

cities, factories and power stations may pollute the water in the river

# The human water cycle

We need fresh drinking water in order to survive, but we also need water for washing, cooking and heating. Most of our fresh water comes from rivers and reservoirs. In many countries, water is cleaned before and after it is used to remove dirt and germs. As there is only a certain amount of fresh water on Earth, we need to keep our rivers clean if we are to continue taking water from them.

## 👫 Taking water from rivers

The cycle begins when we take water from rivers. Sticks, leaves and any large objects are cleared from the water before it is pumped to a reservoir. From the reservoir, the water passes to a treatment plant. It settles in tanks lined with sand and gravel, which trap the dirt. A chemical called chlorine is added to kill the germs, making the water clean and safe to drink. Finally, the water is either stored or pumped directly to homes and factories along pipes under the roads.

## 👫 Cleanup operation

Once it has been used, dirty water goes into huge underground pipes called sewers that carry the water to the sewage treatment plant. The water is cleaned by a kind of **bacteria** that eat the germs and dirt, leaving only gases and water behind. At this stage the water is clean enough to be pumped back into the river. Every glass of water we drink has been used hundreds of times before as part of the endless human water cycle.

▽ *This model shows the "human water cycle": how we take water from the river, clean it, use it, and then clean it again before returning it to the river.*

water-treatment plant, where water is filtered through beds of sand

water is stored, or pumped to homes and factories

pumping station

chlorine is added to the water

storage reservoir

**WATER FILTER TEST**

**You will need** plastic bottle, scissors, sphagnum (garden) moss, sand, gravel, soil, leaves, jug, water, glass, bradawl

**1** Cut the bottom off the bottle. Carefully make a small hole in the bottle top with a bradawl, then replace the bottle top.

**2** Pour some sand into the bottle. Then add some moss. Build up three layers of moss and sand. Finally, add a layer of gravel.

**3** Mix some sand, gravel, soil, leaves and water separately in the jug.

**4** Balance the bottle on top of the glass and pour in the water mixture.

**Result:** the sand and moss will trap most of the debris. The water in the glass should be almost clear, perhaps with some sand particles remaining.

*sewage is treated and clean water is returned to the river*

*storage reservoir*

## 👥 Water around the world

In developed countries, the average person uses up to 132 gallons of water a day. When the rest of the world is included, the average person uses only about 1 1/3 gallons. In some of the **developing countries** of Asia, Africa and South America, only one person in five has access to clean drinking water. People cannot simply turn on a faucet when they want water. They may have to walk long distances to a river or well, and then carry the heavy water back to their homes.

Millions of bacteria live in water. They are too small to see, and most are harmless, but a few can cause deadly diseases such as cholera and typhoid. These diseases spread rapidly where people do not have clean water; in refugee camps for example. Millions of people die each year, from lack of water or from water-borne diseases. By the next century, up to a third of the world's countries may suffer from permanent water shortages.

# Farming on the lower river

Near the end of its journey, a river flows across an almost flat plain toward its mouth. This is part of the lower river. Here, the river is wide and no longer cuts down into the land. It still wears away its banks though, and makes a wide, flat valley floor called a floodplain. At this stage, the river deposits fine mud on the riverbed and riverbanks. When the river floods, the mud spreads all over the floodplain.

### ▲ The fertile floodplain

After heavy rain, or when snow melts in the mountains, more water suddenly pours into the river. All this extra water in the lower river can cause the river to burst its banks and overflow onto the floodplain. When this happens, the water spreads out in a thin sheet over the valley floor.

As the river starts to slow down, it drops the heaviest part of its load (coarse sand) first. This builds up on the riverbanks to form broad walls called levees. Finer sediment, such as mud, is washed out onto the flat valley floor. After many floods, layers of this sediment, called **alluvium**, build up into fertile land that is good for farming.

## FLOOD A RIVER VALLEY

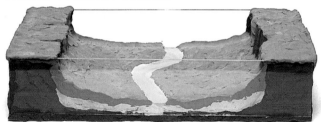

△ *Lower river meandering across a wide, flat floodplain.*

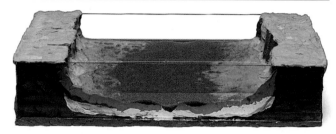

△ *As the river floods, fertile mud spreads over the valley.*

**You will need** baseboard, tape, two sheets of Plexiglass or glass, four bricks, sand, jug, water, blue food coloring, colored plasticine: brown for bedrock, white for river channel, green for vegetation, yellow for sand

**1** Position the bricks on either side of the baseboard. Cover them with layers of plasticine to make a steep-sided valley as shown above.

**2** Carve out a meandering river channel and line it with white plasticine. Add yellow plasticine (for sand deposits) on the inner bends of the river.

**3** Make your river valley watertight by pressing the sheets of Plexiglass or glass into the plasticine at each end. Fix with tape if necessary. Next, fill a jug with water and add a little blue food coloring.

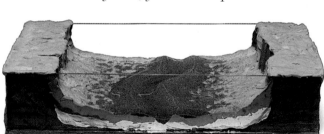

△ *Raised banks, or levees, form on both sides of the river where sand and gravel have been deposited.*

**4** Mix some sand with the water. Pour the mixture slowly into the course of the river, as shown at left. The river will begin to rise over its banks and flood the surrounding land.

**5** Carefully remove one of the Plexiglass sheets and allow the water to drain away. The sand in the water (representing alluvium) should be spread thinly all over the floodplain.

**6** Replace the Plexiglass sheet. Pour some more water into the river channel. This time, the water should flow between the newly formed banks, or levees.

▽ *Flooded rice paddies.*

*floodplain*

*bund*

*irrigation channel*

*lower river*    *raised banks or levees*

## 🏳 Rice farming in China

China has only 7 per cent of the world's farmland, yet it tries to grow enough to feed its huge population which is 20 per cent of the world's total. Rice is the staple food and it is grown near rivers as it needs plenty of water.

River water is fed to the rice fields, or paddies, via a series of irrigation channels. Little walls of stone or soil, called bunds, hold in the water, and small sluice gates control the flow to the fields. As the rice grows, the water level is checked and topped up if necessary. In China, land is never wasted. Flooded paddy fields are sometimes used for fish farming, and crops of sugar cane and mulberries are grown on banks between the fields.

## 🏳 A watering machine

A shadoof is a simple device used in many places to lift water from rivers to fields at a higher level. It is a long lever with a bucket on one end and a weight on the other. The farmer dips the bucket into the river, swings it around and empties the water onto the field.

## 🏳 Danger—flooding!

Many people live on river valley floors despite the risk of flood, either because the land is so fertile or because they have nowhere else to live. In Bangladesh, most of the land is floodplain. Each year many people lose their lives and their homes in floods there.

## MAKE A SHADOOF

*funnel*

**5** Fill the funnel with water. Now swing your shadoof around and pull out the stop to release the water.

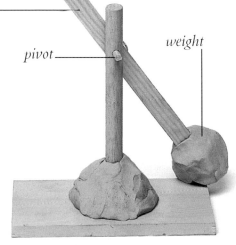

*lever*

*pivot*

*weight*

**You will need** strip of wood 23 in. long, piece of wood 7 x 4 in., 8 in. length of $1/3$ in. dowel, funnel, plasticine, string, 1 in. length of $1/8$ in. dowel, hand drill

**1** Drill a $1/3$ in. hole in the center of the wooden board, and a $1/8$ in. hole through one end of the $1/3$ in. dowel. Drill two $1/8$ in. holes in the long wooden strip (lever) as shown above.

**2** Push the long dowel into the baseboard and secure with plasticine (it should still be able to turn freely). Pass the small dowel (pivot) through the hole in the large dowel and through the hole in the lever as shown at right.

**3** Use a large ball of plasticine to weigh down the end of the lever.

**4** Make two small holes in the funnel as above. Thread string through the holes and tie as shown. Thread the loose end of string through the hole in the lever and tie around the pivot. Make a stop in the funnel with plasticine.

129

# River deltas

Most rivers end their journey when they flow into the sea or a lake. The river slows down and deposits the sediment it is carrying. Heavy grains of sand and gravel drop to the bottom. Lighter particles of fine silt and clay are carried farther out to sea, or into the lake. Gradually, the sediment spreads out to form a new piece of land with gently sloping sides. This is called a delta. This word comes from the Greek letter △ (delta), after the shape of the Nile Delta in Egypt.

## 👫 Farming and settlement

Deltas build up from layers of mineral-rich sediments. For centuries, people have farmed the flat land of deltas. Important cities are often built on or near deltas, such as Shanghai on the Yangtze Delta, Alexandria on the Nile Delta, and New Orleans on the Mississippi Delta. As deltas grow, cities may end up farther away from the sea.

## 🏔 Estuaries

Sometimes the sea level rises and floods the mouth of a river. Seawater drowns the river valley, creating a long funnel shape in from the coast, called an **estuary**. Estuaries are not filled in with sediment like deltas, but they do have lots of rich mud that contains food for wildlife.

▷ *When the river reaches the delta, it splits into branching channels called* **distributaries**. *They carry water over the surface of the delta.*

*farms on the edge of a fertile river delta*

*water spills over the distributaries, dropping sediment that forms levees*

*surface of the delta gradually builds up as more sediment is deposited*

*sediment deposited under the sea beyond the edge of the delta*

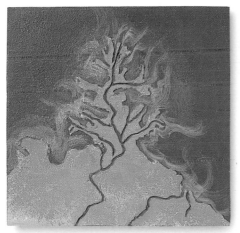

*bird's-foot delta*

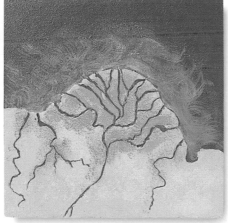

*arcuate delta*

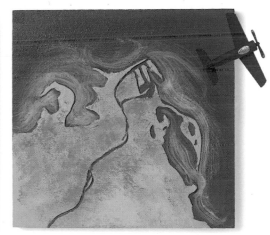

*cuspate delta*

## ⛰ Shapes of deltas

The shape of a delta depends on how much water and sediment is carried by the river, and how fast the water is flowing. It also depends on the speed and strength of the sea's waves, currents and tides.

When a lot of sediment is carried out into calm seawater, a bird's-foot delta forms. The distributaries carry long "toes" of sediment out into the sea. The Mississippi Delta is shaped like this.

An arcuate delta is shaped like a triangle. It forms when a river meets the sea in a place where the waves, currents and tides are not strong. The deltas of the Nile, Indus and Rhône are shaped like this.

When a river drops sediment onto a straight shoreline with strong waves, a cuspate delta is formed. Waves force the sediment to spread outward in both directions from the river's mouth, making a pointed tooth shape, with curved sides.

## DELTA EXPERIMENT

**You will need** large plastic garden tray, bricks, shingle (small stones), sand, water, blue food coloring, jug, two white wooden boards as shown below

**1** Arrange the bricks in the tray as shown at right (they represent the land). Pour the shingle between the bricks. Place the narrower strip of wood on top of the shingle, between the bricks, to form a ramp.

**2** Use the larger piece of wood as a seabed. Place some shingle at the base of the ramp, between the bricks (neck of land), to make a shingle beach.

**3** Half-fill the tray with water (to represent the sea). Mix some sand in a jug with colored water and pour into the back of the tray to create a river.

◁ *The sand deposits have formed a triangular, or arcuate, delta.*

**Result:** as the sediment (sand) flows down the river channel, the delta should grow and spread into a fan shape.

# Flood control

Floods occur when the water in a river suddenly rises and the banks cannot contain it. In large floods, the river may be ten times deeper and carry a hundred times more water than usual. Floods can be caused by natural events, such as high tides, heavy rainstorms or melting snow. They can also be caused by cutting down trees that soak up rainfall, or by draining marshy land into a river.

△ *The Thames Barrier has 10 movable steel gates that can be raised to make a 59 foot-high wall.*

### 👬 Preventing damage

Natural floods are impossible to stop, but it is possible to reduce the damage they cause to people and property. Building walls or levees along rivers and coasts is one solution. Others include dredging the river to make it wider and deeper, and building reservoirs to hold extra water.

### 👬 The Thames Barrier

Mechanical barriers can prevent floodwaters from damaging towns and cities. London, England, is in danger of being flooded when there is a high tide or a storm. This is because the sea level is rising and the land is slowly sinking. Movable barriers can be raised to stop the river water flowing upstream.

## BUILD A THAMES BARRIER

**You will need**
shingle (small stones), plasticine, glass or Plexiglass tank, 8 in. length of dowel, two gutter stops, 13 in. length of rain gutter, hand drill, wood (pine): base: 8 x 3 in., two uprights: 6 x 2 in., paints

**Note:**
measurements of barrier will vary depending on the size of your tank.

**1** Drill two $1/5$ in. holes in the uprights, as shown. For the support, glue the upright pieces to the wooden base, as shown at right. Paint the support.

**2** Cut a 7 in. length of rain gutter. Make a notch in each of the gutter stops as shown above. Attach the gutter stops to the ends of the rain gutter to make your barrier.

**3** Slide the barrier and the dowel into the drilled holes in the gutter stops and uprights. Next, cut a 6 $1/5$ in. section of gutter. Slide it underneath the barrier as shown at right.

**4** Make a watertight seal with plasticine between the second piece of rain gutter and the base. Place the barrier and a bed of shingle in the tank. Make another seal between the support and the tank (as shown opposite). Slip the barrier into the upright position.

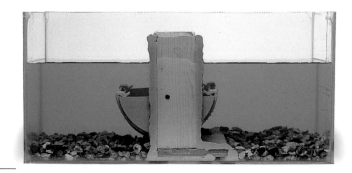

**5** Pour a little water into the left side (to represent the river flowing downstream). Fill the right side of the tank with water (incoming tide). The barrier stops the tide running upstream and flooding the river. Now lower the barrier so that it lies flat (as shown below). When the level of the river is the same on both sides, ships can pass.

## 👫 Holding back the Mississippi

Severe flooding often occurs along the Mississippi River in the U.S. To help control the flooding, 3,600 miles of levees have been built from soil, rock and sand. The soil is usually taken from "borrow pits" around the river. The large pits later fill in with water and become human-made lakes.

In Bangladesh and other developing countries where floods claim many lives each year, there is not much money available for flood control. Levees are often built from whatever materials people can find—soil, wood, old tires and corrugated iron.

## 🏔 Flood-control problems

Building levees can cause problems. If a river does not flood, then fertile sediment is no longer spread over the plain, so the land is not as good for farming. Also, sections of rivers with levees hold more water. This sometimes leads to water being forced into unprotected sections downstream.

*sandbags for extra protection*

*borrow pit*

*raised levee*

*tree and plant roots soak up water and help to bind the soil*

△ *Levees built on the banks of the Mississippi River.*

▽ *The raised barrier holds back the incoming tide.*

# Managing rivers

Rivers and the land beside them are used for farming, industry, energy, transport, water supply and recreation. They are also a home for wildlife. Sometimes people upset the balance of rivers by taking too much water from them, by polluting the water and by overfishing. People also try to control floods by changing the river's course. Often, rivers flow through several countries and people do not always agree on the best way of handling the river's resources.

△ *Keeping rivers clean and free from pollution makes them safe for spawning salmon and other wildlife.*

▽ *This model shows how we use the whole river, in its upper, middle and lower courses.*

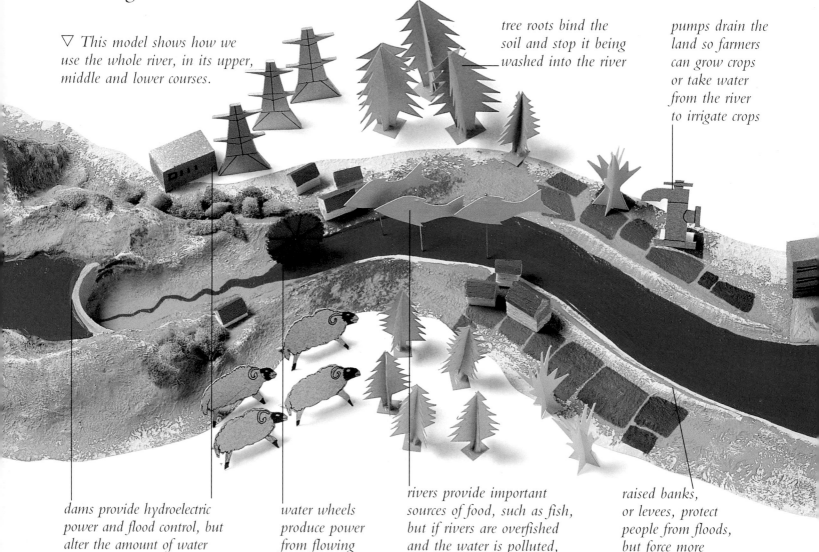

*tree roots bind the soil and stop it being washed into the river*

*pumps drain the land so farmers can grow crops or take water from the river to irrigate crops*

*dams provide hydroelectric power and flood control, but alter the amount of water and sediment in the river*

*water wheels produce power from flowing water*

*rivers provide important sources of food, such as fish, but if rivers are overfished and the water is polluted, the supply will dwindle*

*raised banks, or levees, protect people from floods, but force more water downstream*

## People and pollution

Every day, we take about four-fifths of the world's freshwater that is stored in rivers and in rocks underground. As the world's population grows, water shortages may be more of a problem than food shortages in the next century.

Making sure that people have clean water to drink is another problem. In developing countries, pollution control is very expensive and the river water may be dirty and dangerous to people's health. People may not be able to afford to clean river water before and after they use it. Developed countries also face the problems of pollution—especially if industries are allowed to dump waste into the river.

## Managing the river

People throughout the world depend on rivers, but managing them can cause problems. In order to avoid flooding disasters in the future, it is important to understand why rivers flow the way they do, and what happens when we alter them.

Sometimes, rivers and the sediment they carry are too heavily managed. Dams, barriers and banks control the river in a very unnatural way. They may give protection from floods and other disasters for a while, but over time rivers always fight back, trying to take the easiest path across land. If we are to make the best possible use of rivers, we need to look at the river as a whole, and not just a section at a time.

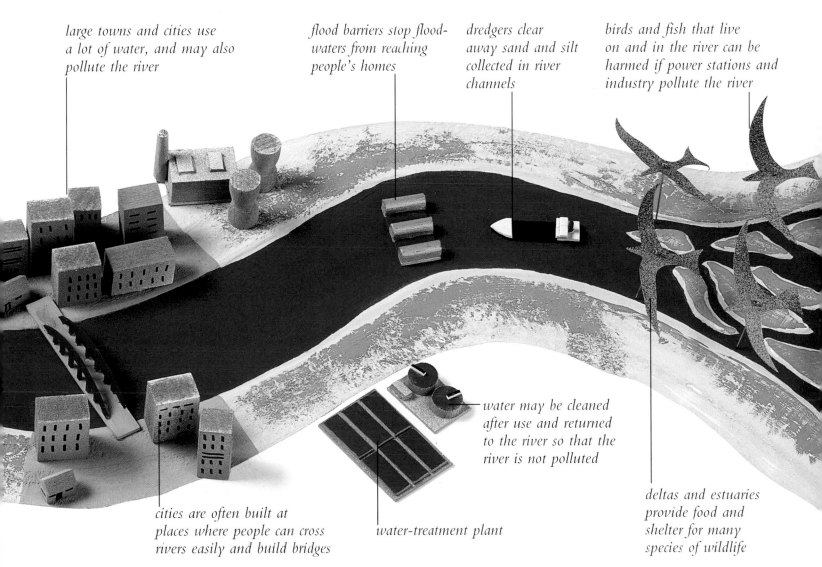

large towns and cities use a lot of water, and may also pollute the river

flood barriers stop flood-waters from reaching people's homes

dredgers clear away sand and silt collected in river channels

birds and fish that live on and in the river can be harmed if power stations and industry pollute the river

water may be cleaned after use and returned to the river so that the river is not polluted

cities are often built at places where people can cross rivers easily and build bridges

water-treatment plant

deltas and estuaries provide food and shelter for many species of wildlife

# Maps

# Being a mapmaker

Geography helps us to understand what happened to the Earth in the past, how it is changing now, and what might happen to it in the future. To try to make sense of our world, people make maps, pictures of the land, to record and share information about the world we live in. Many ancient maps were based more on stories than on facts, but today's geographers have a wealth of information, gathered from **satellite** pictures and computers, to help them to describe our world.

△ *Not all maps are flat. This Inuit coastal map is carved from wood.*

▽ *People make maps of towns, mountains, and even stars in the sky.*

## Why are maps useful?

People first made maps to help find their way across unknown lands or seas, or to record what land belonged to them. Explorers drew maps to record features of the lands they visited. People still use maps to find their way around, but today's maps can also tell us about people—where they live and shop, and how they farm the land.

## Types of maps

You can show almost anything on a map, from weather forecasts to animals of the world. Maps showing natural features of the Earth, such as rivers and rocks, are called **physical maps**. Maps showing how people use the land for farming, transport, homes and so on, are called **human maps**. Some maps are general reference maps; they show a variety of features, such as landscapes, forests, towns and roads.

## A historical record

When someone draws a map, they use the information available to them at that time. Old maps tell us a lot about what people knew of the world in the past, and the ideas they thought were important. Looking at old maps, we can see that people did not know as much about the Earth as we do today. Some mapmakers of the past left out large parts of the world from their maps. They filled the gaps with pictures of monsters or clouds, because they did not know what was really there.

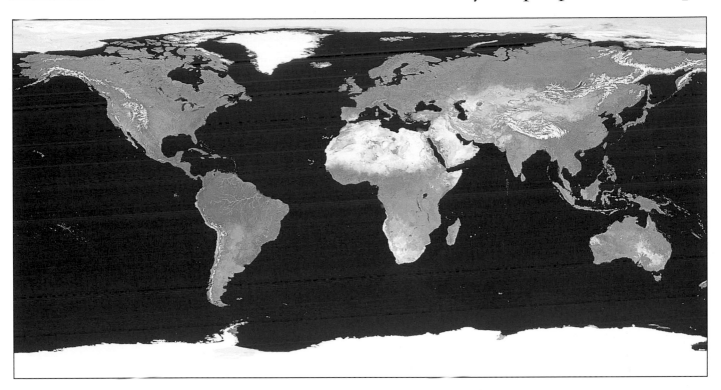

## Using this book

Geographers have to study a wide range of subjects. Throughout this book, we have used **symbols** to show where information relates to particular geographical topics. The symbols are:

🏔 physical      📖 mapmaking, or **cartography**

🌦 weather      ⊗ route-finding

👪 human        🌐 **global**

## Make it Work!

The Make it Work! way of looking at geography is to carry out experiments and make things that help you understand how geography shapes the world in which we live. Just by studying the models and reading the step-by-step instructions, you will be able to see how maps work.

## Safety

You may need to use sharp tools for some of the experiments in the book. Ask an adult to help you. Some of the activities take place outdoors. Be careful near rivers, lakes, ponds, steep slopes, cliffs and busy roads.

△ *This amazing picture is made up of many different pictures taken by satellites out in space. You can see clearly many important features on the Earth's surface, such as the white tops of mountains and green areas of forests.*

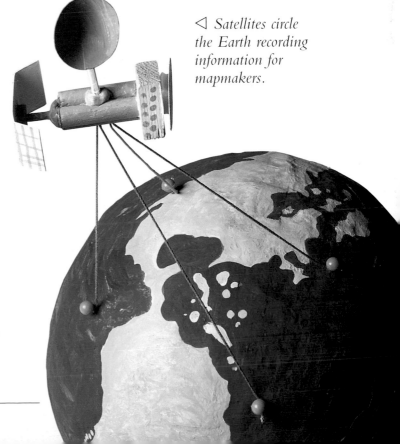

◁ *Satellites circle the Earth recording information for mapmakers.*

# A bird's-eye view

A map is a picture that usually shows things from above, like a bird looking down from the sky. These days, airplanes take pictures from the sky to help people make maps of the land. But maps show many things besides what you see from the air, such as hills and rivers. Weather forecasters may use the outlines of the land to make weather maps. Architects often draw **plans** of the inside of a building, imagining how it will look from above.

### Satellite photography

Satellites hundreds of miles out in space can send back images of the Earth showing amazing detail—sometimes down to areas as small as 100 square feet. Some satellites can "see" groups of trees, or even individual large trees. Satellite images are especially important for mapping places such as mountains or **rain forests**, where it is difficult for people to gather information on the ground.

△ You can see the branching pattern of the Amazon River on this satellite image of South America.

▷ These models show how the view of a valley from a helicopter changes, as the helicopter rises above it.

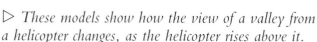

**1 View from the ground**
Imagine you are going for a ride in a helicopter over a river **valley**. Before you take off, you can see how high hills and trees are, but it is difficult to see how far apart they are.

**2 Oblique views**
As the helicopter rises, you can see the valley from a slight angle above the ground. This is called an oblique view and it helps geographers understand the shapes and positions of features.

## looking down

**1** Lay some objects on a low table. Look at the objects from the side and draw them. Now stand on a chair and draw them from above.

**2** Look at how the shapes change. In which picture is it easier to see the positions of the objects?

### ✎ Layers on a map

Maps of places can give us a lot more information than photographs. Although they are usually flat, maps can tell us about the height of the land, show us what buildings are used for, and even reveal what is under the ground. Lines, colors and symbols are used to stand for the different layers of information.

### ✎ Drawing plans

Detailed maps of small areas are often called plans. These are used by people such as architects or builders. Architects draw pictures or plans of what they want a building to look like. Builders use these plans as a guide to tell them exactly where to put the rooms and how a building should look when it is finished.

### 3 Rising up

As you move farther above the valley, everything looks flatter and it's not as easy to see where the land goes up and down. The trees appear to be flat green shapes.

### 4 Looking down from above

It is now easy to see how far apart the different features are, how they connect with one another, and how to move between points. This is why a map showing a bird's-eye view is so useful.

# Scale and grids

On most maps of the landscape you will find two important pieces of information: a **scale** and a **grid**. A scale is something that tells you the actual size of what is on the map. A grid is a network of horizontal and vertical lines drawn over a map. It helps you find places and describe where they are.

### ⚔ Reading grids

Grid lines divide a map into equal squares. Each line or row of squares is labeled along the edges of the map with letters or numbers, so people can describe any point on the map easily. These labels are called grid references. To work out a grid reference, you usually read the labels across the top or bottom first, and then those along the side. This pinpoints a particular square.

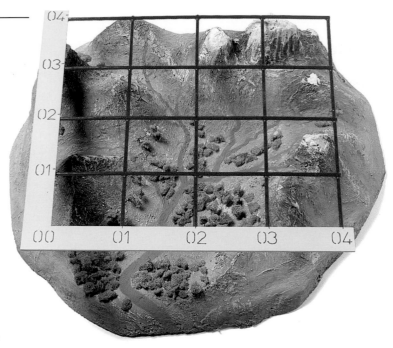

△ On this landscape model you can find certain features, such as the mountain in grid square 0203. The lines cross at the bottom left corner of the square.

1:10,000 or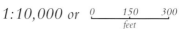

1:6,000 or

1:2,000 or

△ As the scales of these pictures get larger, the view of the airport gets more detailed.

### ✎ Scales on maps

A map that is drawn to scale is the same shape as the landscape it shows, but a different size (nearly always much smaller). The scale tells us how the map size compares to the real size of the landscape. For instance, four inches on a map may represent four feet, or even four miles, on a real landscape.

### ✎ How to write a scale

The scale can be shown on a map in two ways, as shown above. It can be written in figures, such as 1:50,000. This means that one unit on the map stands for 50,000 units on the ground. Another way of writing a scale is to use a bar divided into units. All the units represent the same distance. This is called a linear scale.

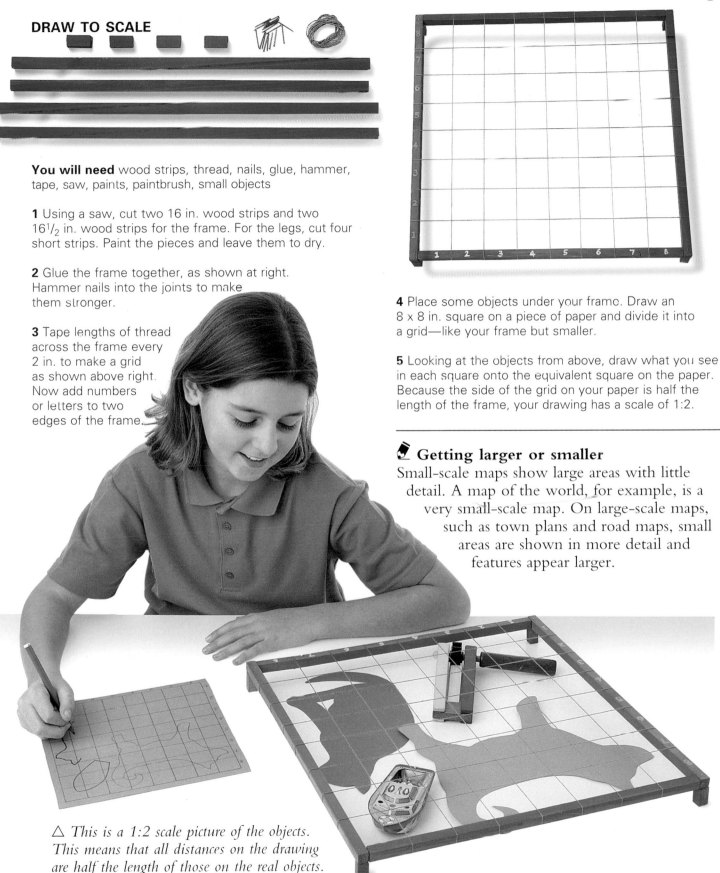

**DRAW TO SCALE**

**You will need** wood strips, thread, nails, glue, hammer, tape, saw, paints, paintbrush, small objects

**1** Using a saw, cut two 16 in. wood strips and two 16$\frac{1}{2}$ in. wood strips for the frame. For the legs, cut four short strips. Paint the pieces and leave them to dry.

**2** Glue the frame together, as shown at right. Hammer nails into the joints to make them stronger.

**3** Tape lengths of thread across the frame every 2 in. to make a grid as shown above right. Now add numbers or letters to two edges of the frame.

**4** Place some objects under your frame. Draw an 8 x 8 in. square on a piece of paper and divide it into a grid—like your frame but smaller.

**5** Looking at the objects from above, draw what you see in each square onto the equivalent square on the paper. Because the side of the grid on your paper is half the length of the frame, your drawing has a scale of 1:2.

✏ **Getting larger or smaller**
Small-scale maps show large areas with little detail. A map of the world, for example, is a very small-scale map. On large-scale maps, such as town plans and road maps, small areas are shown in more detail and features appear larger.

△ *This is a 1:2 scale picture of the objects. This means that all distances on the drawing are half the length of those on the real objects.*

# Measuring height

Maps of the landscape need to show the height of the ground, and mark any hills, valleys, coasts or cliffs. Information about the height and slope of the land is useful to drivers, hikers and cyclists, as well as to builders or engineers planning roads or railways. **Three-dimensional** maps can show clearly how the land goes up and down. Flat maps use **contours**, shading or colors to show height. Hundreds of years ago, mapmakers drew little pictures of hills on their maps, but these were not very accurate.

△ *On this 18th-century map of part of southeast China, the mapmaker has shown height by painting the hills and using colors to show different heights.*

### Contours

Contours are lines joining places of the same height. If the contours are close together, then the slope is steep. If they are widely spaced, it means the slope is more gentle. If there are hardly any contours, the area is almost flat. So contours show both the height of the land and the shape of the slopes.

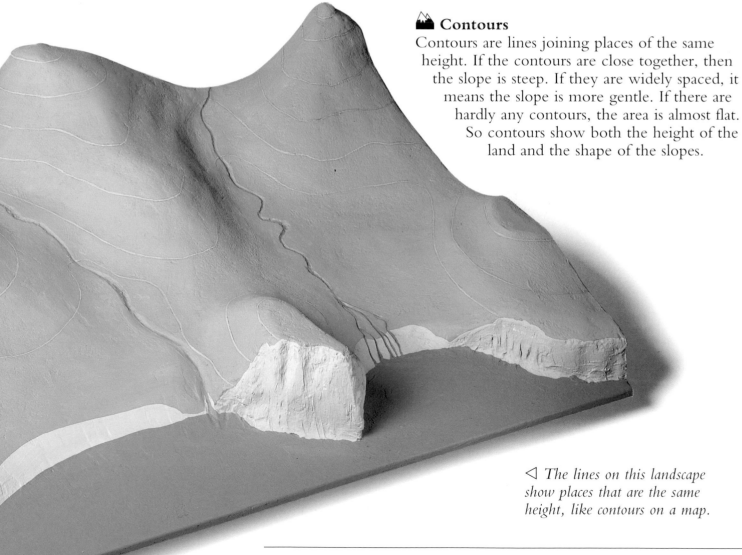

◁ *The lines on this landscape show places that are the same height, like contours on a map.*

## MAKE CONTOURS

**You will need** acrylic paint, plasticine, colored string, toothpick, thick wooden board, glue, cardboard

**1** Build a plasticine landscape on the wooden board. Decorate with acrylic paint. Place the landscape in the tank.

**2** On some card, mark lines ³/₄ in. apart. Glue it to the side of the tank. Pour water up to the lowest mark and scrape a line with a toothpick on the landscape to mark the water level.

**3** Pour water up to the next mark and scrape the next contour in the same way. Repeat until the landscape is completely covered by water.

**4** Remove your contoured landscape from the tank. Now highlight the contours by pushing colored string into the grooves, as shown above.

△ *View the contours from above to see how they would look on a map.*

△ *Mountains and hills like those above can easily be recognized on a map. They are represented by rings of contours inside one another.*

spot height (in yards)

33    45

△ *A cliff is shown by contours ending suddenly. The cliff face is marked using black lines called* **hachures**.

### 🏔 Shading and colors

There are other ways of showing height on maps. Sometimes shading is used. This shows the shadows cast by hills, as if a strong light were shining from a corner of the map. Colors are also used to show height. High ground is usually colored purple or white, and low ground is yellow or green. This method is often used on maps of a large area, such as a whole **continent**.

### 🏔 Spot heights

Some maps also include **spot heights**. These show the height of the land above sea level at certain points on the map. Spot heights are often shown without any contour lines. These points are only marked on the map and do not exist on the ground like **bench marks**. Bench marks on buildings or posts show the height of a point on the ground above sea level

# Signs and symbols

Symbols are the language of maps. They are simple signs that show what and where things are. Symbols are used on maps because there is not enough room to draw pictures of everything on the map. A lot of information can then be presented in a small space. Symbols mark physical features as well as human features. For instance, a blue line may represent a river and a black square may be a railroad station.

### ✎ 🏔 Landscape symbols

On maps of the landscape, symbols are used to stand for physical features, such as woods, rivers, marshes, cliffs, beaches and hills. Hills are often shown as brown contour lines. Marshland may be indicated by small spiky tufts of grass. In a woodland, it is not possible to show every tree, but mapmakers usually have symbols for the two main kinds of tree, deciduous and coniferous. Deciduous trees lose their leaves in autumn, while coniferous trees keep their leaves all year round.

▽ *See how the physical features of this landscape model are shown on the map opposite.*

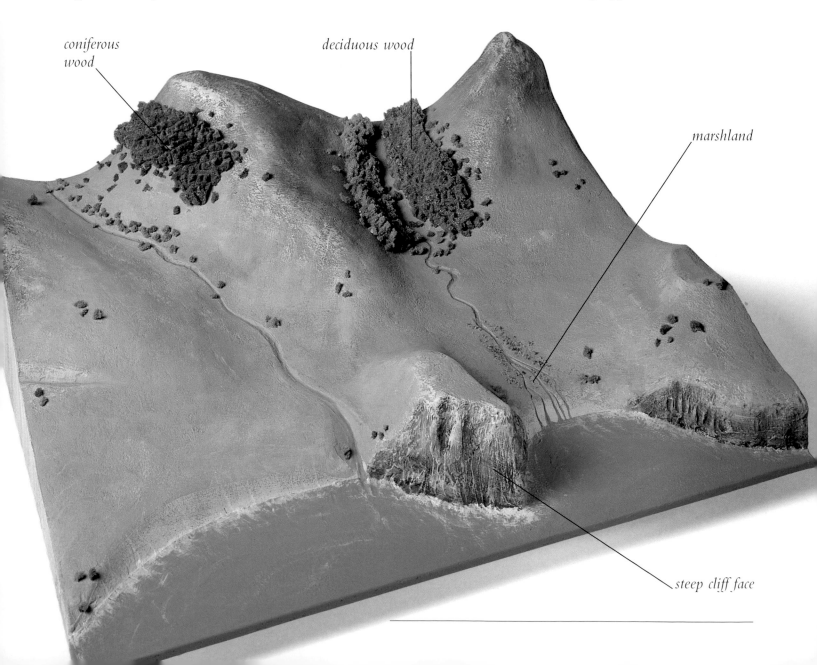

coniferous wood

deciduous wood

marshland

steep cliff face

△ *This photograph of a deciduous tree is simplified into a symbol of a tree with a bushy outline.*

△ *Coniferous trees are taller and more pointed so their symbol is a simple tree with four straight branches.*

### How to design a symbol

A symbol needs to remind people instantly of the real feature it represents. Sometimes a symbol is a less complicated version of the real thing, such as the outline of a tree. Sometimes a symbol just shows the idea of the feature, such as a pair of trainers being used as a symbol for a sports center. It takes a lot of work to design a symbol that can be easily understood by a person looking at the map. When it is not possible to use a symbol, one or two large letters may be used instead, such as T for telephone.

▽ *This map uses symbols and colors to show the features of the landscape simply and clearly.*

### Simple symbols

On a map, the symbols may be very small, so they work best if they are clear shapes with a few, bold lines. Solid shapes are easier to see than outlines when they are very small.

### Unlocking maps

A **key** to a map explains what the symbols stand for. It contains the information needed to unlock the secrets of the map. Although it may be fairly obvious what some symbols represent, it is always worth checking the key to make sure you have understood the map correctly. A key is sometimes called a legend because it tells the story of the map.

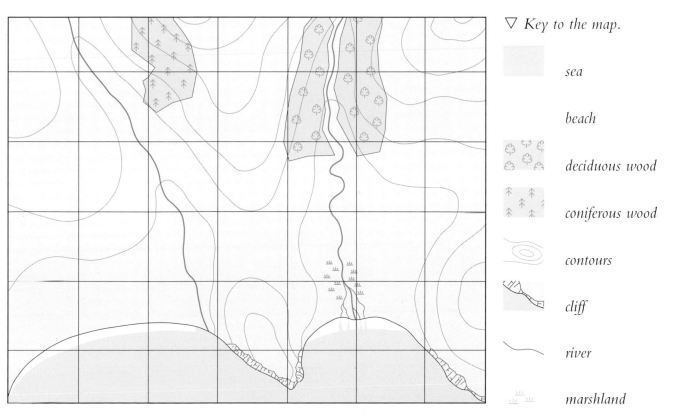

▽ *Key to the map.*

sea

beach

deciduous wood

coniferous wood

contours

cliff

river

marshland

# Signs and symbols

## 📖 🚶 Building up the map

From roads and railroad tracks to towns and historical monuments, symbols for the human features of a landscape have to be added to a map. Maps show roads in different colors depending on their size. Interstate highways, for example, are usually colored red.

## 📖 Symbols and scale

The size of a symbol and the amount of detail it can show depend on the type of map and the scale it is drawn to. For instance, a large city may be shown as only a square or a circle in an **atlas**. But on a large-scale map, the shape of the city can be clearly indicated.

## 🚶 Maps and data

Sometimes, symbols may be used to represent data, or information, on maps. They may stand for numbers of things rather than actual features. For instance, a circle or a symbol of a person may stand for 1,000 people. A shipping map may use the thickness of lines to show how many ships travel from one port to another.

## 📖 Separating the layers

At first glance, maps can appear rather complicated, like a very detailed painting. On the opposite page, we have peeled away the different layers that make up a map so you can see the different features to look out for.

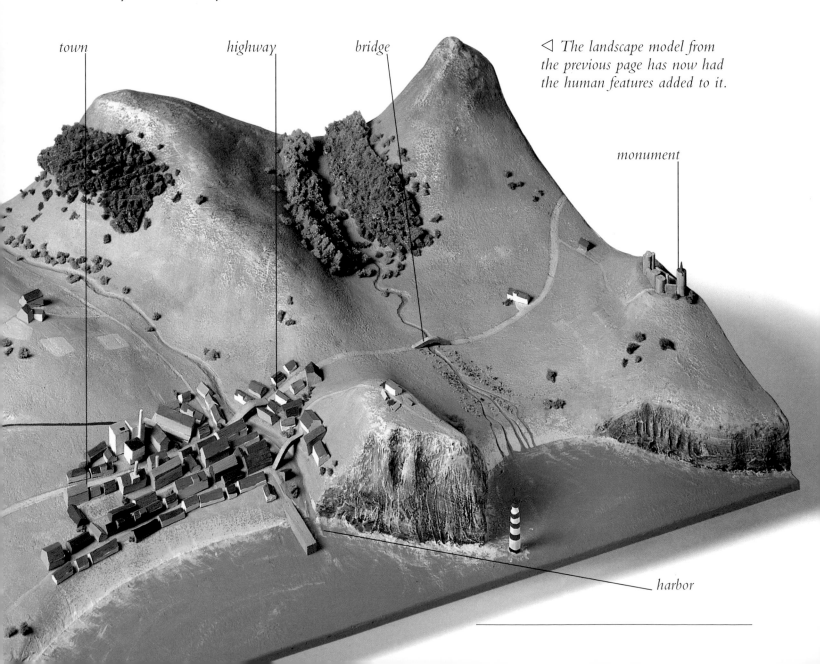

*town*

*highway*

*bridge*

◁ *The landscape model from the previous page has now had the human features added to it.*

*monument*

*harbor*

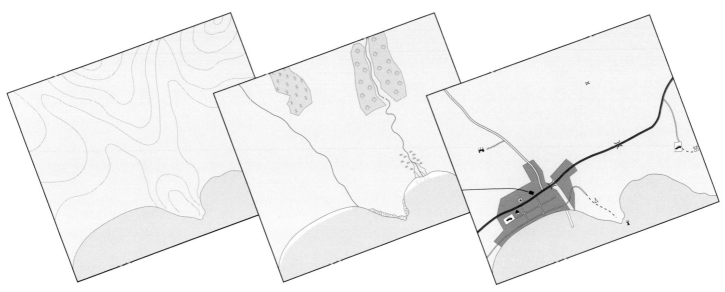

△ The contours show you the hills and valleys and the way the land slopes up and down.

△ Physical symbols show you natural features of the landscape, such as trees and rivers.

△ Human symbols show how people have changed the land by building towns, roads and farms.

▽ The final map shows all the layers placed on top of one another.

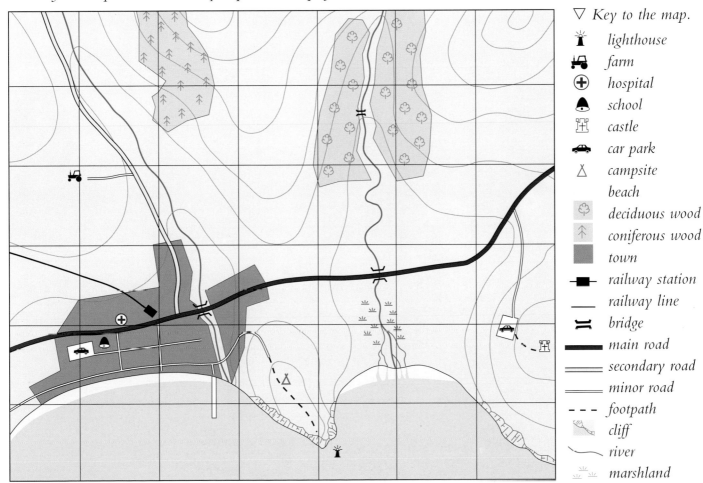

▽ Key to the map.

🗼 lighthouse
🚜 farm
⊕ hospital
🔔 school
castle
🚗 car park
△ campsite
beach
deciduous wood
coniferous wood
town
railway station
railway line
bridge
main road
secondary road
minor road
footpath
cliff
river
marshland

**149**

# Mapping the sea and sky

As well as mapping the landscape we can see, geographers also make maps of places we cannot see, such as under the ground, up in the sky or the deep-sea floor. These maps help people to plan buildings, make weather forecasts and search for fish, oil and minerals under the sea.

## Tracking the weather

Satellites circling the Earth out in space give us an excellent view of how the weather is changing. They can spot a storm, such as a hurricane developing over the sea, and track its path to warn people of the danger that lies ahead. Information from satellites and weather stations on Earth is used to draw weather maps. Weather maps show the invisible movements of air that create the weather.

▷ *This map shows low pressure over the United Kingdom.*

## High and low pressure

Lines called **isobars** join together places with the same air pressure—the weight of air pressing down on the Earth. The higher the number on the isobar, the higher the air pressure. High pressure usually brings dry weather, while lower pressure may bring rain or snow.

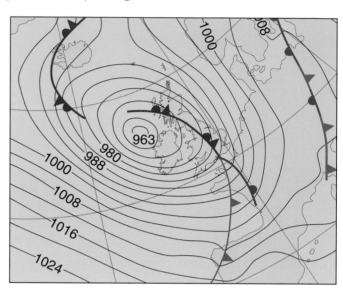

## MAKE AN UNDERSEA MAP

**You will need** tank, wooden skewers, balsa wood, acrylic paints, tape, thick cardboard, bradawl, plasticine, waterproof pens

**1** Cut a piece of cardboard slightly larger than the top of your tank. Draw a grid of ⅔ in. squares on one side. Place the cardboard on top of the tank and use a skewer to poke holes through the center of each square.

**2** Build a plasticine landscape on cardboard and decorate it with paint. Make a measuring stick by marking a skewer every ⅓ in. from its point using a waterproof pen. Mark every fifth line in a different color.

**3** Make a balsa-wood boat. Use a bradawl to make a hole through its center. Slide it onto the stick.

**4** Position the landscape in the tank. Pour water into the tank as shown.

# How do we map places we cannot see?

sound beams ——————— sea floor

### ⛰ "Hearing" the sea floor
Satellites can't "see" through water, so maps of the sea floor have to be made using information collected in a different way. The sea's depth is measured using **sonar**, which stands for "*so*und *n*avigation *a*nd *r*anging." Sonar equipment sends beams of very high sounds called ultrasound down into the water. It then measures the time it takes for the echo of the sound to bounce back.

### ⛰ From beams to maps
We know how far sound travels in a certain time, so we can work out the distance from the surface of the sea to the sea floor. Information from sonar equipment, and from submarines that dive deep into the sea, has revealed that the sea floor has many mountains, volcanoes and valleys, just like dry land.

◁ *Echoes from the sound beams sent down by the ship tell us about the shape of the sea floor.*

**5** Tape your grid on top of the tank. Starting in one corner, push the measuring stick through the cardboard until it touches the plasticine landscape, as shown at left. Now count the number of lines up to the surface of the water and write this number in the square in pencil. Do the same for every square.

**6** To make your map of the sea floor, remove the cardboard from the tank and paint the squares. Areas of the same depth should be the same color. Try and use a gradual scale from white to dark blue, as shown below.

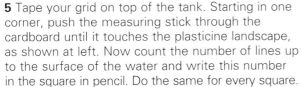

# Human maps

People use land in all sorts of ways, from building roads and towns, to growing crops and raising farm animals. This information can be recorded on maps to help people find places and show how we change the landscape. These maps are called human maps.

*India*

*Australia*

△ *A population map of the world.*

## 👫 Plotting numbers

Sometimes it is useful to turn facts and figures into a map. In this way we can compare places and countries, and make predictions about the future. For example, maps can record population or the amount of energy people use. These are called **statistical maps**.

## 👫 Mapping population

On some world maps, such as the one above, the size of a country or continent relates to the size of its population, not to its real size. India is really smaller than Australia, but it is bigger on this map because more people live there. Compare this map to the world picture on page 5.

## MAKE A STATISTICAL MAP

**You will need** simple local map, pens, pencils, ruler, colored paper, toothpicks, glue or tape, clipboard, watch

**1** Ask an adult to take you to the middle of your town or village. Bring paper, a pencil and a watch with you.

**2** For a traffic survey, stand at a crossroads and note down how many vehicles go down each road in five minutes. Do the same for several other crossroads in your area, as shown on the model opposite.

**3** For a store survey, stand outside a store and count how many people visit it in five minutes. Do the same for other stores.

**4** Indoors, plot your data on a local map. Use colored arrows to represent different numbers of vehicles in your traffic survey. For example, use a yellow arrow for fewer than 20 vehicles, an orange arrow for 20 to 40 vehicles, and so on. In a similar way, make flags of different heights for the different numbers of people visiting each store. Pin your symbols on the map.

▽ *Your final map shows which stores and roads are busiest.*

152

## 👥 Coloring maps

Parts of a town or village are used in different ways. Some areas of land are used for farming, some for stores and offices, and others for places to live. **Land use maps** are colored to show where these different areas are.

People can use these maps to compare different places, such as town and countryside areas. They also help geographers understand how and why places change over time.

▽ *This model of a town shows where surveys were taken for the statistical map below left.*

## MAKE A LAND USE MAP

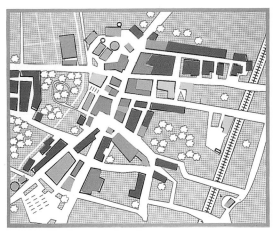

**You will need** local map, colored paper, pens, scissors, glue

**1** Use a map of your town to help you draw a simple map of the area that you want to survey.

▽ *Key to the map.*

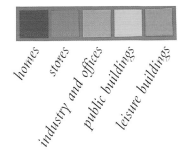

homes
stores
industry and offices
public buildings
leisure buildings

**2** Find out what the different buildings are used for. Make a list of those which are used for stores, homes and so on.

**3** Choose a different color for each type of land use. Then cut and glue colored paper shapes on each building to show how it is used. Finally, draw a key to explain your map.

*yellow triangles show the crossroads where traffic surveys were made*

*blue triangles show where store surveys were made*

# Three-dimensional maps

People are used to seeing the shape of the land in three dimensions (3-D), so it isn't always easy to read a flat map and understand how the land looks. Some maps and **globes** are made with raised surfaces. These maps are used for teaching and also to help people who cannot see well or are blind. The disadvantage of 3-D maps is that they cannot be printed in books or folded up easily to fit in your pocket.

## 3-D symbols

Some flat maps, such as tourist maps or museum plans, include symbols drawn as if they are 3-D. They show buildings, rooms or other features drawn from the side, so they look more realistic. Some people feel this makes the maps easier to understand. But the symbols take up a lot of space and may hide other parts of the map.

▽ *A 3-D map of the Tatra Mountains in Slovakia, eastern Europe.*

## MAKE A 3-D MAP

**You will need** thick cardboard, tracing paper, tape, craft knife, glue, flour, newspaper, paints, paintbrush, maps

**1** Find a map that shows several mountains, hills and other features such as rivers, villages or farms. Trace the contours onto tracing paper. You can enlarge a small part of the map on a photocopier to make the contours easier to trace.

**2** Tape the tracing paper onto a piece of cardboard. Ask an adult to help cut around the lowest contour. Tape the remaining tracing paper onto another piece of cardboard and cut out the next contour. Repeat this for each contour in turn.

**3** Glue the contour shapes in position on a cardboard base so the contours are in order of height, from the lowest to the highest. Contour lines on a map are like the edges of your layers of cardboard.

**4** Cover the cardboard with layers of newspaper strips dipped in a flour and water paste. Leave to dry.

### Computer images

On computer screens, it is possible to produce a 3-D picture of a landscape. These pictures can be moved around so they can be seen from different distances and different angles—from above, from the side, and so on. Now that people can look at the shape of the land so easily on screen, computers will be very useful in the future of mapmaking.

▷ *This is a 3-D computer image of mountains in Corsica, France. Vegetation is shown in red and the sea is dark blue. The sky was added by computer.*

### Touch maps

People who cannot see well, or who are blind, can "read" maps with raised symbols and words that they feel with their fingertips. These special maps are called **tactual maps.**

▽ *Key to the map.*

harbor  campsite  town  school  telephone  hospital  farm  coniferous wood

▽ *This model was made from a map of the Cuillin Hills in Scotland.*

**5** Paint the landscape and make symbols for the various features on the map. List your symbols in a key. Add an arrow pointing north (the grid lines on a map usually point upward to north).

# The globe

The Earth seems flat when you walk around on the surface, but you can see that it is round when you look at pictures taken from spacecraft. The only way to make an accurate map of the world is to build a globe, which shows the true positions of the land and sea. Globes can be made from 12 or more flat segments stuck onto a ball, or sphere. An imaginary line called the **equator** divides the northern half of the Earth from the southern half. Globes usually spin around and tilt at an angle like the Earth.

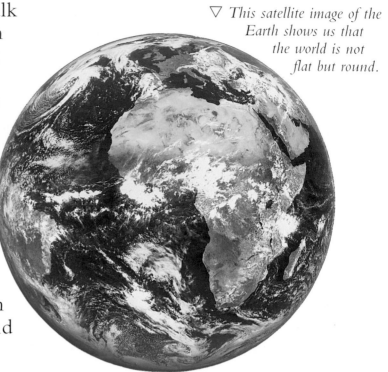

▽ *This satellite image of the Earth shows us that the world is not flat but round.*

**BUILD A GLOBE**

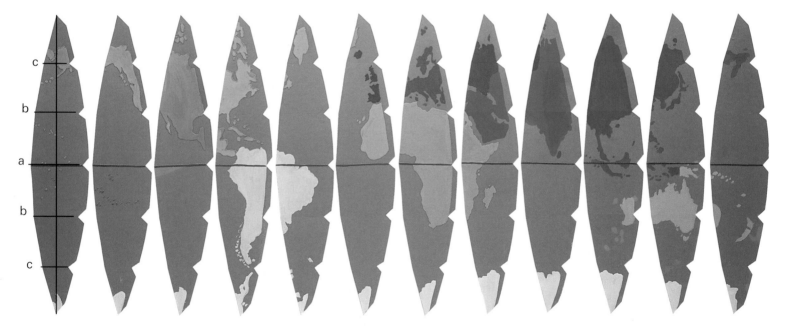

**You will need** glue, atlas, blue paper, cardboard, paints, dowel, plasticine

**1** Draw a 16½ in. straight line on a piece of blue paper. Now draw five lines at right angles to this line to divide it into six equal sections. These lines—a, b and c—above, should be 2⅔ in., 2⅓ in., and 1½ in. long.

**2** Join the end points of these lines together and add six tabs to make a segment, as shown above. Cut out the segment carefully. Cut 11 more segments the same size.

**3** Draw the outlines of the continents on your segments. Use the model shown above as a guide.

**4** Paint the land using appropriate colors. We have painted the seven continents in different colors. Paint the line of the equator in red, as shown above.

**5** Fold each segment along the lines a, b and c, and glue the segments together as shown at right.

## ⊕ Which way round?

In space, there is no up and down or top and bottom, so you can view a globe with any part at the top. If you turn the globe so that the **South Pole** is at the top, you will get a very different view of the world.

## ⊕ Tilted Earth

Globes are usually tilted at an angle because the Earth leans slightly to one side, at an angle of 23.5 **degrees** from the sun. The tilt of the Earth means that some places receive different amounts of light and heat from the sun at different times of year. This produces weather changes that we call the **seasons**.

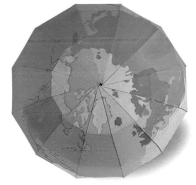

△ *Looking down on the Earth from the **North Pole**, you can see that many continents are clustered together at this end of the world.*

△ *One side of the Earth is nearly all blue—the Pacific Ocean. All the continents together would fit into an area the size of the Pacific Ocean.*

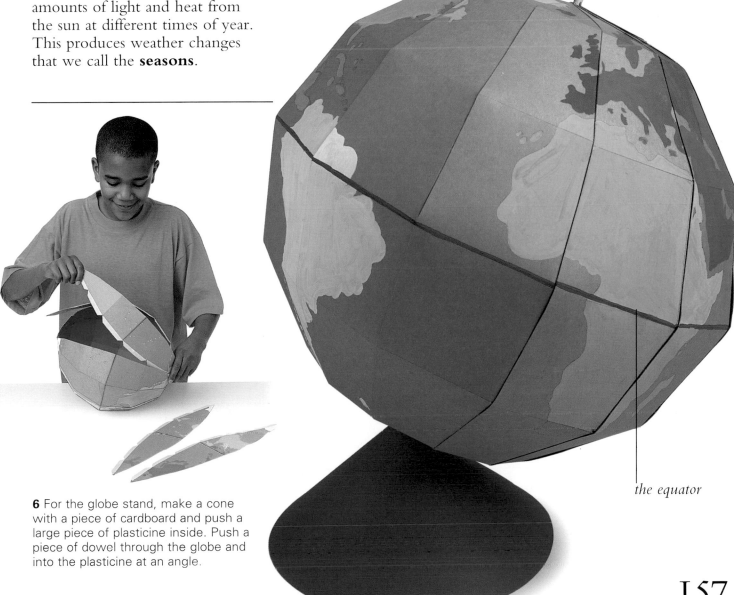

**6** For the globe stand, make a cone with a piece of cardboard and push a large piece of plasticine inside. Push a piece of dowel through the globe and into the plasticine at an angle.

the equator

# Dividing up the world

A grid of imaginary lines helps people to pinpoint different places in the world. The grid lines are called **longitude** and **latitude**. On a globe, lines of longitude meet at the poles, while lines of latitude run parallel to the equator. On a map, longitude lines go from top to bottom and latitude lines from side to side. Every place in the world can be located using longitude and latitude. For instance, New York is 40 degrees north (latitude) and 73 degrees west (longitude).

⊕ **Where is north?**
The true North Pole is right at the top of the world, in the middle of the Arctic Ocean. A **compass** needle, a tiny **magnet**, doesn't point to true north but to an area in northern Canada, called **magnetic north**. There is also a magnetic south pole. The magnetic poles move slightly from year to year.

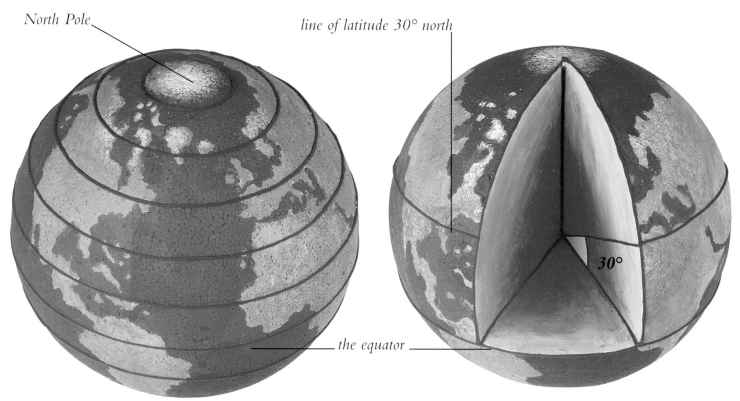

magnetic north

true north

latitude lines

longitude lines

North Pole

line of latitude 30° north

30°

the equator

⊕ **Latitude**
The latitude of a place tells us its position north or south of the equator. The equator has a latitude of 0 degrees (0°). There are 90 "slices," or degrees, on each side of the equator, so the North Pole has a latitude of 90° north while the South Pole has a latitude of 90° south.

⊕ **Moving north and south**
Lines of latitude are measured in degrees because they are angles. Each line is the angle between two imaginary lines drawn from the center of the Earth to the surface. One line goes to the equator and the other to the line of latitude. This model shows the line of latitude 30° north.

## MAKE A COMPASS

**You will need** magnet, needle, cork, plastic tub and lid, plasticine, bradawl, toothpick

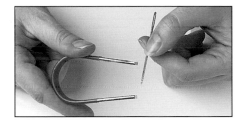

**1** Place a large piece of plasticine in the tub and push a toothpick into the middle. Cut away most of the lid, leaving only the rim. Glue a ring of paper to the top side of the rim.

**2** Use a bradawl to dig a hole ⅕ in. deep in the center of one end of the cork. Balance the cork on the end of the toothpick. Fill the tub with water until the cork floats. The toothpick stops the cork from floating to the side.

**3** Make a needle into a magnet by stroking a real magnet toward the tip of the needle about 50 times.

**4** Paint the tip of the needle and place it on the cork. The needle should now swing round to point north.

**5** Put the rim in place. Mark north with a yellow triangle, as shown at right.

**6** Place the compass on a local map and turn the map until the needle points to the top of the map. Your map now shows you the true direction of features in your area.

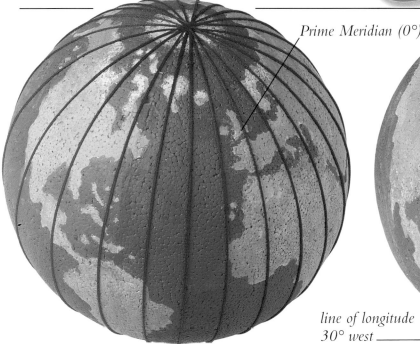

*Prime Meridian (0°)*

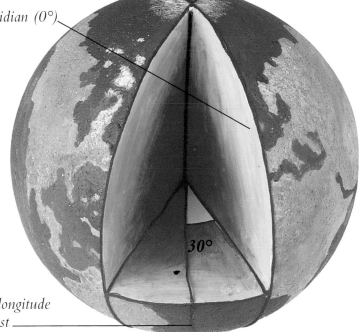

*30°*

*line of longitude 30° west*

### ⊕ Longitude

The longitude of a place tells us its position east or west of an imaginary line called the **Prime Meridian**. This line is drawn from the North Pole to the South Pole through Greenwich, in London, England. Lines of longitude divide the world up like segments of an orange.

### ⊕ Moving east and west

Lines of longitude are measured in degrees between two imaginary lines drawn from the center of the Earth to the equator. There are 180 degrees west and 180 degrees east of the Prime Meridian (0°). This model shows the line of longitude 30° west.

# Mapping the globe

A drawing of the Earth's curved surface onto a flat surface is called a **map projection**. First the lines of latitude and longitude are drawn from a globe onto a sheet of paper. Then the continents and oceans are added. There are many different ways of projecting a globe onto a flat surface, but all of them distort the Earth in some way. Mapmakers have to choose carefully between projections, to find one that will best suit their purpose.

### Stretching the world

No projection is ever as accurate as a globe map. It might distort the shape or size of the land, or show the wrong distances between continents. But projections do show parts of the world fairly accurately. There are three main kinds of projections: planar, conic and cylindrical. These are done by geographers using mathematics.

### Planar projections

A planar projection makes a circular map and shows only half the world at a time. It is made as if one point on the globe is touching a flat surface and light is shone from the center of the globe. Most planar projections have the North or the South Pole in the middle, but the middle of the map can be anywhere on the globe.

## MAKE MAP PROJECTIONS

**You will need**
large plastic bottle, scissors, black string, paper, flashlight, glue, tracing paper, bulb and bulb holder, paperclips, wires, flat battery

**1** Cut off the top of the bottle. Ask an adult to help you. Then cut off the neck to make half a globe.

**2** Glue lengths of string onto the half globe to make lines of latitude and longitude.

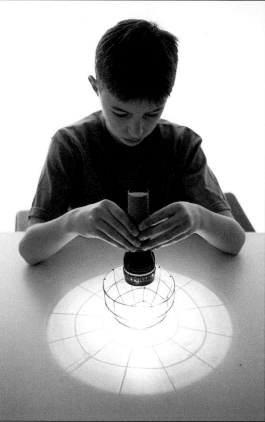

**3** For a planar projection, place your half globe on a piece of paper. Shine the flashlight into the middle of it, as shown. You will see the shadows of the latitude and longitude lines thrown out, or projected, onto the paper.

**4** Connect the bulb to the battery using the wires and clips. Rest the bulb on the flat side of the battery.

**5** For a conic projection, place the half globe upside down over the bulb and battery. Make a cone from tracing paper, so that it just fits over the half globe. The shadows show rings of latitude and straight lines of longitude.

*conic projection*      *cylindrical projection*

**6** For a cylindrical projection, fit a tube of tracing paper around the base of the half globe as shown above. The shadows produce horizontal lines of latitude and vertical lines of longitude.

**Be careful!** Don't let the tracing paper get too hot or it may burn. Ask an adult to help you.

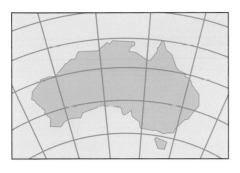

*planar projection*

*conic projection*

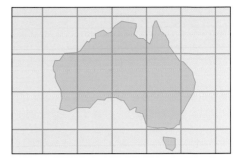

*cylindrical projection*

△ *These pictures of Australia show how various projections make maps look different. Map projections stretch the shape of a country in different ways.*

### ✎ 🌐 Conic projections

A conic projection creates a fan-shaped map. It is made as if light is shining through a globe onto a cone of paper wrapped around it. The most accurate part of the map is where the cone touches the globe. The map gets less accurate as you go farther from this line. It is useful for mapping countries in the middle of the globe, such as the United States.

### ✎ 🌐 Cylindrical projections

A cylindrical projection will give you a rectangular map. It is made as if a light shines through a globe onto a tube of paper wrapped around the globe. This projection can show almost the whole world, but it makes countries near the poles, such as Greenland, too big and stretched out. Countries farther from the poles, such as India, appear too small.

▽ *This cylindrical projection has been stretched and squashed so that areas are the right size but their shapes are distorted. Compare this map with a globe.*

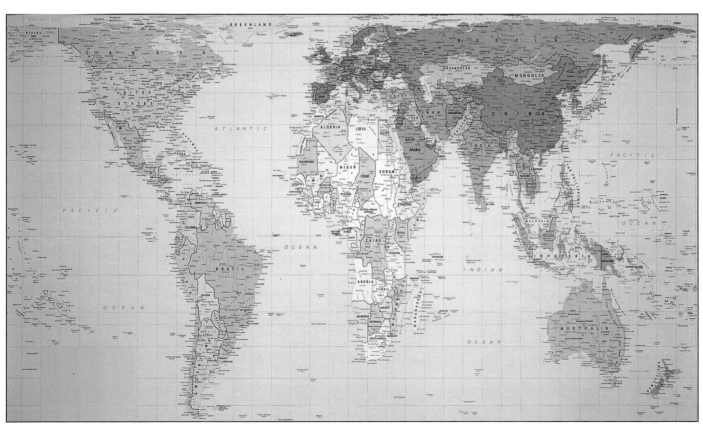

# Early maps

People have been drawing maps for thousands of years. Over 4,000 years ago, people in Babylon (modern-day Iraq) drew maps on clay. Ancient Egyptians made maps from papyrus, a type of paper, and also developed ways of **surveying** the land.

△ *Inuit coastal maps were carved out of pieces of driftwood.*

### 📖 Building and carving maps

Over 500 years ago, people living in the Marshall Islands in the Pacific Ocean needed to be able to move between islands easily, for hunting and trading. They made maps out of sticks and shells. The sticks stood for the pattern of the ocean currents, and the shells marked the positions of islands. The Inuit, native people of Greenland and Canada, carved accurate wooden maps of the coastline. They used these maps to navigate on fishing and hunting trips.

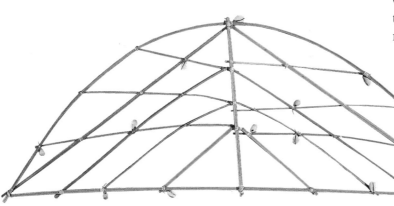

△ *This Marshall Islands stick map was used to teach navigation as well as to plan journeys.*

### 📖 ⊕ Maps of the world

The first world map was drawn by the Greek scholar Ptolemy in AD 160. At that time he did not know that America, Australia or Antarctica existed. During the Middle Ages—about AD 400 to the late 1400s—mapmaking progressed in China and the Arab world. The Chinese printed the first map in 1155, more than 300 years before maps were printed in Europe.

▷ *Compare this naval map of the Atlantic, drawn over 400 years ago by a mapmaker from Portugal, with a map in a modern atlas.*

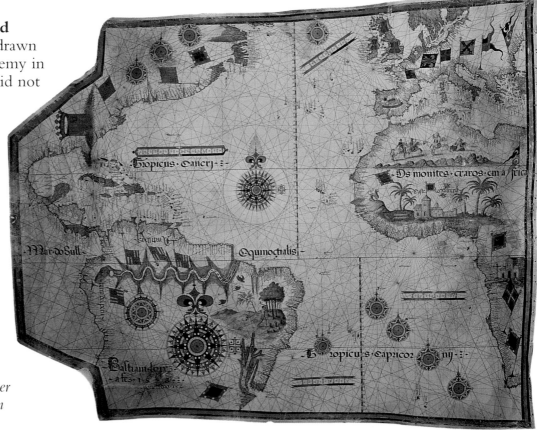

## ✎ Route maps

Religious pilgrims in the Middle Ages used strip maps with their routes across the country shown in straight lines. They read the maps from the bottom to the top of each column.

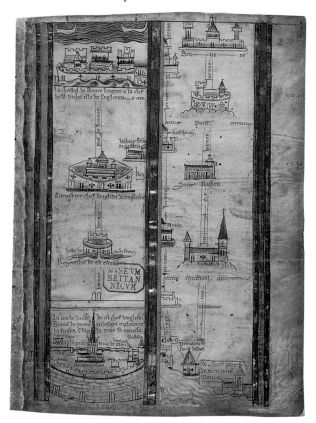

△ *This 13th-century route map shows the journey from London to Dover Castle, and then across the waves of the English Channel to two French towns.*

### MAKE A ROUTE MAP

**You will need** paper, scissors, colored pens, cardboard

**1** Write a list of the different stages of a journey you have been on recently, or of an imaginary journey. Make a note of interesting landmarks, such as towns and forests, and the time as you passed each one.

**2** Draw a road going down the middle of a large piece of paper. Add clocks to show the start and finish times of the journey. On the map shown at right, lines are marked for every five minutes of the journey.

**3** Starting at the bottom of the paper, add cardboard symbols for the different stages of your journey. Don't worry about drawing things to scale. The main point is to get all the different stages in the right order.

# Surveying and measuring

To draw a map, mapmakers need to know about the shape of the land and the distance between points on the ground. People who gather this information are called land surveyors. Today, many of the measurements for maps come from pictures from satellites or **aerial photographs**, photographs taken from aircraft.

### Angles and triangles

Many surveyors today still have to take measurements by walking across land. A good way to map a piece of land is to divide it into triangles. Surveyors use triangles because they can work out the lengths of the sides of a triangle by measuring mainly angles. This method is called **triangulation**. Surveyors use instruments called **theodolites** to measure angles between points of these triangles. A theodolite contains a small telescope and a level, and is mounted on a tripod.

## Measuring with triangles

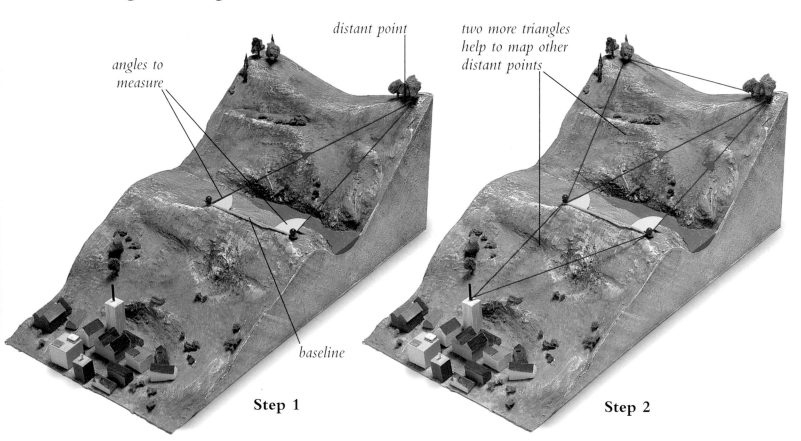

*distant point*

*angles to measure*

*baseline*

**Step 1**

*two more triangles help to map other distant points*

**Step 2**

### 1 Using a baseline

Surveyors first measure a short distance called a baseline. Standing at one end of the line, they measure the angle to a distant point—in this case, a tree. They then go to the other end of the baseline and measure the angle to the same point. Surveyors then use mathematics to work out the distances from the baseline to the tree.

### 2 Adding more triangles

The sides of this triangle are used as new baselines to work out other distances. Triangles are linked to the first, covering the whole area. This is useful because surveyors have to measure only one distance, the baseline, and from then on they measure only angles. In large areas, it is easier to measure angles than distances.

*satellite*

## Mapping with photographs

Aerial photographs are taken with a special camera fitted to the floor of an aircraft. The aircraft flies above chosen strips of land and the camera takes photographs automatically at regular intervals. Each photograph in every strip overlaps the next by 60 per cent, so that no details are lost. Aerial photographs are particularly useful for updating existing maps and for plotting contours.

△ *A satellite can produce pictures covering a very wide area. These satellites are thousands of times higher up than the aircraft that take aerial photographs.*

▽ *This model shows how a surveying aircraft takes overlapping photographs of the landscape.*

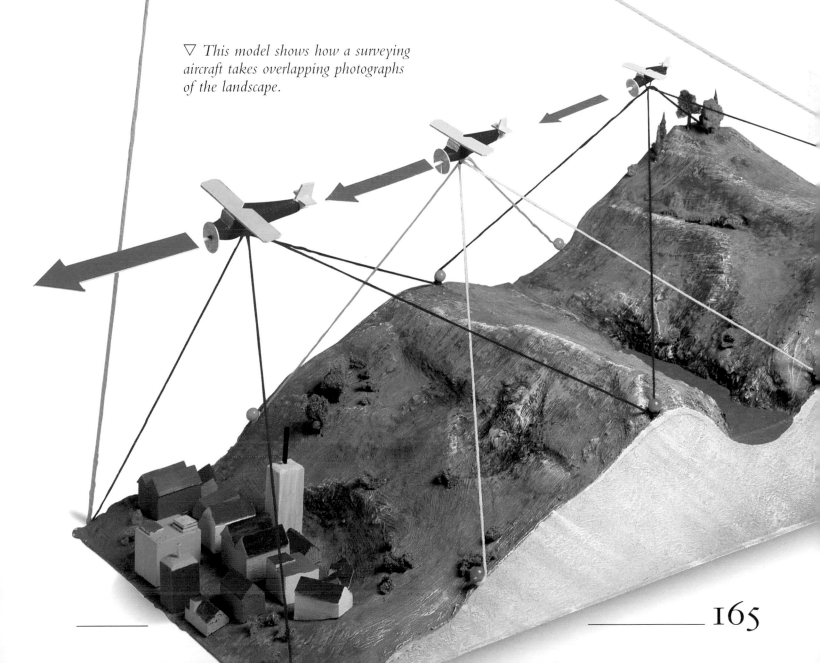

# Plotting maps

The art, science and technology of making maps is called cartography, and the people who draw maps are called cartographers. Having collected as much information as possible from surveyors, a cartographer has to decide what to include on the map and what to leave out. It is important to make sure the map is as clear and easy to read as possible.

## Map drawing

The conventional way of drawing maps is called **scribing**. The cartographer carefully scrapes lines onto a film that is then used as a photographic stencil to print the layers of a map. Nowadays, instruments scan plans and aerial photographs, and turn them into information for drawing a map on a computer. Using a computer is much faster than scribing, and the maps can be easily updated if new information needs to be added.

△ The hand control on this computer is used to scan maps so that they can be copied onto a screen.

## MAKE A 3-D VIEWER

**You will need** tracing paper, thin cardboard, thick cardboard, two small lenses, camera and tripod, tape, slide film

**1** Load your camera with slide film. Then take a photograph of an object. Move the camera round slightly and take another photograph. You then need to have these pictures developed and made into slides.

**2** Cut a cardboard shape like the one above. Each edge of the wide end of the viewer should measure 2 in. Cut a hole slightly smaller than your lens. Now fold and glue the cardboard to make the viewer. Glue a lens to the small end of the viewer.

▷ *Cartographers use very accurate images of the Earth which are produced by satellites in space.*

## 🌐 Curved Earth, flat maps

Small areas of the Earth are mapped as though the Earth is flat. But for large areas, mapmakers must allow for the fact that the surface of the Earth is curved. Mapmakers use mathematics to change the curved surface to a flat surface.

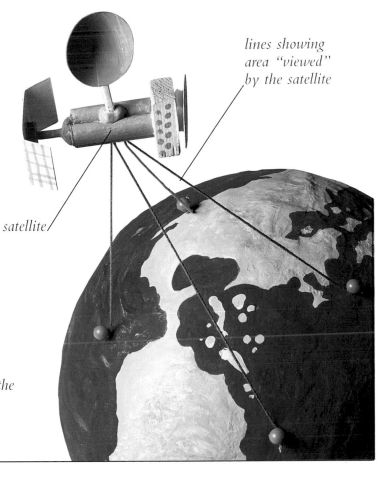

*lines showing area "viewed" by the satellite*

*satellite*

△ *This is a curved section of the Earth, as viewed by the satellite shown at right. Mapmakers correct distortions, especially in the corner areas, to make an accurate map.*

**3** Cut thin cardboard and cardboard pieces as shown. They should be slightly larger than the slides. Tape tracing paper to the card window and glue the pieces on top of each other in the order shown.

**4** Tape the slide holder to the wide end of the viewer with the rectangular window facing outward.

**5** Now make another viewer in the same way. Place one of the slides in each viewer, and put a viewer to each eye. Hold the viewers close together and relax your eyes. You should see the pictures slide together. The object will pop up in 3 D. You may have to look at the object for some time before it works for you.

## 📷 Seeing in 3-D

When cartographers look at overlapping aerial photographs through a **stereoscope**, they see a 3-D picture of the land—even though the photographs are flat. They see the view as if they were looking down from the plane that took the photograph. Seeing in 3-D helps them to pick out features and show how the land goes up and down.

## 📷 How stereoscopes work

When we look at an object, each eye sees a slightly different view. Our brain combines these views to make a 3-D image. In the same way, a stereoscope combines the two views so that we see the picture in 3-D

**167**

# Making your own map

Over the next six pages, you will find out how to survey and map a small local area, such as a park. This will help you to understand the different stages involved in making maps. After making your measuring tools, turn to pages 170-171 to learn how to use them outdoors to survey a piece of land. Finally, look at pages 172-173 to learn how to draw your map to scale.

## Types of tools

Surveyors measure distances with instruments that use lasers or sound waves. These tools are very accurate and make it easy to measure distances over rough ground. You can measure distances with a trundle wheel that clicks every yard as it rolls. Theodolites are complicated tools for measuring angles. You can measure angles more easily using a bearing board, a tube that moves around on a board with degrees marked on it.

## MAKE A TRUNDLE WHEEL

**You will need** thick cardboard, glue, length of $1/5$ in. dowel, two corks, drill, strips of wood, paints, nail, hammer, tape, bradawl, thin cardboard, drawing compass

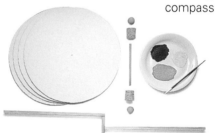

**1** Cut three long strips of wood and one short strip, as shown above. Drill a $1/5$ in. hole at the end of two long pieces. Glue the pieces together to make a fork shape. The holes should be at the ends of the fork prongs. Cut four thin cardboard circles. Each circle should be 6 in. from the center to the outside.

**2** Glue the circles of thin cardboard together to make the wheel. Divide each side into quarters and paint them in two colors as shown below.

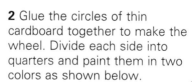

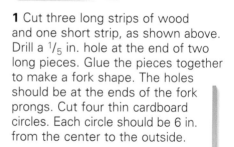

**3** Make holes through the corks with a bradawl. Push the dowel through one of them, as shown above.

**4** Make a hole through the middle of the wheel and push the dowel through. Slide the other cork onto the other side of the dowel. Glue the corks to the wheel and dowel. Now stick a folded piece of thin cardboard near the edge of the wheel as shown. Tape around the edge of the wheel.

**5** Hammer a nail into the inside of one fork prong about $5\frac{1}{2}$ in. above the hole. Slip the wheel into the fork. As the wheel turns, the nail should click against the cardboard. Wind tape around the wood for a handle.

## MAKE A BEARING BOARD

**You will need** thick cardboard, paper fastener, colored paper, protractor, magnetic compass, drawing compass, scissors, glue, tape, broom handle

**1** Cut out a 12 in. square of thick cardboard and a square of colored paper the same size. Glue the cardboard and paper together to make the base of your bearing board.

**2** Using a drawing compass, draw a ring of different colored paper slightly smaller than the base. Cut it out and glue it to the base.

**3** Use a protractor to divide the colored ring into 360°. Label every 10° on the yellow ring and write the number next to each line. Glue a magnetic compass into the board with the north arrow pointing to 0°/360°.

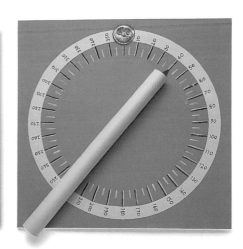

Now turn the page to see how to use your tools to make a map.

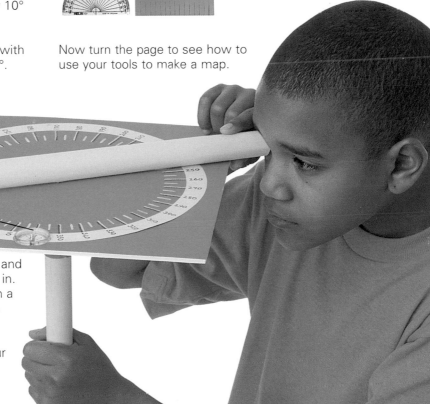

*pointer*

*compass*

**4** Roll up a sheet of colored paper and tape the edges to make a tube 12 in. long. Cut a small triangle pointer in a different color and glue this in one end of the tube.

**5** Make a hole in the center of your board and push a paper fastener through it. Cut a small slit about a third of the way along the tube. Slip the round head of the fastener through the slit. Make sure the tube can turn right round the circle.

**6** Now cut a small piece of cardboard to fit around the broom handle. Cut slits into the top of the cardboard, then roll it up into a tube and glue it onto the broom handle, making sure the cut end sticks up above it. Press the slits outward to make a flat surface. Glue to the underside of the bearing board.

# Making your own map

## Taking measurements

Once you have made your measuring tools, the next step is to choose a small area to map. An area of about 8,000 square feet is a good size. Make sure the area has several fixed features such as paths, trees, a slide or a pond. A fairly open area is best so you don't get confused between features. To work out where to plot the features on your map, you will need to measure angles and distances to each feature.

## Planning your survey

Surveyors need to choose a suitable base point from which to take measurements. Find a position roughly in the middle of your area that has a clear view of most of the main features. You need to choose a place you can easily find again. If you don't finish all your measurements, you may need to return there another day.

Make a sketch of the area including all the features you want to plot on your map. Draw lines to each feature from your base point, as on the model below. Distances are not important at this stage. You are now ready to take your measurements. Use a magnetic compass to mark a north arrow on your sketch.

*distances to measure*

*take measurements from this base point*

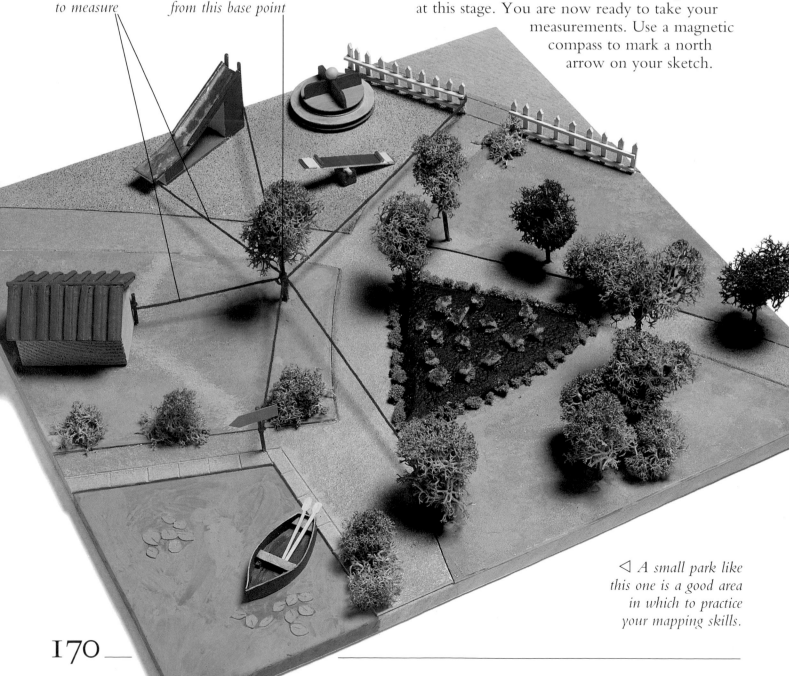

◁ *A small park like this one is a good area in which to practice your mapping skills.*

## MEASURE ANGLES

**1** Start at the base point. Hold the bearing board you made on page 169 in a level position. Looking at the compass, turn the board until 0° is pointing north.

**2** Look through the tube at the feature you want to plot on your map. The arrow at the end of the tube will be pointing at one of the angles around the edge of the board.

**3** Write down the angle next to the feature on your sketch map. Do the same for each of the features in your area.

## MEASURE DISTANCES

**1** Start at the base point. Hold the trundle wheel you made on page 168 upright so the nail sits behind the folded piece of cardboard, as shown below.

**2** Push the trundle wheel in a straight line from the base point to the first feature. Count how many times it clicks. The wheel you have made clicks every yard. So if the wheel clicks five times, it has measured 5 yds.

**3** Write down the distance to each feature next to the distance lines on your sketch map.

Turn to pages 172-173 to see how to use these measurements to plot a map.

# Making your own map

### ✎ Plotting your measurements

To plot an accurate map of your area, you will use all the measurements that you marked on your sketch map. You need to decide on a scale for your map, as explained below. The map should include as much information as possible, but still be clear and easy to read. Choose colors that stand out well.

### ✎ Showing height

You can also show where the land goes up and down by using shading or a color code for high and low ground. Look carefully at a local map of your area and read the contours to work out how high the land is above sea level.

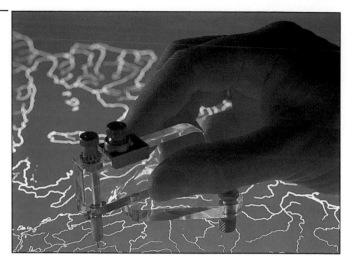

△ *This cartographer uses a sapphire-tipped scriber to scrape fine lines in film when plotting a map by hand.*

## DRAW YOUR OWN MAP

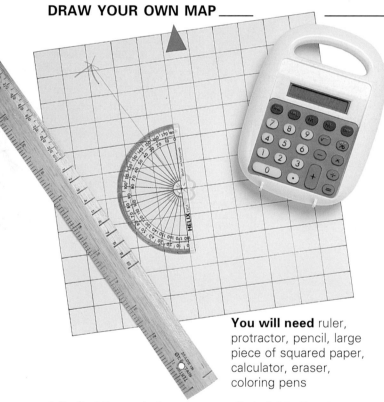

**You will need** ruler, protractor, pencil, large piece of squared paper, calculator, eraser, coloring pens

**1** To find the scale for your map, first divide the size of the area you are mapping by the size of your paper. For instance, if your area is 100 ft. along one side and your paper is 10 in., you need to divide 100 ft. by 10 in.

**2** You can't divide the two numbers because one is measured in feet and the other in inches. But by knowing that there are 12 in. in 1 ft., you can work out that 100 ft. is the same as 1,200 in. You are now able to do the sum. 1,200 in. divided by 10 in. is 120, so the scale is 1:120. This means that 1 in. on the map equals 120 in. (10 ft.) on land.

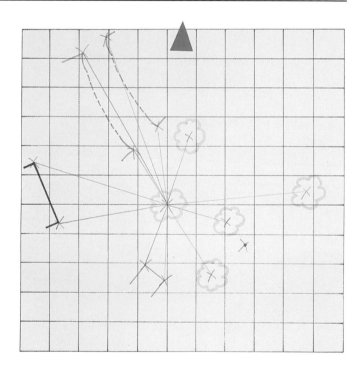

**3** With a calculator, work out your own scale and change the distances on your sketch map to this scale. In the center of your paper, mark the base point with its symbol. Mark the direction of north with an arrow. North is at 0°.

**4** With a protractor, plot the angle of the first feature from the base point. The angle marked above left is 330°. Draw a line of correct length in the direction of this angle.

**5** At the end of each line, put a small dot or cross. Then draw in a colored symbol for each feature in the correct position. For larger features, you will need to draw two or more lines to fix their positions accurately.

## ✾ Making a grid

You could use the lines on squared paper to make a grid. Write numbers between the grid lines along one edge of the map and letters along the other edge. If you wanted to meet a friend at a point on the map, you could give them a grid reference for how to get there.

## ✎ A record of the past

Maps are a useful record of the history of a place. If new roads, houses, paths or other features are built, they must be added to a map of the area. Every month, update a map of your area to see the changes that take place over a whole year.

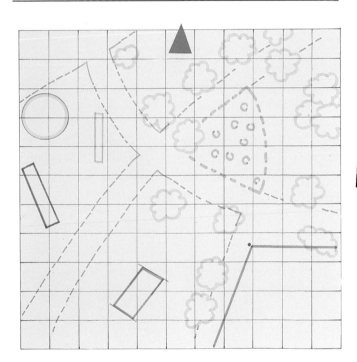

**6** Erase the pencil lines from the base point to each feature. You could also add a border to the map or any colored shading in the background that makes the map easier to read. For instance, you could color the water in a pond. Finally, draw a key at the side of the map to explain the symbols and colors you have used.

You could also plot your map on a computer. This is useful as the map can be updated if the area changes. New features can be added or old features taken away. Names can be changed easily. Several copies of the map can also be printed out and the map scale changed without drawing the map all over again.

▽ *This map was drawn on a computer. Some computer programs for drawing simple maps have small symbols like these already prepared for you to position.*

▽ *Key for the map shown above.*

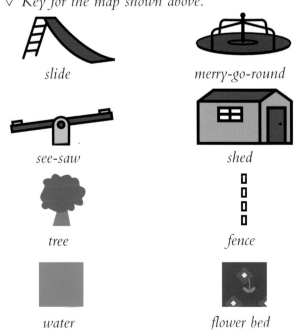

slide

merry-go-round

see-saw

shed

tree

fence

water

flower bed

# Finding your way

Maps help you find your way to places, especially if you have never been there before. To prepare for a journey, it is a good idea to work out the best route on a map. Most cities have street maps showing the roads, important buildings and park areas in detail. You can use the scale of a map to measure the distance of your journey.

△ *This aerial photograph shows the grid pattern of the streets in New York City.*

### ⌖ Maps and settlements

Some modern cities, such as New York and Los Angeles, are built in a series of squares. This grid pattern makes it easier for people to find their way around. The roads have numbers and directions, such as north, south, east and west—East 64th Street, for example. Older cities often have more winding streets, especially in the center, which sometimes make places more difficult to find.

## USING A STREET MAP

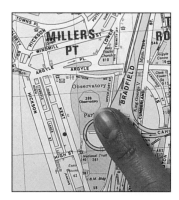

**1** The first step is to look in the index. This gives you the grid reference for the right square on the map. For instance, the Observatory in Sydney, Australia, is in square D4.

**2** Find the letter on the sides of the map and the number on the bottom or top of the map. You can now follow the lines into the map until your fingers meet.

**3** This is the square you want. Look carefully within the square to find the road or feature you need. Use the same steps to find out where you are on the map at the moment.

**4** Figure out the best way to get to your destination. If you look at the scale on the map, you can calculate how far you have to travel. Then you can decide on the best way to get there.

## ⚓ Other route maps

Some maps are not drawn to scale. If they were they would be too confusing. On subway maps, the systems of lines and stations are spread out neatly and drawn in straight lines so it is easy to find a station and plan a route. The distances between stations are not accurate. Sometimes bus-route maps and road maps are also drawn like this to make them easier to read.

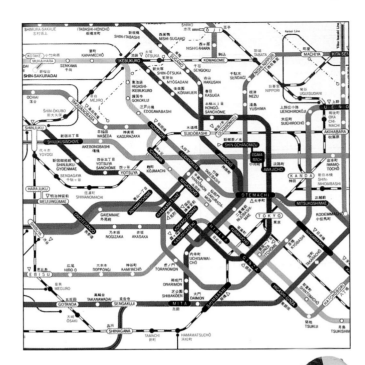

▷ *This map of the Tokyo subway system is not drawn to scale. Each route is a different color to make the lines easier to follow.*

## ⚓ How far is your journey?

To measure distances on a map, you may be able to use a ruler. For curved routes, you need a piece of string or wool, the edge of a piece of paper, or a special mini-trundle wheel.

## MAKE A MINI-TRUNDLE WHEEL

**You will need** cardboard, pin, maps, paint, drawing compass, strip of wood

**1** Draw two circles on the cardboard. To make a wheel for a 1:25,000 scale map, the radius of the circle should be 1 in. For a 1:50,000 scale map, make the radius 1/2 in. This will give you a wheel that turns once every 2 1/2 mi. on your map. Or you can draw any size circle and simply roll the finished wheel along the linear scale (see page 142) to see how far it measures in one turn.

**2** Divide the circles into quarters and paint them as shown. Glue them together. Mark a start line on the edge between two quarters.

**3** Now pin the wheel through its center to a short wooden strip as shown, so that the wheel moves round freely.

**4** To use the wheel, line up the start line with the upper edge of the handle and roll it along your chosen route. Count the number of turns the wheel makes.

**5** To work out the distance, multiply the number of turns by the distance covered in one turn. If your wheel turns once every 2 1/2 mi. on the map and your wheel turns five times, the total distance of the route is 12 1/2 mi

# Finding your way

## ⊕ Plotting a route

The map below is being used to plan a walking route. The colored figures show sights to visit. The orange figures mark a castle and a beach, sights to visit on a short walk from the campsite. The red figures show sights for a longer river valley walk that includes a view from a hill. It is best to work out the distance of a walk before you start so you know how long it might take. You can cover 2-3 miles in an hour. Knowing how to use a compass will help to keep you on the right track.

▽ *Look at this map and think about routes you might take on a walk from the campsite.*

## HOW TO USE A COMPASS

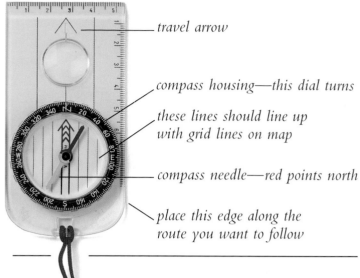

*travel arrow*

*compass housing—this dial turns*

*these lines should line up with grid lines on map*

*compass needle—red points north*

*place this edge along the route you want to follow*

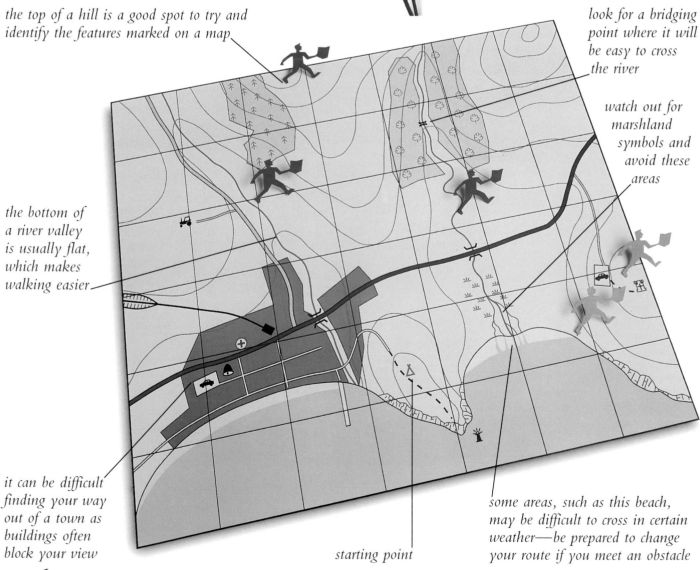

*the top of a hill is a good spot to try and identify the features marked on a map*

*look for a bridging point where it will be easy to cross the river*

*watch out for marshland symbols and avoid these areas*

*the bottom of a river valley is usually flat, which makes walking easier*

*it can be difficult finding your way out of a town as buildings often block your view*

*starting point*

*some areas, such as this beach, may be difficult to cross in certain weather—be prepared to change your route if you meet an obstacle*

# How do you plan a walking route?

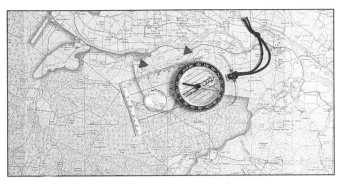

**1** Place the straight edge of the compass on the map so that the travel arrow points along the route you want to follow.

**2** Turn the compass housing so the lines in the circle line up with the grid lines on the map. The red arrow points to the top of the map. Ignore the compass needle for now.

**3** Hold the compass and map horizontal, at about waist height, and turn yourself around until the compass needle swings above the red arrow in the circle. This is the north/south line.

**4** Holding the map and compass, move off following the direction of the travel arrow on the edge of the compass—not the direction of the compass needle.

*red route*

*yellow route*

### ⌖ The chosen routes

The yellow route marked on this model follows a road or path where possible and avoids steep hills. Most of the red route is across rough countryside and there are some steep climbs. Think of other routes you could take.

### ⌖ Before you go

If you set out on a long walk, remember to take your map and compass with you. Take warm and waterproof clothing, food and drink. Always go with an adult.

◁ *This model shows two routes: the yellow route is easier, the red route is more challenging.*

# Changing maps

People will always need new maps because the world is changing all the time. New roads, towns and airports, as well as natural changes to the surface of the Earth, must be recorded. Satellite images are becoming more useful to mapmakers for updating maps, as well as for making new types of maps. Satellite images of other planets are now being used to map surfaces people have never even walked on.

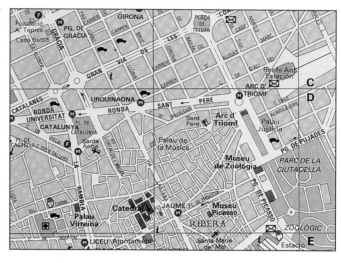

△ On this map of Barcelona in Spain, the straight lines of the newer streets fill the space around the shorter, denser streets of the old city.

## Birth of an island

Sometimes new pieces of land, such as volcanic islands, appear on the Earth. When a volcano erupts under the seabed, the hot lava cools to form land that may rise above the surface of the water. The resulting island now has to be added to a map so that sea travelers can plan their routes accurately.

▷ *This model shows the three stages of a volcanic eruption that produce a new island.*

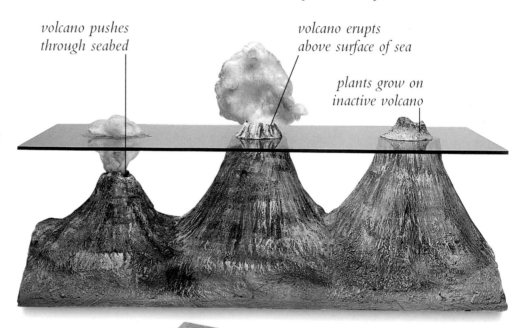

*volcano pushes through seabed*

*volcano erupts above surface of sea*

*plants grow on inactive volcano*

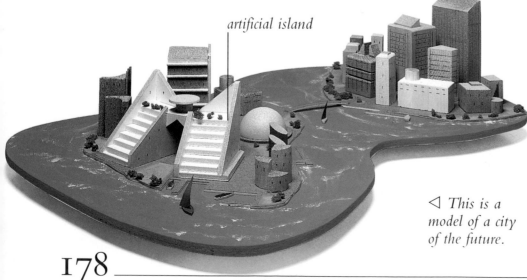

*artificial island*

◁ *This is a model of a city of the future.*

## Artificial land

In places where there is not much land for building, such as Hong Kong or Japan, people plan to build artificial islands. Airports may be built on these islands so that the noise of the aircraft is farther from places where people live. Whole cities may even be built on artificial land one day. Maps will have to record these new pieces of land and the buildings on them.

### 🌐 Satellite sensors

Satellite technology is advancing all the time. As well as being able to "see" smaller pieces of land, satellites now have special sensors to detect different types of land. These satellite pictures are usually taken with special infrared film that shows vegetation in red and roads and buildings in blue. Nowadays, satellites can even tell us where to drill for oil.

▷ *This picture of Tokyo, Japan, was taken with infrared film. Plants are red and buildings are blue so mapmakers can clearly see the types of land use.*

### 📐 New kinds of maps

In the future, computers will be used more often to record data for maps and to draw maps. Advances in technology have already led to "talking" maps in cars. These computer maps show drivers the best routes, avoiding traffic jams and road construction. Instead of paper maps, electronic maps of the future could appear on a pocket TV screen at the touch of a button.

▽ *This is a computer-generated map of one side of the moon. It shows the different types of minerals that make up the moon's surface.*

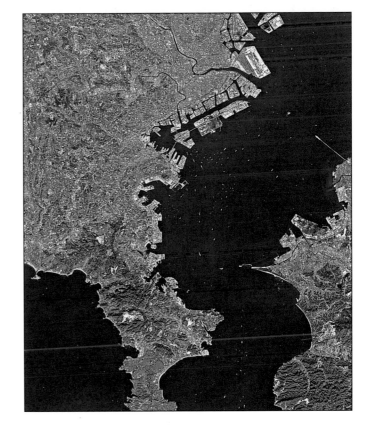

### 🌐 Mapping space

Maps are not limited to features here on Earth. Satellites and other spacecraft have sent back information that enables us to map distant stars and the surfaces of planets. These maps help scientists to understand the universe and investigate the geography of other worlds.

*blue areas show a mineral found in low land*

*this part of the moon shows its natural color*

*red areas show a mineral found in high land*

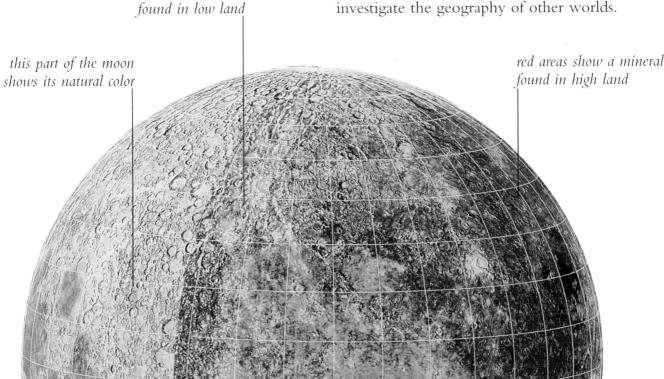

# Glossary

**abyssal plain** The vast, flat ocean floor beyond the continental slope and continental rise. It is covered with a thick layer of sediment.

**aerial photograph** A picture taken from the sky, usually from an airplane. Aerial photographs may be taken from directly overhead, or at an angle.

**alluvium** Material such as fine sand, silt, and clay that is deposited by a river over the land, especially in the lower river, and on the delta.

**Alvin** A submersible (small submarine) able to work at depths of up to 15,000 feet (4,600 meters) and for up to eight hours. Alvin was the first submersible used to explore deep-sea vents in the Pacific.

**anemometer** An instrument used to measure the speed of the wind.

**aquifer** An area of underground permeable rock that absorbs and stores water.

**atlas** A book of maps.

**atmosphere** The air that surrounds the Earth. It is made mainly of nitrogen and oxygen gases.

**bacteria** Tiny organisms that can only be seen under a microscope. They are used to break down soil and sewage, but they can also cause serious diseases in people, animals, and plants.

**barometer** An instrument used to measure air pressure.

**bathymetric map** A map showing ocean depth, and ocean peaks and valleys.

**bench mark** A mark cut in rocks, posts, or buildings to mark the height of the land above sea level.

**canyon** A large, deep river valley with steep sides.

**cartography** The science and art of mapmaking. A cartographer is someone who draws maps.

**climate** The pattern of weather for a place. The climate is similar from year to year.

**compass** A magnetic compass is an instrument used to find directions. It has a needle that points to magnetic north.

**condensation** The process by which a gas changes into a liquid when it cools down. For example, water vapor turns into liquid water when it cools down.

**continent** One of the big land masses of the world. There are seven continents: Africa, Europe, North America, South America, Asia, Australia, and Antarctica.

**continental shelf** The gently sloping shelf along the edges of the continents. It ends in a steep slope called the continental slope. Sediments dropped at the bottom of the continental slope form the continental rise.

**contour** A line on a map that joins places that are at the same height above sea level.

**coral reef** A structure built up in warm waters from the hard remains of small animals called polyps, or corals. There are three kinds of reef: a fringing reef, a barrier reef, and an atoll.

**Coriolis effect** The way that the spin of the Earth makes the world's winds and ocean currents bend. They bend to the right in the northern hemisphere, and to the left in the southern hemisphere.

**dam** A large wall or bank that is built across a river to hold back water. A dam can be used to control the water flowing in a river and prevent flooding. It can also be used to direct the water towards water wheels or turbines in order to generate power.

**deep-sea vent** A crack in the seabed with very hot water and minerals pouring out of it. Vents are usually found along mid-ocean ridges. They are sometimes called black or white smokers.

**degree** A unit for measuring angles. Lines of latitude and longitude are measured in degrees. A symbol is usually used in place of the word "degrees."

**delta** An area of flat land by the sea or a lake that is made up of sediment deposited by a river.

**developed countries** Wealthy countries, such as those in North America, or those in parts of Europe or Australasia, which have developed a strong industrial base, and a high standard of living for most of the people there.

**developing countries** Poor countries in parts of Africa, Asia, and South America, which are trying to create an industrial base and improve the economic and social conditions for their people.

**distributaries** Small, shifting river channels on a river delta that carry water and sediment away from the main river and spread it over the delta.

**drainage basin** The total area of land that is drained by a river and its tributaries.

**drainage pattern** The way a river and its tributaries are arranged on land, seen from a bird's-eye viewpoint.

**Earth's plates** The Earth's outer crust is broken up into about 30 moving pieces, called plates. The continents and oceans sit on top of these plates.

**energy** The power to make things happen. The Sun releases two forms of energy: light rays and heat rays.

**Equator** An line on a map around the middle of the Earth, that divides the Earth into two equal halves – the northern hemisphere, and the southern hemisphere.

**erosion** Wearing away of the Earth's surface by wind, ice, and water.

**estuary** The wide mouth of a river where fresh water meets the sea.

**evaporation** The process by which a liquid changes into a vapor or a gas when it is heated. For example, liquid water becomes water vapor when it is heated,

**fjord** A narrow, steep-sided inlet of ocean formed when the ocean floods into a coastal valley dug out by a glacier.

**floodplain** A broad, flat area of land on either side of the lower river. It is covered with sand, silt, and clay deposited by the river when it floods.

**food chain** A group of living things arranged in the order in which they feed on each other.

**fossil** The hardened remains of either a plant or animal that lived long ago, in prehistoric times. Over time, the remains undergo a chemical change and become preserved in rock. By looking at the remains of the creatures that lived in the past, geographers can work out what the climate was like thousands of years ago.

**front** The boundary between two air masses with different temperatures. There are three types of weather front: warm, cold, and a mixture of the two, which is called an occluded front. All types of front tend to bring rain.

**geology** Studying the Earth's history by looking at the rocks that make up the Earth's crust.

**glacier** A large mass of ice that forms when snow is packed down hard in a hollow on a mountainside. Glaciers can form large "rivers" of moving ice on land, and flow slowly downhill.

**global** If something is said to be global, it is "of the whole world." A global problem is one that is faced by the whole world.

**globe** A sphere that shows the true positions of the land and sea areas on the Earth. A globe is usually tilted at an angle and spins around just like the Earth.

**GLORIA** A type of sonar device that is towed under water. It is used to make maps of large areas of ocean floor.

**gravity** An invisible force that pulls things down to the ground and gives them weight.

**grid** A pattern of equal-sized squares arranged in columns and rows on a map. A grid reference tells people which rows and columns to follow to find any point quickly and easily.

**groundwater** All the water underneath the ground that fills cracks, crevices, and pores in rocks and soil.

**guyot** A seamount (underwater volcanic mountain) with a flat top.

**gyre** A vast circle of moving water. There are five main gyres in the oceans, all of which are made up of the paths of ocean currents.

**hachures** Short, black lines used to show very steep slopes on maps. They are often used to represent steep cliffs on maps.

**hemisphere** One half of a sphere. The Equator divides the Earth into two halves: the northern and the southern hemispheres.

**human map** A map showing information about how people living on the land use it. A human map would show homes, travel, shopping, farming areas, and so on.

**humidity**  The amount of water vapor or moisture in the air.

**hurricane**  A violent tropical storm with heavy rain, strong winds, and thunderclouds swirling around a calm "eye." They form over warm seas near the Equator, and are sometimes called typhoons, or tropical cyclones.

**hydroelectric power**  Electricity that is generated by turbines driven by water falling down from a height.

**ice age**  The Earth's climate changes over time, and has not always been as it is now. An ice age is a period of time in the Earth's history when the climate is very cold. Glaciers and ice sheets cover large areas of the land during these periods. There have been several ice ages, and may be others in the future. The most recent ice age ended around 10,000 years ago.

**interlocking spurs**  Tongues of land on the sides of a river valley around which the river winds. When the points of the spurs are eroded by the river, they become truncated, or "cut off."

**irrigate**  To carry water to crops and pastures by artificial means. Almost 20 per cent of the world's cropland is now irrigated.

**isobar**  A line on a weather map that joins points – places on the map – with the same air pressure.

**key**  When found on a map, a list explaining all the symbols on the map. It is sometimes called a legend.

**lagoon**  A shallow stretch of seawater partly or completely separated from the open ocean by a narrow strip of land, such as a reef.

**land use map**  A map that shows how people use the land. Each activity is usually shown in the form of a color code.

**latitude**  Imaginary lines that run horizontally around the world parallel to the Equator. They are sometimes referred to as parallels.

**load**  The sediment carried by a river. There are three types of load – solute load (material that is dissolved in the water), suspended load (fine particles floating in the water), and bedload (large, heavy particles that move along the river bed).

**longitude**  Lines on a map that run at right angles to the Equator and meet at the North and South poles. They are also called meridians.

**lower river**  The last section of a river, where it flows across an almost level plain to its mouth (the point where the river meets the sea). At this point, the river deposits much of the material that it has picked up from the land along its course.

**magma**  Hot liquid rock below the Earth's surface. Sometimes magma rises up through the Earth's crust. When the hot rock cools, it forms new land, or new ocean floor.

**magnet**  A material which produces a magnetic force that attracts some metals, such as iron. The Earth behaves like a giant magnet because of the dense core of iron in the center of the planet.

**magnetic north** The point to which the needle on a compass always points, allowing us to take compass readings. The magnetic north pole is near the true North Pole of the Earth, but its position slowly changes over the years.

**mantle** This is a layer of hot, flowing rocks that lies between the Earth's outer crust and the inner core.

**map projection** A way of showing the surface of the Earth as a flat map. There are three main types of projection: planar, conic, and cylindrical.

**meander** A natural curve or bend in a river, often occurring in the middle course.

**meteorologist** A geographer who studies the atmosphere and the weather. The word comes from the Greek word "meteoron" meaning "phenomenon in the sky."

**middle river** The central section of a river's course linking the upper and lower river. The river cuts sideways into the land, carries finer sediments, and also deposits some material.

**mid-ocean ridge** A long, narrow chain of underwater mountains formed where two of the Earth's plates are moving apart and magma spills out onto the ocean floor.

**monsoon** A wind that draws warm, wet air from an ocean onto a continent, causing a rainy season.

**neap tide** The tide with the smallest difference between high and low tide.

This tide happens when the Sun, Earth, and Moon are at right angles to each other.

**North Pole** A point at one end of the Earth, usually taken to be the very top. It lies within the Arctic Circle. The North Pole is sometimes called "true north."

**ocean basin** A great depression in the Earth's crust that is filled with ocean or sea. An ocean basin does not include the continental shelf.

**ocean current** A "river" of water flowing in the oceans. There are two main types of currents: surface currents carry warm water from the Equator to the poles; and deep-water currents carry cold water from the poles to the Equator.

**oceanographer** A person who studies the science of the oceans.

**ocean trench** A long, narrow valley under the sea, usually near a continental shelf, where old ocean floor is being pushed down inside the Earth.

**oxbow lake** A meander that has been cut off from the river to form a horseshoe-shaped lake.

**ozone** A form of oxygen gas. A layer of ozone in the atmosphere absorbs most of the harmful rays from the Sun, preventing them from reaching the Earth.

**permeable** A rock that allows water to pass through it is called permeable. Some rocks, such as limestone, let water pass through them easily. Impermeable rocks, like slate, do not allow water through.

**physical map** A map showing natural features of the Earth, such as rivers and hills.

**plan** An outline drawing of an object or a place as seen from above. A plan usually shows a smaller area than a map.

**plankton** Plankton are a vital link in ocean food chains, and there are two main types. Phytoplankton are tiny, plantlike organisms that drift near the surface of the oceans. Animal, or zooplankton, can swim, and are found at all levels in the ocean.

**poles** The points at the top and bottom of the Earth. The North Pole is in the Arctic and the South Pole is in Antarctica. The polar climate is cold and dry all year round.

**porous** A rock or soil that can hold water is known as porous. This depends on the number of pores in the rock or soil. Chalk is a porous rock.

**precipitation** Water that falls from clouds to the ground. It may be in the form of rain, hail, or snow, depending on the temperature.

**Prime Meridian** The line of 0° longitude that passes from the North Pole to the South Pole through the South London borough of Greenwich in England, UK.

**rain forest** Areas of dense forest near the Equator where it is hot and wet all year round.

**raised beach** A rocky platform above a beach, formed when the sea level falls or the land rises.

**rapids** A stretch of rough and fast-flowing water in the upper river. A series of rapids are called cataracts.

**reservoir** An artificial lake storing water for drinking, making electricity, or irrigation.

**resources** A stock or supply of something that can be used if necessary. The oceans are full of natural resources, such as food and minerals.

**river valley** A long, narrow hollow in the Earth's surface in which a river flows. In the upper river, valleys are narrow and steep-sided. Lower down the river's course, valleys are wider, with gently sloping sides.

**satellite** A remote-controlled spacecraft placed in orbit around the Earth, or any other planet. Satellites are vital for mapping the surface of the oceans, and are an essential source of information to today's mapmakers. In addition, pictures and measurements from satellites help meteorologists to forecast the weather.

**scale** The number of units on the ground shown by one unit on a map. On a 1:120 map, 1in represents 120in (10ft).

**scribing** A method used to scrape the lines needed on a map onto a piece of plastic film.

**scuba** This stands for Self-Contained Underwater Breathing Apparatus. Divers carry a tank of air that is kept at the same pressure as sea level, so that they can breathe underwater.

**sea level** The average level of the sea around the world. We usually say that sea level is at zero feet.

**seamount** A large, underwater volcanic mountain. If a seamount erupts or rises above the ocean surface, it forms a volcanic island.

**seasons** Changes in the weather throughout the year. Some places on Earth have four seasons – spring, summer, the fall, and winter. Others have wet and dry seasons. Seasons are caused by the Earth leaning at an angle as it moves around the Sun.

**sediment** Loose particles of rocks or living things that stick together to form mud, sand, or silt. Sediment is carried along and deposited by rivers and tides on the ocean floor or continental shelf.

**sedimentary rock** A type of rock, such as chalk or sandstone, formed from loose sediments, vegetation, or fossils, that have been deposited in layers on the Earth's surface over millions of years.

**silt** Very fine grains of sediment that are carried and deposited by a river.

**sonar** A way of using sound echoes or very high sounds, called ultrasounds, to measure distances and pinpoint the position of objects. Also an instrument that uses sound echoes to measure distances and locate objects.

**South Pole** A point at one end of the Earth, usually the very bottom. It lies in the continent of Antarctica.

**spot height** The exact height of a point marked on a map.

**spring tide** The tide that has the greatest difference between high and low tide. This tide happens when the Sun, Earth, and Moon are all in a line.

**stalactite** An icicle-shaped deposit of minerals that hangs down from the ceiling of a cave.

**stalagmite** A cone-shaped mass of minerals deposited on cave floors, often directly below a stalactite.

**statistics** Information, or facts, given in the form of figures.

**statistical map** A way of showing numbers in the form of a map. Statistical maps can be used to compare towns or countries.

**stereoscope** A device used to view aerial photographs so they appear in three dimensions (3-D).

**submersible** A special vehicle that can withstand the extreme pressure and cold water in the deep ocean. It looks like a small submarine and is used by scientists to work in the ocean depths.

**subtropical climate** A warm climate that is cooler than the tropics but warmer than temperate areas.

**surveying** Measuring distances and angles to work out the size, shape, position, and height of the land. The person who carries out this work is a surveyor.

**symbol** A small picture or special shape on a map that stands for a real feature.

**synoptic chart** A weather chart that is drawn using observations made at the same time in different places. Synoptic means "seen together."

**tactual map** A map with raised symbols that blind people can read by touch.

**temperate climate** The mild, rainy climate of places that are neither too hot, nor too cold. These places are between the hot tropics and the cold poles.

**temperature** How hot or cold something is, for example, the weather.

**theodolite** An instrument used by surveyors to measure angles.

**thermometer** An instrument used to measure temperature. Most thermometers measure temperature in degrees Celsius (°C) and degrees Fahrenheit (°F).

**three-dimensional (3-D)** Something having height as well as length and width. A flat map only has two dimensions.

**tide** The rise and fall of the oceans each day caused by the pull of the Moon, the Sun's gravity on the water, and the spin of the Earth.

**tornado** A violent whirlwind that extends from a cumulonimbus cloud to the ground.

**triangulation** A method used for surveying the land by measuring a series of triangles.

**tributary** A stream or small river flowing into a larger river or stream.

**tropical climate** The hot climate of countries close to the Equator. Tropical climates may be wet all year round, or have wet and dry seasons.

**troposphere** The lowest layer of the atmosphere, nearest the ground, where the weather happens.

**turbidity current** A huge current of sediment flowing down a continental slope. This usually occurs close to where a river flows out onto the continental shelf.

**upper river** The first part of a river's course, starting at the source of the river. The river cuts down deeply into the land and may form gorges.

**upwelling** The process by which winds move warm surface waters offshore, allowing cold, nutrient-rich waters to rise up from the ocean floor to the surface.

**valley** A long, low area mainly enclosed by hills. A valley often has a river running through it.

**water table** The level to which the ground is full, or saturated, with water. The water table rises after rainfall and falls during dry weather.

**water vapor** Water that is held in the Earth's atmosphere in the form of a gas.

**weathering** The process by which rock is broken up into soil and sand by heat, water, ice, plants, or chemicals.

# Index

**A**byssal plain   56, 57, 80, 88
acid rain   44
aerial photographs   164–165, 167, 174
air masses   32–33
air pressure   20–21, 22, 38, 39, 40, 150
alluvium   128
*Alvin* submersible   58, 86–87
Amazon River   140
anemometers   24, 25
aquifers   104, 105
architects   140, 141
Arctic Ocean   52, 53, 60–61, 63, 85, 158
Atlantic Ocean   52, 53, 61, 62, 76
atlases   148, 162
atmosphere   6, 10–11, 12–13, 46, 47, 98–99
atolls   74–75
auroras   11

**B**arometers   21, 38
bathymetric map   89
bathyscaphe, *Trieste*   58
Beaufort scale   24–25
bench marks   145
Black Sea   91
blizzards   31
blue whale   50, 90
braided river   106
breezes   12, 23, 24
bunds   129

**C**anyons   118–119
Caribbean Sea   52
cartography   139, 166–167, 172

cataracts   110–111
caves   94, 104–105
chalk   100, 101, 105
cities   96–97, 124, 125, 130, 135
cliffs   145, 146
climate   14–15, 46–47
clints   104–105
cloud cover   39, 40
clouds   10, 12, 13, 19, 26, 28–29
coasts   50, 70–73, 74, 84, 90, 91, 144
compasses   158–159, 170, 176–177
computers   138, 155, 166, 173, 179
condensation   20, 26, 27, 28, 37
conic projections   160–161
coniferous wood   146, 147, 149
continental rise   56
continental shelf   56, 57, 79, 80, 83, 88, 91
continental slope   56, 80
continents   152
contours   102, 144–145, 146, 147, 149, 165, 172
coral   52, 74–75, 81, 82, 90
Coriolis effect   22, 62
Cousteau, Jacques   86
*Cousteau Diving Saucer*   58
cylindrical projections   160–161

**D**ams   107, 114–115, 116, 125, 132, 135
deciduous wood   146, 147, 149
deep-sea cores   81

deep-sea vents   76–77, 86
deltas   96–97, 130–131, 135
developed countries   124, 127, 135
developing countries   127, 133, 135
distributaries   130, 131
diving   58, 87, 90
diving bell   86, 87
drainage basins   102, 103, 107
drainage patterns   102–103
dredging   124, 125, 132, 135

**E**arth (planet)   46, 94, 111, 116, 117, 118, 119, 122, 123, 126, 138, 139, 140, 150, 156–157, 158, 167, 178–179
Earth's crust   54–55, 82
Earth's mantle   54–55
Earth's plates   55, 76
earthquake   52, 55, 64, 65, 68
electricity   113, 114, 115
energy   13, 19, 34, 35
Equator   8, 9, 14, 15, 22, 37, 156, 158
erosion   44–45, 94, 104, 106, 108–109, 110, 117, 118–119
estuaries   130, 135
evaporation   26, 27

**F**arming   94, 96, 106, 116, 121, 124–125, 128–129, 130, 133, 134, 135
fishing   84, 90, 91
flooding   6, 44, 95, 96, 106, 109, 118, 121, 122, 124, 128, 129, 130, 132–133, 134, 135

food chains   78, 90
forecasting   6, 38, 40, 42–43
fossils   46, 95, 119
fronts   28, 32–33, 34, 40

Gagnan, Emile   86
geographers   94–95, 97, 103,
   108, 109, 138–139, 150,
   153, 160
geology   94, 95, 105, 118–119
glaciers   98, 99, 100, 101, 111,
   116, 117
global warming   47
globes   154, 156–157, 160,
   161
GLORIA   89
gorges   107, 111
granite   95, 101
Great Barrier Reef   52, 74
greenhouse effect   46
Greenwich   159
grid references   142, 173
grids   142, 158–159, 173,
   174
groundwater   98
grykes   104–105
guyots   57, 80
gyres   62

Hachures   145
hail   30–31
Halley, Edmund   86
Hawaiian Islands   52, 57, 74,
   85
human maps   138, 139,
   152–153
humidity   28
humpback whale   60
hurricanes   9, 25, 36–37, 65

hydroelectric power   114–115,
   134
hydrometer   59

Ice   60, 61, 68, 87
ice age   46, 68, 81
icebergs   52, 53, 60, 61
impermeability   100–101
Indian Ocean   52, 53, 62, 74
industry   96, 113, 125, 126,
   134, 135
interlocking spurs   106–107
Inuit maps   138, 162
irrigation   112, 114, 121, 129,
   134
isobars   40, 150

Keys   147, 149, 155, 173

Lagoon   72, 74, 75
lakes   94, 96–97, 98, 99,
   100, 114, 116–117, 125,
   130
land use maps   153
landslides   44
large-scale maps   143, 148
latitude   158–159, 160
legends   147
levees   128, 130, 132, 133, 134
lightning   34–35
limestone   100, 101, 104, 105,
   118, 119
limestone pavement   104, 105
linear scale   142
longitude   158–159, 160
lower river   94, 128–129,
   134, 135

Magma   54, 57
magnetic north   158
magnetic south   158
map projections   160–161
mapmakers   138–139, 144,
   146, 160, 162, 164, 167, 178
mapping   51, 88–89
maps   94, 95, 138–179
   human   138, 139, 152–153
   Inuit   138, 162
   land use   153
   large-scale   143, 148
   physical   138, 139
   small-scale   143
   three-dimensional   144,
      154–155
   underground   175
   undersea   150–151
   weather   25, 31, 39, 40–41
Mariana Trench   52, 58
marine life   50, 51, 63, 67, 74,
   76, 77, 78–79, 87, 90, 91
Marshall Islands map   162
marshes   100, 101, 124, 132
meanders   94, 121, 122–123,
   125, 128
measuring tools   168–169,
   170–171
Mediterranean Sea   53, 67
meteorologists   6–7, 42, 43
middle river   94, 120–125,
   134, 135
mid-ocean ridge   51, 53, 54,
   55, 56, 57, 76, 81, 88
minerals   50, 58, 59, 74, 76,
   77, 79, 82, 83, 104–105,
   109
Mir 1 submersible   58, 77, 87
Mohs, Friedrich   105
monsoons   9, 17
Moon   179
mountains   94, 95, 99,
   106–107, 118, 128, 145, 151

**N**eap tide   66
North Pole   157, 160
North Sea   69, 91


**O**blique views   140
ocean basins   53, 54, 55
ocean currents   56, 60, 61,
    62–63, 65, 87
ocean floor   50, 51, 54, 55,
    56–57, 59, 63, 68, 76, 78,
    79, 80, 81, 86, 87, 89
ocean trench   52, 54, 55, 57,
    58, 79, 81, 88 (see also
    seabed)
oceanographers   50, 79, 81,
    86, 87, 88, 90, 91
oceans   50–91
oil and gas   50, 82–83, 90,
    91
oxbow lakes   122
ozone   11


**P**acific Ocean   51, 52, 53,
    57, 62, 65, 76, 77, 85,
    157, 162
permeability   100–101, 104,
    105
physical maps   138, 139
pine cones   42
planar projections   160–161
plankton   50, 60, 78, 79, 82
plans   140, 141
plunge pool   110–111
poles   14, 15, 16, 17, 22
pollution   90–91
population maps   152
porous rocks   105
ports   84–85, 91
potholes   104, 105

precipitation   30–31, 40
prevailing winds   22
Prime Meridian   159
Ptolemy   162


**R**adiometers   13
radiosondes   42
rain gauges   30, 31
rainbows   30
rainfall   6, 8–9, 12, 20, 26, 27,
    29, 30–31, 37, 38, 44
rainforests   120–121, 122,
    140
rapids   110–111, 120
Red Sea   53
Remote Operated Vehicles
    (ROVs)   87
reservoirs   107, 114–115, 126,
    127, 132
rice farming   129
river profiles   102–103,
    108–109
river terraces   123
river's load   108–109, 120,
    122, 123, 129
rivers   53, 56, 59, 72, 73, 80,
    84, 91, 94–135
route maps   163
route-finding   139


**S**altation   109
sandstone   95, 101, 118
satellites   6, 7, 11, 40, 42, 43,
    50, 87, 88, 89, 138, 139, 140,
    150, 151, 155, 156, 164–165,
    167, 178–179
scale   142–143, 174, 175
scribing   166, 172
scuba   86

sea   94, 96, 98, 99, 108, 109,
    111, 116, 118, 119, 123,
    130, 131
seabed   50, 51, 58, 65, 73, 77,
    79, 81, 82, 87, 88 (see also
    ocean floor)
sea level   67, 68–69, 74, 86, 89
seawater   51, 58–59, 61, 73,
    76, 86, 87, 90
seamount   57, 64, 65, 74
SEASAT   88
seasons   16–17, 157
sediment   56, 71, 72, 73,
    80–81, 82, 83, 87, 91, 94,
    97, 106, 108, 115, 118, 119,
    128, 129, 130, 131, 133,
    134, 135
sedimentary rock   81, 82
seep   100
shading   145, 172
shadoof   129
silt   109, 120, 121, 124,
    130, 135
slate   95, 101
small-scale maps   143
snow   30–31
sonar   57, 88–89, 151
sources (of rivers)   96,
    100–101, 102, 116,
    120, 135
South Pole   157, 160
Southern (Antarctic) Ocean
    52, 53, 59, 60, 63
space   139, 179
spacecraft   156, 179
spot heights   145
spring tide   66, 69
springs   101
stalactites   104, 105
stalagmites   104, 105
statistical maps   152
stereoscopes   167
Stevenson screen   38

storms   34–35, 36–37
street maps   174
submarine canyons   80
submarines   151
submersibles   58, 77, 86–87
   *Alvin*   58, 86–87
   *Cousteau Diving Saucer*   58
   *Mir 1*   58, 77, 87
subtropical climate   14–15
Sun   10–11, 12–13, 14, 15, 16,
   17, 19, 26, 46, 47, 157
surveying   162, 164–165, 168,
   170–171
surveyors   164, 166, 170
swallowholes   104, 105
symbols   139, 141, 146–147,
   148–149, 154, 155, 173
synoptic charts   40–41

**T**actual maps   155
temperate climate   14, 15,
   16, 34
temperature   8–9, 18–19, 30,
   38, 40, 47, 51, 52, 59, 60,
   62, 68, 76, 79, 87
Thames Barrier   132–133
theodolites   164, 168
thermometers   6, 18, 38
three-dimensional maps   144,
   154–155
thunder   34, 35
tidal range   67
tidal zone   67
tides   50, 64, 66–67, 82, 83, 91
   neap tide   66
   spring tide   66, 69
tornadoes   9, 36
trade winds   22
transport   96, 107, 121,
   124–125, 134
tree rings   46

triangulation   164
tributaries   102, 103, 107,
   116, 120
tropical climate   14–15, 17, 34
troposphere   10–11, 13
truncated spurs   106–107
tsunamis   65
turbidity currents   80, 81
turbines   113, 114–115

**U**ltrasound   151
underground maps   175
undersea maps   150–151
upper river   94, 106–107, 110,
   113, 115, 120, 135
upwelling   79

**V**alleys   94, 103, 106–109,
   114, 117, 118, 120, 122–123,
   124, 125, 128, 130, 140, 144,
   151, 176
volcanic islands   74, 75
volcanoes   46, 47, 151, 178

**W**ater cycle   26–27
water table   104, 116, 123
water treatment   126–127, 135
water vapor   12, 20, 26–27, 28,
   37, 98–99
water wheels   112–113, 134
waterfalls   94, 96, 97, 107,
   110–111, 120
waves   50, 57, 64–65, 66, 70,
   71, 72, 73, 83, 91
weather   6–47, 139, 140, 150,
   157
weather maps   25, 31, 39,
40–41
weather satellites   6, 7, 11, 40,
   42, 43
weather stations   38, 40–41, 42
weathering   44–45
whales   60, 61, 85, 91
   blue whale   50, 90
   humpback whale   60
wildlife   96, 115, 116, 119,
   130, 134, 135
wind   6, 12, 20, 22–25, 34,
   36, 37, 39, 44
wind chill   19

# Notes